Why Read PASCAL?

Why Read?

Michael J. Root
The Catholic University of America
SERIES EDITOR

Bruce D. Marshall
Southern Methodist University
SERIES EDITOR

James J. Buckley
Loyola University Maryland

Michael Gorman
The Catholic University of America

Paul J. Griffiths

Christopher Ruddy
The Catholic University of America

PAUL J. GRIFFITHS

 # Why Read PASCAL?

THE CATHOLIC UNIVERSITY OF AMERICA PRESS
Washington, D.C.

Library of Congress Cataloging-in-Publication Data
Names: Griffiths, Paul J., author.
Title: Why read Pascal? / Paul J. Griffiths.
Description: Washington, D.C. : The Catholic University of
America Press, [2021] | Series: Why read? | Includes bibliographical
references and index.
Identifiers: LCCN 2021006202 | ISBN 9780813233840 (paperback)
Subjects: LCSH: Pascal, Blaise, 1623–1662.
Classification: LCC B1903 .G75 2021 | DDC 194—dc23
LC record available at https://lccn.loc.gov/2021006202

This book is for the afflicted

Le Dieu des chrétiens ne consiste pas en un dieu simplement auteur des vérités géométriques et de l'ordre des éléments; c'est la part des païens et des épicuriens. Il ne consiste pas seulement en un dieu qui exerce sa providence sur la vie et sur les biens des hommes pour donner une heureuse suite d'années à ceux qui l'adorent; c'est la portion des Juifs. Mais le Dieu d'Abraham, le Dieu d'Isaac, le Dieu de Jacob, le Dieu des chrétiens, est un Dieu d'amour et de consolation; c'est un Dieu qui remplit l'âme et le coeur de ceux qu'il possède; c'est un Dieu qui leur fait sentir intérieurement leur misère et sa miséricorde infinie; qui s'unit au fond de leur âme; qui la remplit d'humilité, de joie, de confiance, d'amour; qui les rend incapables d'autre fin que de lui-même.

CONTENTS

PROLOGUE

My principal purpose in this book is to encourage you, its reader, to read Pascal for yourself. To this end, I provide a conspectus of the central themes in his work by way of engagement with and frequent quotation of it. Pascal's writing speaks for itself, loudly: among the exegete's tasks is to get out of its way. I hope at least to have done that. But I don't intend to have done only that. This book is neither a florilegium nor the work of a ventriloquist. It is, rather, a kind of commentary: I offer a reading of Pascal's texts, sometimes by way of explanation (here's another way of saying that), sometimes by way of extension (here's how we might take that further), sometimes by way of disagreement (here's why that's surely wrong), and sometimes by way of admiring endorsement (what a lovely thing that is, and here's why). Pascal's words provoke, and mine are what's provoked; that's how commentary works. I hope in doing these things to convey something of the flavor of reading Pascal, which is a matter of interest to him: he thinks of himself as a writer, is attentive to literary style in theory and practice, and often shows concern about how he is or might be read and the ways in which his writing is different from, and better than, as he takes it to be, that of his contemporaries.

I don't engage Pascal on all the topics he wrote about. I focus on his philosophical and theological thought, and respond to his writing on topics in mathematics or physics only in so far as it illuminates what he writes about theology and philosophy—which, sometimes, it does, especially when he considers what it is to design an experiment in physics, or to think about a problem in geometry. I'm concerned throughout to take Pascal as an interlocutor: to let him speak, and then to respond to what he says, sometimes affirmatively, and sometimes not. In doing that I treat his thought topic-wise, not historically. That is, I'm concerned to show not how his thought developed but rather how the texts of his corpus can be read together as a whole; I occasionally indicate points of internal tension, some of which are explicable by developments in Pascal's thought, or by his practice of writing under pseudonyms; but those are never the focus of my interest.

I also eschew, almost entirely, indication or discussion of Pascal's dependence upon or use of sources, which entails also eschewal of questions about the adequacy of his readings of work by others. Asking, for example, whether what he writes about the late anti-Pelagian works of Augustine rightly represents them, or whether his reading of the decrees and canons of the Council of Trent is defensible, would divert from my major purpose, which is to show the contours of his thought by way of engagement with them. There's much of interest to say about all these things, but it won't be said here. Edward Gibbon wrote of Augustine that his learning was too often borrowed and his arguments too often his own, which wasn't meant kindly.[1] I'd say the same of Pascal, but as a compliment: he largely depends for his historical and theological learning on contemporaries more learned in those matters than he, and he shows no independent interest in scholarship of that kind; but that liberated him precisely for argument, in which he is deeply interested and at which he is very good.

1. Edward Gibbon, *The History of the Decline and Fall of the Roman Empire*, 6 vols (London, 1776–89), ch. 28, n. 79.

My first debt of gratitude is to Blaise Pascal for writing as he did: his work has been for me a source of nourishment and stimulus for forty years. My second is to those, listed in the bibliography, who've edited, commented on, explained, and engaged Pascal's work: without what they wrote I couldn't have written this. And my third is to those I know personally who've been kind enough to talk with me about Pascal at various times during the past several decades, to suffer through my halting attempts to teach Pascal to them, or to read some or all of this book in various stages of its composition. They include, and with apologies to those I'm forgetting: Brendan Case, John Heyhoe-Griffiths, Tom Hibbs, Derek Jeffreys, Del Kiernan-Lewis, Stephanie Ladd, Jean-Luc Marion, Bruce Marshall, Tom Morris, Philip Porter, Mike Root, Bill Wainwright, Lauren Winner, and Bill Wood. Susan Needham copyedited a somewhat chaotic manuscript and improved it greatly; I'm grateful to her. I am grateful, too, to the editors of *Commonweal*, for permission to re-use some material I published in that journal in May 2020 in chapter 5 of this book.

CONVENTIONS

All quotations from Pascal in this book are in English, translated by me from the French (occasionally Latin) given in *Oeuvres complètes*, edited by Le Guern (*OC*). Words in italics in my translations from Pascal indicate that what I've translated is in some language other than French—almost always Latin. My English doesn't always, or often, reflect the punctuation and paragraphing of *OC*, but it does follow that text in every other way.

I assume Le Guern's decisions, given in *OC*, about authorship and date of particular works, and thus about the extent of the *oeuvre* as a whole; and I follow his division and enumeration of the parts of individual works, though where he uses roman numerals for parts of some works and arabic numerals for others, I always use arabic. In the case of some works, *Pensées* notably, but also *Grace*, parts are divided, ordered, and enumerated differently by different editors and translators; I use the divisions and numbers given in *OC*. For *Pensées* I provide, at the end of the book, a concordance to the two other most widely-used systems of enumerating the fragments in order to make it easier to locate *pensées* discussed here in other editions and translations.

When writing in my own voice, I use "LORD" to designate the god of Christians and Jews, the one who called Abraham, self-named to Moses, and is incarnate as Jesus-Christ, who is also

LORD; I don't use pronouns for the LORD, unless the reference is particularly to Jesus-Christ, and then I use masculine pronouns. I use "god" to indicate all other gods, and as an epithet of the LORD. When translating Pascal, I follow his usage, which is most often to indicate the LORD by "Dieu," which I render "God." When Pascal uses "Seigneur," which is rare, I represent that as LORD. And I write of Jesus of Nazareth, the second person of the Trinity, as Jesus-Christ, in this following standard French (and Pascalian) style; the hyphenated compound usefully pushes thought toward conceiving of a single person with two natures, which is to say, toward thinking of Jesus-Christ as he is.

ABBREVIATIONS

Advocate   *Lettre d'un avocat au parlement à un de ses amis*

Comparison   *Comparaison des chrétiens des premiers temps avec ceux d'aujourd'hui*

Conferences   *Récit de deux conférences*

Conics   *Essai pour les coniques*

Conversion   *Écrit sur la conversion du pécheur*

Cycloid   Various pseudonymous [Amos Dettonville] works on the cycloid

Denzinger   *Enchiridion Symbolorum*, 43rd edition, ed. Hünermann, cited by section number

Discourses   *Trois discours sur la condition des grands*

Geometry   *Introduction à la géométrie*

Grace   *Écrits sur la grâce*

Instruction   *Projet de mandement contre l'Apologie pour les casuistes*

Jesus-Christ   *Abrégé de la vie Jésus-Christ*

Logic   Pascal's contributions to the Port-Royal *Logique*

Maladies   *Prière pour demander à Dieu le bon usage des maladies*

Mind   *De l'esprit géometrique*

Nevers   Various documents from the clergy of Nevers, partly drafted by Pascal

OC	Pascal's *Oeuvres complètes*, edited by Le Guern, cited by volume/page
Paris	*Écrits des curés de Paris*
Pensées	*Pensées*
Provincials	*Les Provinciales*, attributed to Louis de Montalte
Sacy	*Entretien de Pascal avec M. de Sacy sur Épictète et Montaigne*
Signature	*Un écrit sur la signature*
Sorbonne	*Reflexions d'un docteur de Sorbonne*
Triangle	Various works on number theory and probability theory
Vacuum	Various works on the vacuum

Why Read PASCAL?

LIFE AND WORKS

Blaise Pascal was born on June 19, 1623, in Clermont (now Clermont-Ferrand) in the Auvergne, and was baptized on June 27; he died on August 19, 1662, in Paris, at the age of thirty-nine. His father, Étienne (1588–1651), was a bourgeois who worked as a civil servant; at the time of Pascal's birth he presided over the local tax court. His mother, Antoinette (née Begon, 1596–1626), was a merchant's daughter in Clermont. She died when Pascal was not yet three years old, after a decade of marriage; Étienne did not remarry. Of the children she bore, three were living at the time of her death: Pascal, his older sister Gilberte (1620–1687), and his younger sister Jacqueline (1625–1661). Gilberte married Florin Périer in 1641, and bore him four children; after the early deaths of her two siblings she wrote biographies of them,[1] and devoted energy to the preservation and editing of their papers and the burnishing of their images, as well as to controversies surrounding Jansenism. Jacqueline entered the convent of Port-Royal in Paris in 1652 and was professed in 1653, after controversy with Blaise and Gilberte about the proper disposition of her share of Étienne's estate; she wrote poet-

---

1. *La vie de M. Pascal* (*OC* 1/63–94); *La vie de Jacqueline Pascal* (*OC* 1/44–54).

ry as a young woman, as more than an amateur (Corneille took an interest in her work), and after her profession works of theology and philosophy; she held various positions of authority in the two Port-Royal convents from 1653 until her death.[2]

Pascal's education was largely at home according to a pedagogical plan of his father's, overseen at first by a governess, Louise Delfaut. The plan provided for training in classical languages, history, and literature, and in the philosophical, mathematical, and scientific questions and controversies of the time—Étienne was himself an accomplished mathematician. After 1631, when the family moved to Paris from Clermont (Pascal was then eight), the household was often visited by eminent mathematicians and scientists. This formation contributed to the development of Pascal's mathematical interests, as well as to his characteristic habit of abstraction—that is, of analyzing whatever topic he wrote about into its fundamentals, with attention to questions of method and approach, as well as to substance.[3]

During his late teens and early twenties, Pascal—still living with his father and sister (Gilberte left when she married in 1641), though in Rouen from 1639 onwards because of Étienne's appointment there as supervisor of taxation—developed his interests in physics and mathematics: he designed and had performed experiments showing that a vacuum can be established and observed, and he designed and had made the first mechanical calculating machine. He also became increasingly interested in and passionate about the practice of Christianity, in part as a result of reading Jean Duvergier de Hauranne, the Abbé of Saint-Cyran (1581–1643), Cornelius Jansenius (1585–1638), and others who would

2. A recent and good study of, inter alia, the life and work of Gilberte and Jacqueline is John J. Conley, *The Other Pascals: The Philosophy of Jacqueline Pascal, Gilberte Pascal Périer, and Marguerite Périer* (University of Notre Dame Press, 2019). See also his *Adoration and Annihilation: The Convent Philosophy of Port-Royal* (University of Notre Dame Press, 2009).

3. See chapter 3 below, on order.

later become influential in the broadly Augustinian reform movement within French Catholicism that would come to be called Jansenism. Étienne died in 1651; Jacqueline entered Port-Royal in 1652; Gilberte had married in 1641; and so, by the time he was twenty-eight, Pascal was no longer living with any of his immediate family.

During the first half of the 1650s, in Paris, Pascal worked mostly on topics in physics and mathematics. Late in 1654, when he was thirty-one, he had a vision of the LORD, and recorded it in the *Mémorial*, discovered after his death sewn into the lining of his jacket, and now ordinarily included as part of the *Pensées*.[4] That event was a turning point; following it, early in 1655, he spent some weeks in retreat at Port-Royal-des-Champs, and for the last seven years of his life he spent much of his intellectual and literary energy on the defense of the Port-Royalists, by now called Jansenists, though never to the exclusion of concern with scientific and technical matters. One of the last enterprises he undertook was the planning and establishment of a mass-transit system in Paris;[5] this was intended as a commercial venture as well as a charitable one, and he left shares in it as part of his estate.[6]

From boyhood on Pascal was often ill, and by 1661 he was largely incapacitated.[7] At the end of June 1662, expecting death, he went to live with Gilberte and her family. He died there six weeks later. Gilberte provides an affecting picture of his last days, and writes that his last words, on receiving the sacrament of extreme unction, were, "Que Dieu ne m'abandonne jamais!"—May God never abandon me![8] Those words are as likely to be pious fabrica-

---

4. *Pensées* 711 (*OC* 2/851–52); Le Guern also provides a reproduction of the autograph of the *Mémorial* at *OC* 2/1562.

5. See *Les carosses à cinq sols* (*OC* 2/525–37).

6. *Testament* (*OC* 1/11).

7. He had violent headaches and severe stomach problems. No exact diagnosis in terms of twenty-first-century medicine seems now possible.

8. *Vie de M. Pascal* (*OC* 1/94).

tion on Gilberte's part as sober record, but they show affinity with the Christian sentiments evident in works Pascal wrote during the last decade of his life.[9]

Pascal had, then, a short, atypical, and privileged life. He never married, and so far as is known fathered no children and had no sexual relations with anyone; he had friends, certainly, and many acquaintances; he was close to his father, his sisters, and, eventually, to Gilberte's children; and worldly life was important to him—he appears never seriously to have entertained living as a solitary at Port-Royal-des-Champs, as some of those he esteemed did. Mostly, his was a life of intellectual work on problems in mathematics and physics, and of polemical writing in the service of what he took to be orthodox Catholic Christianity. It was also a Catholic life, begun by baptism eight days after his birth, ended by extreme unction shortly before his death, and marked throughout by an abiding concern with what it meant to be and live as a Christian. His privilege, of which he was aware, is evident in the education he was given and in his freedom from material need. When his father died in 1651, his estate, both liquid and illiquid, was significant; Pascal's share permitted him to live modestly without needing to earn money.[10]

*

What did Pascal write? That's a difficult question to answer with precision, for three reasons.

The first is transmission. Most of what Pascal wrote wasn't published in his lifetime, and the course of events that led to its eventual publication, in some cases centuries after his death, was sometimes tortuous in ways that make it impossible to be sure what

9. I have in mind especially *Maladies* (*OC* 2/183–93), and the letter of October, 17, 1651 to Florin and Gilberte Périer in response to the death of Étienne Pascal (*OC* 2/14–25).

10. On this see Conley, *Other Pascals*, 24–26, and Régine Pouzet, *Chronique des Pascal: "Les affaires du monde" d'Étienne Pascal à Marguerite Périer (1588–1713)* (Paris: Champion, 2001), 129–52. Assessing the value of Pascal's own estate is difficult for many reasons, not least among which is the unclear value of the mass-transit company he established.

is from him and what isn't. For example: in 1655 Pascal had a more or less formal oral discussion of Epictetus and Montaigne with Isaac Le Maistre de Sacy (1613–84) at Port-Royal-des-Champs; a record of this was made by Nicolas Fontaine (1624–1709), one of Port-Royal's solitaries, which languished among Fontaine's papers until a version of it was published in 1728; only in 1994 was a critical edition, based upon Fontaine's autograph, published; and even with that to hand there are obvious difficulties in determining whether to take what the work contains as a verbatim record.[11] Another example: in 1647 Pascal and two of his friends had oral debates about theological and epistemological matters with Jacques Forton, a controversial, and by Pascal's standards heretical, ex-Capuchin. We have a manuscript that presents itself as a verbatim record of what was said, of which the concluding paragraph is in Pascal's hand, and which is signed by him and the two friends who participated with him in the debate. But it is difficult to say, especially given the principal purpose of the written text, which was to persuade the local bishop not to give Forton charge of a parish in the diocese of Rouen, how much of the text should be regarded as a verbatim record.[12] There are other examples of difficulties produced by complex chains of transmission.

The second is collaboration. Pascal contributed to works compiled and published by others, and he composed work in which he drew upon materials (dossiers, notes, sketches) provided him by others; it's often difficult to discern the boundaries of his contribution. Parts of *Provincials*, for example, are based closely upon materials provided Pascal by Antoine Arnauld (1612–94) and Pierre Nicole (1625–95), his friends and mentors in matters theological

---

11. The text is at *OC* 2/86–98, and a discussion of transmission at *OC* 2/1154–56. The most detailed study seems still to be Pierre Courcelle's *L'Entretien de Pascal et de Sacy, ses sources et ses énigmes* (Paris: Vrin, 1960).

12. *Conférences*, of which the text is at *OC* 1/547–65, and a discussion of occasion and purpose at *OC* 1/1111–13.

and historical; it's likely that in some cases Pascal reproduced what they'd given him with only minor changes, and those demanded by style.[13] Another example: in 1658 *Paris* appeared. It was a collection of documents notionally from the priests of Paris protesting the moral theology and pastoral practice recommended in the Jesuits' *Apologie pour les casuistes*, which had been published the year before in response to *Provincials*. Pascal contributed to the final redaction of *Paris*, as did Arnauld and Nicole; and it's likely that some of the work was directly composed by Pascal. But determining precisely who wrote what is not now possible, and the question may in any case be the wrong one—it's probably better to think of *Paris* as a collective composition.[14] There are similar difficulties with other works.

The third is pseudonymy. A high proportion of what Pascal wrote was composed, and some of it also published, under names other than his. We know what these pseudonyms were, and so this doesn't ordinarily lead to puzzlement about whether Pascal composed the works in question; but he seems to have used pseudonyms not only for self-protection but also as mouthpieces for views in some respects distinct from his own. That is, when writing as Louis de Montalte, over whose name *Provincials* appeared, he makes arguments and claims that, when writing over his own name and in his own voice, he wouldn't make and sometimes contradicts. The same is true when he writes as Amos Dettonville, over whose

13. See the discussion of the composite nature of *Provincials* by Le Guern (*OC* 1/1122–25). Pascal was called by some of his Jesuit opponents *secrétaire du Port-Royal*, which suggests that his function was to redact and make more vivid materials given him by others, and thus minimizes his contribution as author. In fact, it is no longer possible cleanly to separate what he wrote from what his mentors provided him; but the unity of style evident in *Provincials* shows that at the very least there's a strong and single stylistic hand at work there.

14. The text of *Paris* is at *OC* 1/833–934. Le Guern discusses the compositional questions at *OC* 1/1298–300, and although he is more optimistic than I would be about the possibility of disinterring Pascal's contributions, even he writes that "il n'est guère possible de déterminer avec exactitude le rôle de chacun des collaborateurs" (it's scarcely possible to determine exactly what each of the collaborators did) (*OC* 1/1298).

name the works on the cycloid appeared. And arguably, though the case is more difficult because the work is unfinished, the same is true for Salomon de Tultie, to whom (some of) the apologetical parts of *Pensées* are attributed.[15] In all these cases Pascal writes the words, but he is, or may be, doing so as amanuensis for a fictional double. Assuming that Pascal endorses what Dettonville or Montalte or de Tultie writes may be as misleading as assuming that Jane Austen endorses what Elizabeth Bennet says.

The upshot of these three areas of difficulty is that the boundaries of Pascal's *oeuvre* are fuzzy in spite of several centuries of editorial work trying to sharpen them. It's good to keep this in mind, but for the purposes of this book it doesn't matter much. "Pascal" here means simply what's printed as his in the two volumes of the *Oeuvres complètes* edited by Michel Le Guern. I assume, without further comment, Le Guern's conclusions on all these matters, and treat the written corpus as a whole, any part of which can reasonably be taken to illuminate or stand in tension with any other part.

*

What, then, once again, and with those difficulties in mind, did Pascal write?

In terms of quantity: about half a million surviving words, mostly in beautiful and polemical French, with a little in Latin.

In terms of genre: letters, of which there are forty or so to real people and another twenty or so to imaginary people; an incomplete collection of aphorisms, apothegms, and sketches for an apologetic; two quasi-verbatim records of discussions or debates with others; a short life of Jesus-Christ; an extended prayer to the

15. See, for example, *Pensées* 628 (*OC* 2/798). For discussion of Pascal's pseudonyms see Le Guern, *Études*, 197–207; and *OC* 1/xv–xxiii. See also Duchêne, *Imposture litteraire*, on literary personae in *Provincials*. It's worth noting that each of the three pseudonyms mentioned is an anagram of the other two, if we allow the ordinary substitution of "u" for "v" in the case of Dettonville. Each of them is also an anagram of the Latin phrase, *talentum Deo soli*—"[my] talent for God alone." Pascal, so far as I can tell, mentions none of these facts; I no longer recall where I came across the suggestion that each of the names anagrams *talentum Deo soli*.

LORD; a half-dozen or so quasi-legal briefs and other interventions in ecclesiastical-political matters of the day; and a dozen or so treatises of varying length.

In terms of topic: mathematics, especially number theory, probability theory, and geometry; philosophy, especially epistemology and logic; theology, especially theological anthropology, moral theology, the nature of conversion and of faith, and the theology of grace; political theory; ecclesiology, especially magisterial authority; experimental and theoretical physics, especially the nature and possibility of a vacuum and the nature and effects of atmospheric pressure.

It's a notable, but not large, literary output for a working life of about twenty years. About half of it was published during Pascal's lifetime, and most of that was pseudonymous. Under his own name there appeared during his life only five short works, taking about eighty pages in Le Guern's edition. The rest appeared gradually after his death, and it's only since the beginning of the twentieth century that the work of editors has made clear the full extent of his writing.[16]

More remarkable is the range of topics Pascal addresses. It was more common in the seventeenth century to be a polymath than it is now—Leibniz (1646–1716), for example, who commented on Pascal's work on conic sections, had a range of interests that makes Pascal's seem parochial—but even by the standards of the time, Pascal was unusual in the catholicity of his concerns, and in his ability to extend and reshape many of the areas of thought to which he contributed. He could do this because of an unusual capacity for dialectics and abstraction: he could see the structure of a problem in theology or philosophy or mathematics, and could, with relative ease, lay out the range of possible ways of thinking

16. See, especially, the edition done by Brunschvicg at the beginning of the twentieth century, and the incomplete one begun by Mesnard.

about it, show, typically by dialectical opposition, where the difficulties lay, and then resolve them.[17] That kind of thinking doesn't require, and is perhaps incompatible with, precise and extensive historical or textual knowledge. That's very evident, for example, in Pascal's treatment of theological topics. He had vastly less textual and historical knowledge than did his friends and mentors Arnauld and Nicole, and was happy to let them provide him what he needed in that way. He is not a knowledgeable or nuanced guide to the Augustinian or conciliar texts he quotes and discusses. They are, for him, counters in the game of truth, deployed to make clear what the truth is and must be about, whatever is under consideration; they're there to provoke thought, not as objects of independent exegetical interest. And that approach to intellectual work made it possible for him to contribute to a much wider range of topics than would have been the case if he'd taken the time to develop wide and deep historical and textual knowledge.

17. For a more detailed discussion of Pascal's dialectics, see chapter 2 below, on style.

2

STYLE

The fundamental question of this book is: Why read Pascal? An answer to that question might reasonably begin with a depiction of what it's like to read Pascal. What are the pleasures and annoyances of his text? What's the feel of reading him? Those questions, however, can't be answered in any straightforward way because readers vary. Your pleasures might be my annoyances; you may find in the text things I don't see there; and your body of knowledge, assumptions about the world, and intellectual interests will lead you to focus on some aspects of Pascal and ignore, or be blind to, others, just as is the case for me. But that doesn't mean that nothing can be written about what it's like to read Pascal now. All it means is that anything written about those matters must be partial and incomplete.[1]

One thing, however, that may be of some use to anyone thinking about reading Pascal, as well as to those who've read this or

1. On Pascal's style I've benefited especially from: Dominique Descotes, *L'Argumentation chez Pascal* (Paris: Presses Universitaires de France, 1993), which treats Pascal's rhetorical and argumentative tactics; Michel Le Guern, *Études sur la vie et les Pensées de Pascal* (Paris: Honoré Champion, 2015), 237–57; and Andrew Hui, *A Theory of the Aphorism: From Confucius to Twitter* (Princeton, N.J.: Princeton University Press, 2019), 121–50.

that by him already, is the question of style: How does Pascal order his words? What are the characteristic patterns, lexical and syntactic, of his writing? What, deeper below the surface, is the prose's skeleton: its length of leg, and therefore its characteristic gait; its distance between cheekbone and lip, and therefore its idiosyncratic smile; its combination of salt, fat, acid, and heat, and therefore its peculiar savor; its balance of impasto and hair-delicate touch, and therefore its distinctive texture; its light-dark, umbra-penumbra contrasts, and therefore its particular radiance? These deep-structural features of prose style, though they're appropriately classifiable as rhetorical features of a text, can also, and equally well, be considered as attitudes or stances toward the act of writing.[2] They're things the writer does in order to begin, continue, and bring to completion a piece of writing; they're stances toward composition evident in the texture of the whole of what is written. A number of these attitudes toward writing are evident in Pascal, and he explicitly addresses some of them.

2.1 Natural Style

Pascal is himself interested in literary style, and when he writes about it he tends to advocate what he calls a natural style. For example:

    ≪ When natural discourse paints a passion or an effect, we find within ourselves the truth of what we hear without knowing it was there. The result is that we're drawn to like those who've made us feel this because they've shown us not their good things but ours. This

---

2. Also, I suppose, toward thinking; but the proper object of this book is what Pascal wrote, which is available, not what he thought, which isn't. As far as possible, which isn't as far as I would like given the almost ineluctable pressure of English toward mentalese (the language of thought, intention, belief, purpose, hope, and so on) when writing about someone's writing, I eschew writing about what Pascal thought in favor of writing about what he wrote. I eschew also, so far as is in me, writing about what I think. I rarely know what that is, and have no interest in knowing more. I find it more instructive to observe what I say and what I write than to introspect, which is what trying to find out what I think seems to require.

kindness makes them likeable to us; the shared understanding we have with them inevitably moves our hearts to like them. (*Pensées* 551, *OC* 2/777)

Natural style—Pascal uses *discours naturel* here, but *discours* and *style* are largely interchangeable for him—represents things in such a direct and recognizable way that those who read what's written in such a style are convinced that what's shown them is real and that it's something they've already seen and have now been given words for. If what's shown is an emotion, readers are convinced they have it or know what it is; if a mode or state of being, likewise; and so on. What the text gives them is the gift of language for depicting something they've already seen and can now recognize more fully because of the style—the lexicon and syntax—of the text they've read.

One upshot is that readers come to like those who write like this. They don't, Pascal implies, feel belabored or argued with or dazzled; they don't feel asked to be impressed by the virtuosity of the writer; rather, it seems to them that they've been done a kindness, a *bienfaisance*. They've been shown something (Pascal's verb here, *montrer*, finds echoes in "demonstration" and "monstrance," both vessels for showing something clearly) in such a way that they see it clearly and are convinced by it.

The metaphor of painting is important to Pascal in writing about literary style.[3] He writes, for instance, that eloquence provides a painting of thought, and that if a writer (or speaker) continues to add ornaments after the painting is done, the result is a tableau rather than a portrait.[4] Portraits are better than tableaux; a portrait shows what's there, in part if not in whole, while a tab-

3. He likes to use the metaphor of painting also in writing about the figures of the New Testament in the Old, as in *Pensées* 503 (*OC* 2/761), where the six days of creation "paint" the six ages of the world that lead to the incarnation.

4. I paraphrase *Pensées* 495 (*OC* 2/758).

leau ornaments what's there, obscuring it by stylizing it. Prose—
or poetry—thus ornamented is like a pretty woman loaded with
gewgaws; she doesn't need them, and those who see her will be
distracted from her beauty by her ornaments, with the result that
they won't see her as she is.[5] Rather than speaking of small things
with big words, the literary painting done by natural stylists ought
to use just the words needed to show what's being painted, no
more and no less.

For example: "Quench sedition's flaming torch—excessively
luxuriant. The restlessness of his genius—two strong words too
many."[6] Pascal doesn't explain this example further, but it's easy
enough to see what he means. Writing of sedition as a *flambeau*
is excessive, overblown like a blowsy peony, aimed at inflaming
readers rather than showing them something. Painting someone's
intellectual capacities as those of a restless genius (*l'inquiétude
de son génie*) draws attention to the depiction rather than to the
thing depicted. And what natural style is supposed to do is paint a
picture that shows—draws attention to, demonstrates—the thing
painted rather than the painter's skill at painting it. The reader's
response to something written in the natural style is supposed to
be a look at what the writer writes about rather than at the particulars of the writing.

A slightly different way of putting the same point:

≫ When we find natural style we're entirely astonished and delighted because we expect to see an author and find a person. People with
good taste, by contrast, expecting to find a person when they read a
book are entirely surprised to find an author. *You've spoken more as a
poet than as a person* [they'll say]. (*Pensées* 569, *OC* 2/781)

5. I elaborate upon parts of *Pensées* 500 (*OC* 2/759–61).
6. *Pensées* 543 (*OC* 2/774–75).

Authors (*auteurs*), in Pascal's usage, are make-believe artists, virtuosos of style, masters of illusion. They seek applause rather than truth. When you read them, you can't see them and aren't addressed by them; you see only their tricks and devices. If you're a person of good taste, an *homme de goût bon*, you don't like the writing of *auteurs*; what you're looking for is to be addressed by a person and shown something about the world by that person. The Latin tag (*plus poetice quam humane locutus es*) from Petronius with which the excerpt just quoted ends is, by Pascal's lights, nothing but an insult. Good writers, those who use a natural style, address their readers conversationally, without artifice, giving them a word-gift whose lucidity carries conviction and brings gratitude. They don't write poetically.

A final instance, and I suggest reading this one with the thought that Pascal here describes the person he aspires to be:

> ⇒ No one passes in the world as skilled in verse without identifying as a poet.... But universal people want no such badge and make almost no distinction between the skills of poets and those of embroiderers. Universal people don't call themselves poets or geometers or the like; but they are all of them, and they judge all of them. They can't be pigeonholed, and they'll talk about whatever was being talked about when they came in. One quality isn't more evident in them than another, unless there's some necessity to show it; and in that case we remember it. For it's equally characteristic of them that we don't say they speak well when the question of language doesn't come up, and that we do when it does. It's therefore false praise of people to say of them when they come in that they're very skilled at poetry; and it's a bad thing when we don't have recourse to them in a question of judging some particular verses. (*Pensées* 500, *OC* 2/760–61)

This passage isn't perhaps as pellucid as we might expect of someone who advocates the natural style—though it should be kept

in mind that it's from *Pensées*, most of which, including probably
this passage, weren't much revised or edited or polished. But its
central point is clear enough: it's a mistake to seek and find reputation as possessor of particular skills, so that when you walk into
a room (the setting of the passage, as so often in Pascal, is social—
the salon) people say, "Ah, here's the poet—the wit—the mathematician—the theologian." To hold such a reputation, I imagine
Pascal would say, though he doesn't, quite, here, would be the result of presenting oneself in person and on the page as an author
rather than as a person, which in turn would be tantamount to
turning poetical tricks in order to be admired—and perhaps paid
like a *meretrix* for behaving meretriciously. You'd be Oscar Wilde
in full bon-mot mode, having nothing to declare but your genius.
Better to be among the *gens universels*, the universal people, who
can discourse with equal facility upon everything and anything
(*ils parleront de ce qu'on parlait quand ils sont entrés*), who refrain
from showing any particular skills until occasion demands, and
whose judgments about some particular poem (*quelques vers*) are,
when they're called upon to make them, just and memorable. For
it to be said of you that you speak (or write) well in general is of no
interest, as Pascal sees things; what is of interest is that you speak
well about what's under discussion when occasion suggests that
you might, and that when you do, people recall what you said as
demonstrating to them something of importance about the topic
or object you're addressing. Natural style and good taste, for Pascal, aren't detachable from particular objects and particular occasions; and when they're evident, they're responsive to what's at
hand by providing a word-portrait of it without freezing it into a
tableau by the blunt force of literary virtuosity.

I prefer to leave aside Pascal's advocacy of universality. There
are no universal people (*gens universels*) in his sense of the phrase,
and even he, possessed of an unusually wide range of skills and
knowledge as he was, wasn't one. Universality was more plausible

as an aspiration in the seventeenth century than it is now, though even then it was fast receding as a possible one. But even with that aspiration left aside as a grandiose gesture, there's the appropriate thought that good (plain, natural) style isn't a single, recognizable thing, but varies, instead, according to the kind of thing being written about. The palette and brushstrokes appropriate for rendering the crest of the piliated woodpecker aren't the same as those good for a storm at sea or the wounds of Jesus-Christ. What the appropriate styles have in common, if they're to continue to be properly categorized as natural in Pascal's sense, is the renunciation of rhetorical and ornamental excess ("quench sedition's flaming torch," recall) in favor of close and careful responsiveness to the particulars of what's at hand and before the eye. Pascal's mention of embroiderers (*brodeurs*) is relevant, and perhaps also revelatory, here. They are practitioners of a craft, we'd be likely to say, and as such need to attend closely to the weave of the fabric they're embroidering, the strength of the thread appropriate to that fabric, the colors best for the design being embroidered, and so on. So also for poets, and prose writers, and mathematicians, and theologians, and so on: they too practice a craft, and when they do it well the result is an artifact that carries its own conviction. That's what Pascal aspires to with his prose.

2.2 Style and the Order of Things

Pascal's thought that good, natural style is not always the same but varies in response to what's being written about and to particular occasions of writing fits well with his impulse to divide what there is in the world, and, correspondingly, discourse responsive to what there is, into different orders.[7] There is, for example, the mathematical/geometrical order of things, which has its corresponding style: the *esprit géometrique*, or geometrical mind, pro-

---

7. On order and orders in more detail, see chapter 3, below.

duces a style proper to geometrical thought and writing. There is the order of the abstract sciences, including but not limited to mathematics, and, by contrast, the anthropological order: the topic of the former is abstract objects and that of the latter human persons, and the style appropriate for the depiction of items in the one is distinct from that appropriate to the depiction of items in the other. There is, too, a distinction important to Pascal between matters of fact and matters of doctrine, the former best addressed by empirical method with its corresponding prose, and the latter by exegetical method with its corresponding prose. And there is the order of love, whose norms and actions are incommensurable with and have no necessary implications for what goes on in, say, the order of political power.

Pascal is prolific in his taxonomies of order and shows little interest in reducing them to a system. Instead, he deploys them occasionally, in response to particular polemical or apologetical pressures. What he calls orders do, however, share common features. Each treats a particular kind of thing or a particular kind of relation among things, and is therefore an order of being; each order of things or relations is also known by us in a particular way (you don't get to know a person in the same way as a number, or a Christian doctrine in the same way as the boundaries of *arrondissements* in Paris), which is to say that it is also an order of knowing; and, ordinarily, there is a mode of writing (and speaking) appropriate to each order, which is to say that it is also a stylistic order, at the level of the sentence and paragraph as well as at the level of an entire text: a treatise in physics is different in sentence-level style and in overall structure from one in politics, for example.

Pascal's *oeuvre* treats a wide variety of topics: mathematical, physical-experimental, theological, pastoral, devotional, philosophical, ethical, ecclesial, familial. If his literary work is to reflect his theoretical convictions about style, it ought to exhibit significant stylistic variation just because it treats such a wide range of topics; it ought also to have a deeper-going unity, given it by its adherence to whatever might best count as plain/natural style in connection with whatever it is that's being written about. Natural style aspires to translucence to object and occasion by way of renunciation of ornament. There is no complete realization of such a goal; but it seems fair to say that Pascal's literary work at least approaches it.

For example: One large part of that work is devoted to topics in mathematics, principally number theory and geometry.[8] In *Mind*, a work in part devoted to the principles of reasoning in geometry, by which Pascal means, roughly, the mathematics proper to the measurement and location of objects extended in space,[9] he shows and argues for what he takes to be the proper method of reasoning and exposition in that discipline. Geometry, he says, treats its objects first by way of primitively worded axioms, such as "a number, whatever it is, can be augmented."[10] That's an axiom because it's sufficiently clear to reason's natural light (*lumière naturelle*) that, once understood, its truth is evident.[11] It's primitively worded because it deploys a word, *nombre*/number, that isn't defined, but rather deployed in axioms. That's what makes it primitive. Like *temps*/time, it's a word that moves the thought of everyone who uses it into the same order or sphere, even though—or perhaps just because—most who use such words can offer no definition of them and may disagree, even vehemently, about particular definitions when they're put forward.[12] The first device of geometry, on this view, is the listing of primitively worded axioms; its second

8. I have in mind *Conics* (*OC* 1/111–28), *Cycloid* (*OC* 2/319–524), *Geometry* (*OC* 1/140–42), and *Triangle* (*OC* 1/169–328).

9. *Mind* 1.8–9 (*OC* 2/161–62).

10. *Mind* 1.11 (*OC* 2/163).

11. See *Mind* 1.3 (*OC* 2/157).

12. Pascal takes the claim that numbers are entities that can be augmented not as definitional of them but rather as picking out a feature of them that can't be denied without contradiction. This seems right. *Peut être augmenté* is neither an exhaustive definition of numbers, nor a feature possessed only by them.

device is the deployment of such axioms in arguments to show what follows by entailment from them,[13] as when Pascal deploys the mentioned axiom to show that everything located or extended in space, and hence subject to mathematical measurement, is to be found between nothingness and infinity.[14] This must be so because if every number can be increased (added to), and if all spatio-temporally located objects are locatable by measurement the instrument of which is number, then where any particular thing is must be neither nowhere (nothingness—if it were there then it wouldn't be measurable and hence wouldn't be located) nor everywhere (infinity—if it were there then it also wouldn't be measurable, because since any set of numbers used to measure/locate is augmentable, nothing measured by any set of numbers could be in a place-time beyond further extension, which is just what it would be to be located at infinity).

On this view of the broadly mathematical disciplines, treatises concerned with them should have a particular shape and a corresponding style. They should begin with a list of axioms, given as succinctly as possible; entailments of those axioms should then be provided, with only as much argument as is needed either to elucidate the conclusion or, more commonly, to show the incoherence of its denial.[15] Pascal's treatises on these subjects indeed have this shape.[16] And their sentence- and paragraph-level style is, accordingly, abstract and definitional. An instance chosen almost at random, from the work in number theory: "In a series of natural num-

13. Pascal's most extended treatment of logic, which included delineation and analysis of necessary and sufficient conditions, and the beginnings of a treatment of modes (necessity, possibility) of entailment, is to be found in *Logic* (*OC* 2/108–53).

14. *Mind* 1.11 (*OC* 2/163). See also *Pensées* 185 (*OC* 2/397–298[au??]).

15. On the importance of the *reductio* as a pattern of reasoning in all disciplines (not just the mathematical), for creatures constituted cognitively as humans are, see *Mind* 1.12 (*OC* 2/164). We're better, Pascal says, at discerning falsehoods entailed by incoherence than at comprehending truth, especially when the topic at hand is abstruse, as often in mathematics—and theology.

16. This is most evident in *Cycloid* and *Triangle*.

bers beginning from any number you like, the difference between the square of the number immediately higher than the last item in the series and the square of the lowest number in the series, less the number of items in the series, is double the sum of all the numbers in the series."[17] This is an instance of natural style in the order of mathematics—it's the lexicon and syntax, the grammar that is, of discourse prompted by close attention to relations among abstract objects.

By contrast, there's the theological order of things. Arriving at, and expounding, truths in this order is different in almost every respect from arriving at and expounding truths in the mathematical order. About this, Pascal writes:

> ⇥ [Divine truths] are infinitely above nature. God alone is able, at pleasure, to place them in the soul. I know that he has willed that they enter the mind from the heart and not the heart from the mind, so as to humiliate the proud power of reasoning that pretends it must judge what the will chooses, and to heal the infirm will that is entirely corrupted by its filthy attachments. And so it follows that in speaking of human things we say that they must be known before they're loved, a view that's become proverbial; the saints say the contrary in speaking of divine things—that it's necessary to love them in order to know them, and that we can only enter into truth by way of love. (*Mind* 2, *OC* 2/171)

This view of how truths about the LORD are arrived at suggests a style for expounding and defending such truths different in almost

---

17. *Triangle* (*OC* 1/264). The example that Pascal gives is the series 5-6-7-8. The square of 9 (*quadratum numeri qui proximi major est ultimo termino*) is 81; the square of 5 (*quadratum minimi termini*) is 25; the difference between them is 56; which is 52 when the number of items in the series is subtracted (*minuta numero qui exponit multitudinem*); the sum of the numbers in the series 5-6-7-8 is 26; and 52 is indeed twice 26. This is an application of a method laid out earlier in the treatise, which also proves the validity of the method; and the application has use in particular, inter alia, in the calculation of odds in games of chance, a matter of continuing interest to Pascal.

every way from that required for geometry. Theological truths aren't translucent to the natural light of reason in the way that geometrical ones are, and so theological style ought not to present them as if they were; the patterns of argument, too, in theological demonstration, ought to be different from those in geometrical demonstration, and different again from those used to address anthropological or political or literary matters.

On this view of theology, which for Pascal is the same thing as *vérités divines*, the LORD is the agent of conviction: only by what the LORD does can we see that theological truths are true. Our reasoning capacities are of no use in this, theological, order.[18] Instead, we must rely upon authority: "Authority alone can enlighten us here,"[19] Pascal writes; and in the case of theology, that means the authority of the Church, and of the books judged authoritative by the Church—paradigmatically the canon of Scripture, but also the works of those judged to be teachers of the Church (*doctores ecclesiae*), and the texts promulgated by the Church's teachers, the bishops and the pope. A simple reading of such books won't, however, on Pascal's view, bring assent to what they contain. That is evident from the fact that many who have read the books do not believe what they teach. The LORD's further and direct action is required if theological truths are to be embraced with faith and acted upon. That is one aspect of the mystery of grace.

But some care is necessary here. It might seem, for Pascal, that if theological discourse is always and necessarily responsive to the ecclesially guaranteed and textually transmitted body of texts that preserves scriptural revelation and authoritative churchly teaching, reason would be irrelevant to it. But this is not so. He also writes that true Christianity consists in submission together with

18. Pascal is characteristically extreme here, for dialectical and polemical purposes. On reason's capacities see chapter 3, §3.4, and chapter 5, below.

19. *Vacuum* (*OC* 1/453). This theme is taken up at length in parts of *Provincials*. The passage quoted is applied by Pascal not only to theology, but to all testimony-based disciplines.

the use of reason.[20] The submission part is clear enough: that's what you do to authority. But how is reason to be used in theology? First, exegetically: what the authoritative sources contain needs always to be restated and ordered and commented on and explained. These tasks require the use of reason. Second, argumentatively: misconstruals of the content of the faith need to be engaged and shown for what they are; and, in-principle objections to the possibility of theological truth, prior in the order of argument to any engagement with the content of putatively authoritative texts, may need sometimes to be addressed and rebutted. This, too, is a work of reason, and one of special interest to Pascal.[21] In a letter to his older sister, Gilberte, Pascal lays out some of these points as early as 1648, at the age of twenty-four—he's reporting a conversation he'd had with Antoine de Rebours (1592–1661) at Port-Royal:

> ≫ I then said to him [Rebours] that I thought it possible, following the same principles of common sense, to demonstrate many things that his adversaries say are contrary to it, and that good reasoning would lead to assent to those things even though it's necessary to assent to them without reasoning's help. That's what I said, and I think there's nothing in it damaging to the most severe modesty. But as you know, all our actions can have two sources, and what I said might have been founded on vanity as well as confidence in reasoning. Suspicion of this, increased by the knowledge he [Rebours] had of my studies in geometry, sufficed to make him find what I'd said strange, and he showed me this by a response so full of humility and modesty that it would certainly have confounded the pride he wanted to refute. I nevertheless tried to make him understand my motive, but my attempt increased his doubt, and he took my excuses for obstinacy. I acknowledge that what he said was so beautiful

---

20. *Pensées* 156 (*OC* 2/601).
21. For more on the apologetical enterprise, see chapter 3, §3.4, and chapter 4, §4.5, below.

that if I'd been in the condition he imagined me in it would have removed me from it. But since I didn't take myself to be suffering from that disease, I resisted the remedy he offered. (Letter of 1648 to Gilberte Périer, *OC* 2/6)

Pascal's interlocutor, a confessor at Port-Royal and a follower of Saint-Cyran,[22] doubts that the (largely Jesuit) opponents of what both he and Pascal took to be a soundly orthodox Augustinian Christianity could be convinced of their errors by reasoned argument. Pascal is more optimistic. He agrees, or at least acknowledges, that the truths of the faith ought to be assented to without reasoning's help—by faith, that is to say. But he also thinks it possible that decisive and possibly convincing arguments can be offered against theological errors by following the *principes de sens commun*. Pascal doesn't here specify what these are; but from his later attempts to do just this, in the *Provincials* and other works, it's reasonable to assume that he means methods of argument accepted and used by the adversary, coupled with bodies of evidence also so accepted—"common" in the sense of "shared," that is. Reasoning undertaken in that way, he implies here, can work in the double sense of identifying error as such (which in some cases will entail showing also what the truth is), and of convincing those to whom it's shown that it is indeed that. Rebours, the interlocutor, isn't, according to Pascal's report, convinced that reason has such powers, and takes Pascal's confidence that it does to be evidence of pride. Pascal acknowledges that it may indeed be such evidence, and that what he'd said might have been based in part upon *vanité*; but, not without a hint of the *amour-propre* he later spends so much time identifying and criticizing as among the principal

22. Saint-Cyran had been spiritual director of the Port-Royal nuns, and a friend of Cornelius Jansenius, author of the *Augustinus*. Although Saint-Cyran died before the controversies about Jansenius's book became warm (the *Augustinus* wasn't published until 1640), he was among the revered ancestors and formative forces of what came to be called Jansenism.

marks of the Fall, he ends by writing to his sister that he wasn't, in what he'd said to Rebours, suffering pride-sickness, but, rather (or, at least, as well), showing a proper confidence in what reason can do, which is, with respect to divine truths, at least to identify and rebut error. That is, for Pascal, among the ways in which the maxim that the Christian life involves both submission to authority and the use of reason finds purchase. He maintains this degree of trust in reasoning about theological questions throughout his life.

Given this conviction about the place of reason and reasoning in theology, it's natural to expect that Pascal's argumentative theological works would be agonistic and polemical. And it is indeed the case that many of them are, paradigmatically *Provincials*, but also *Conferences*, and to some degree *Grace*. *Provincials*, especially, is polemical from beginning to end, and is written in an easy and bitingly satirical style in which Pascal's opponents and their views are as often mocked as rebutted. On this, Pascal writes:

> ⇒ On this topic [the right uses of mockery and ridicule] it's remarkable that in the first words God speaks to humans after their fall there's mockery, what the Fathers call a piquant irony. For after Adam had disobeyed in the hope that the devil would make him like God, Scripture shows that God punished him by making him subject to death, and that, after reducing him to that miserable condition due to his sin, God mocked him in that state with words of ridicule: "Behold the man who has become like one of us." According to St. Chrysostom and the exegetes, those words are a bitter and wounding irony by which God stung Adam. (*Provincials* 11, *OC* 1/698–99)

And, in words reported by Pascal's niece:

> ⇒ People ask why I used a pleasing, bantering, and diverting style [in *Provincials*]. I reply that if I'd written in a dogmatic style, only the learned would have read, and they have no need to because they

know as much about these matters as I do. And so I saw that it was necessary to write what could be read with pleasure by women and worldly people, so that they might understand the dangers of the easily persuasive maxims and propositions everywhere current at that time. (From Marguérite Périer's "Récit de ce que j'ai ouï dire à M. Pascal mon oncle, non pas à moi, mais à des personnes des ses amis en ma présence," quoted by Le Guern at *OC* 2/1091.)

The satirical flavor of Pascal's polemical theological works, which is what made them then and makes them now such astringent fun to read, is in these excerpts given a double justification. The first is that mockery and ridicule are scriptural: the Lord's words to Eve and Adam immediately after the Fall are replete with them—with piquant, wounding, and bitter irony. Pascal thinks it clear that the Lord's words to the fallen couple in Genesis 3:22 are ironic: there is no sense in which creatures about to die, as they now are, can be like gods, *quasi unus ex nobis*—like one of us (Pascal provides the Latin as well): that is, either like one among the gods, as the Lord also is, typed, for example, as a "great god / a great king above all gods" in Psalm 95—but still with the gods as the proper reference class; or like one among the three persons of the Trinity—which is a long-lineage Christian interpretation of *nobis*. It can only be a taunt to say that mortal creatures are like the Lord.[23] To use rhetorical devices like this himself, then, Pascal claims, is to do no more than imitate what Scripture and the Fathers do—and in the eleventh *Provincial* he provides many more examples.

The second justification, from the second excerpt, is to do with audience: those without technical theological knowledge won't read treatises written in dogmatical style—treatises, that is, writ-

---

23. It's far from clear that the words are best, or even possibly, read as a taunt. They're immediately followed in Genesis by "knowing good and evil," and in that respect, clearly, Genesis is better read to say that Eve and Adam post lapsum are, nonironically and without taunt, like the Lord as they hadn't been before the Fall. Here, as in other respects, the serpent spoke the truth to Eve when persuading her to eat the forbidden fruit.

ten didactically or exegetically, setting out the Church's teaching as an axiomatic system, as, for instance, in the manuals used for the training of priests, which are, in these respects, not unlike manuals for auto repair. For nonsavants, then, something more accessible and entertaining is needed, and a bitterly satirical style, weaving together wit-leavened mockery with the heat of righteous anger, is what's needed and what Pascal provides.

But not all Pascal's theological work is stylistically polemical and satirical in the mode of *Provincials* or *Conferences*. Some, though properly theological in that it addresses its topic theologically in light of the LORD of Christian confession, is devotional or pastoral in approach. The pastoral style, solemn and didactic, is very evident in the letters of spiritual advice to Charlotte de Roannez, composed at about the same time as *Provincials*,[24] and in the remarkable letter to his elder sister and brother-in-law following the death of Étienne Pascal in 1651.[25] If satirical mockery is the right style for rebutting theological error, then, it seems, the rhythmic periods of prose marked more than anything else by the style of the collects and prayers of the order of the Mass is the style natural to the meeting of pastoral and devotional need.[26] Consider the following example, from *Maladies*, a work on the right use of illness framed as a prayer to the LORD:

> ≫ Touch my heart to repent of my offenses, for without that interior suffering the exterior pains with which you touch my body will be a new occasion of sin. Make it clear to me that the pains of the body are nothing other than a figure for and punishment of the pains of the soul. Make them their remedy by making me consider by way of the sufferings I sense those I'm insensible of in my soul, even though it is entirely sick and ulcerated. For, LORD, the greatest of maladies

---

24. Letters of 1656 to Charlotte de Roannez (*OC* 2/26–39).

25. Letter of 1651 to Florin and Gilberte Périer (*OC* 2/14–25).

26. For a useful study of the appearance in various works by Pascal of liturgical formulae, see Philippe Sellier, *Pascal et la liturgie* (Paris: Presses Universitaires de France, 1966).

is that insensibility, that extreme lassitude which has removed from the soul all sense of its real miseries. Make me sense these in a lively way; and let what remains to me of life be a continual penitence to wash away the offenses of my earlier life. (*Maladies* 7, *OC* 2/187–88)

This is a plea to the LORD ordered around a dialectical contrast between the sufferings of the body in its illness, and those of the soul in its sickness. The importance of the former is that they can remind us of the latter, and that is good, indeed essential, for it's only when we're properly aware of the soul's sickness that the distance between the LORD and us can diminish. The paradigmatic soul-sickness is exactly our insensibility to that distance; and bodily pains can, with grace, overcome that insensibility. But bodily pain isn't only a figure and reminder; it's also a punishment for the soul's sufferings, so understood. This is striking and worrying as a piece of theology—it can't be said that every instance of my or your bodily suffering is direct punishment for the parlous condition of our souls. Neither is *punition* the best, or even a defensible, category for labelling the nature of the LORD's relation to our bodily sufferings—but my interest in the passage is stylistic rather than substantive at this point, and on that there are two points to make. The first is that even here, in spite of the elevated liturgical tone of pastoral solemnity, and of the framing of the text as direct address to the LORD, Pascal writes in something close to *style naturel*. Modifiers, whether adverbial or adjectival, are few, and essential when present—*vivement* / in a lively way, for example, isn't there to gin up affect, but to make an essential point. The whole is condensed, sad, restrained, and dignified, and in all those features also liturgical. It's a style natural to its topic, not calling attention to itself (no *auteur* here) but, rather, exactly to its topic—that, recall, being the hallmark of *style naturel*. The second point about the style of this excerpt is that it's dialectical in its treatment of inner and outer sufferings and sicknesses, and that dialectical approach has broad and deep ramifications for Pascalian style.

2.3 Polemic

Another attitude to writing, of considerable importance to Pascal, is the polemical. Pascal's works are, in very many cases, instruments of battle: he has opponents and he wants to vanquish them. His goal is scorched earth: to remove his opponents and their errors from the field, and to leave standing there only the truth and its proponents.[27] His prose, therefore, is honed, sharpened to draw blood. This also means that his work is occasional in the sense that it's provoked by and responsive to a particular occasion: Jesuit moral theologians defend probabilism; the magisterium conflates claims about what Jansenius wrote with claims about how grace's workings should be delineated; various theologians defend the thought that there are some actions exclusively ours, independent of the workings of grace; some theorists claim that a vacuum is impossible in nature;—and Pascal enters the lists against these confusions, as he sees them.

All writing is occasional and agonistic to some degree. None drops from heaven without a history, without opponents in mind, and without concern to overcome adversaries and remove errors. But there are great differences in the degree to which those interests are explicit and central, and on that spectrum Pascal is toward the far end. Most of his works are almost entirely ordered around those interests, and that has considerable effects on what it's like to read them. Readers are drawn into the field of battle, where, typically, the opponents are named and their errors expounded, ridiculed, and rebutted; they are pressed to take a position on the field themselves; and they are, according to temperament, either exhausted or invigorated by their impressment.

Pascal is aware of these features of his writing, and of objections to them. Consider this:

27. For further discussion of Pacal's awareness of, and reservations about, these aspects of his own writing, see chapter 6, §6.1, below.

↠ It's therefore beyond doubt that those who always rely on the pretexts of love and peace to prevent criticism of those who destroy both show that they are friends only of a false truth and true enemies of real peace and of truth. Also, it's always under the pretext of peace that those who persecute the Church have veiled their horrid violence, and that the false friends of peace have consented to the oppression of the truths of religion, and of the saints who defend them. (*Paris*, Réponse, *OC* 1/850–51)[28]

Or, more briefly said: error demands rebuttal; attempts to prevent rebuttals in the name of peace are themselves violent; the (rhetorical) violence of polemic is both unavoidable and required when error is promulgated. This excerpt is taken from the *Écrits des curés de Paris*, a work to which Pascal contributed significantly, though to an extent that is still debated. *Paris* was prompted by the publication in December 1657 of a work titled *Apologie pour les casuistes contre les calomnies des jansénistes* by Georges Pirot, a Jesuit. That work responded in part directly to Pascal's *Provincials*, and in part more generally to critiques of Jesuit laxism in moral theology.[29] That is the field of debate; and one element in it was the thought that the *Provincials*, especially, were unseemly because of the rhetorical violence with which they treat their opponents.[30] Here's an instance of that:

↠ O abominable theology, so corrupt in all its principles that unless it were both probable and sure in conscience that one may offer calumnies without crime in order to preserve one's honor, scarcely any of its decisions would be so! It is very likely, Fathers [Pascal addresses the Jesuits], that those who hold this principle will sometimes put it into practice! The corrupt inclinations of humans carry them so impetuously along that path that, once the obstacle of conscience is

28. Compare *Provincials* 12 (*OC* 1/722), and *Pensées* 78 (*OC* 2/566–67).
29. For more on these debates see chapter 4, §4.3, below.
30. This topic is discussed *in extenso* in *Provincials* 11 (*OC* 1/697–709).

lifted, it's unbelievable that it won't spread itself with all its natural vehemence. (*Provincials* 15, *OC* 1/750–51)

Pascal here writes about the Jesuits' view that it's permissible in conscience to slander one's opponents when honor is at stake. Our inclinations, being corrupt, lead us to want to do this and other things like it in any case; and once the barrier to these inclinations—the thought "this is a wrong thing to do," grounded by the Church's teaching and the work of confessors—is removed by jesuitical probabilistic casuistry, we'll do that thing energetically, perhaps all the more energetically. Pascal doesn't merely indicate that this is a wrong view. He castigates it as an abomination. His goal is to remove it as a possible view, forthwith and without remainder, and to make those who've defended it ridiculous. It's that polemical tone, mocking, sarcastic, and violent, that Pirot and others responding to the *Provincials* objected to. Pascal, as in the excerpt from *Paris* quoted above, responds *tu quoque*: you're as rhetorically violent as I am; the only difference between us is that I show my violence while you hide yours.

2.4 Dialectic

Another rhetorical stance is dialectical, and this is perhaps the most significant and fundamental among the attitudes informing Pascal's prose. He writes:

>> If people lift themselves up, I bring them down; if people bring themselves down, I lift them up. I always contradict them until they understand that they're incomprehensible monsters. (*Pensées* 121, *OC* 2/578–79)

This provides an instance of an aspect of the dialectical stance—that of contradiction, in this case in the sphere of anthropology. Self-exaltation and self-abasement are contradictory practices, at least in the sense of being noncompossible: you can't do them both at the same time; perhaps, depending on their further definition, they are contradictory in other ways as well. Whichever of these you do, Pascal writes, I'll contradict your doing of it. Should you move from the one to the other—perhaps, ashamed of your self-glorification, you begin to denigrate yourself—Pascal will contradict you in that, too. The outcome should be that you find yourself without a place to stand in the tension between uplift and bringdown. You become to yourself *un monstre incompréhensible*. The dialectic in this case, as typically, constructs a contradiction that intends to exclude any middle: either you're for *p* and are doing it; or you're for *not-p* and you're doing that; and whichever of those is the case, Pascal will contradict you, showing you that in the one case you're *not-p* and in the other *not(not-p)*. But if so, then … ?

Another example:

> ↠ Two contrary reasons. We must start with those. Otherwise, we understand nothing and everything is heresy. And even at the conclusion of each truth, we must add that we're bearing in mind the opposed truth. (*Pensées* 493, *OC* 2/757–58)[31]

This excerpt provides a more abstract and generalizable statement of the dialectical stance and its corresponding method. Take a position—Pascal here writes *raison, deux raisons contraires*, but the point can be extended to claims—and then take another that opposes it—whether in the strict sense of contradiction, or in the more relaxed one of contrariness or incompatibility Pascal doesn't here specify. That's the proper beginning for one crouched at the dialectical starting block, stylistic and conceptual muscles tensed. Not to begin there, with that attitude, is to be heretical (*tout est hérétique*) and therefore to get nothing right in the sphere of theology, which is what Pascal here writes about. This isn't to

31. Compare *Sacy* (*OC* 2/96).

say that no resolution of the assertion-and-denial of each of the two contrary reasons is possible (there'll be an instance of such a resolution in a moment); but it is to say that it's something close to a rule of thought to keep in mind the contrary (and perhaps also the contradictory) of any truth in theology you wish to assert. This rule of thought is also something approaching a rule of writing for Pascal. In composing prose about almost anything, he commonly begins by constructing and contradicting an affirmation about the topic; constructing and contradicting a contrary (and sometimes a contradictory) affirmation about the same matter; and then resolving the resulting difficulty by indicating what its presence and unavoidability tells us, or where its unavoidability places us. This feature of Pascal's writing is, more than any other except possibly the presence of memorable aphorisms in it, what gives it its drama and intensity.

Another instance:

> ≫ Were God to continually show himself to us there'd be no merit in believing. If God never showed himself there'd be little faith. So, God ordinarily hides himself and shows himself rarely, to those he wants to place in his service. This strange secrecy into which God has retired, impenetrable to our gaze, is a great lesson to draw us into solitude, far from human eyes. (Letter of 1656 to Charlotte de Roannez, *OC* 2/30)

This is from a letter of advice, and is entirely typical of the dialectical stance at work. The dilemma: either the LORD self-reveals all the time, or never. These, obviously, are contraries rather than contradictories: they can't both be true, but they can both be false: the LORD might self-reveal sometimes, which is what Pascal affirms—the LORD self-reveals *rarement*, and then only to some. Why not simply state the final position? Because when the final position is arrived at dialectically, by way of the statement and denial of the two opposed positions whose rejection it resolves, the meaning and importance of the final position is shown with a depth and under an aspect otherwise unavailable. The aspect emphasized in this excerpt is strangeness: *Cet étrange secret* ... It's not only that the LORD's self-revelation is exceptional; it's also that it isn't what you'd expect, and that it's puzzling. The alternatives of the dilemma aren't strange in this way. They're clear and explicable and predictable. Denying them shows something unclear, inexplicable, and unpredictable—namely, the LORD's hiddenness, a fundamental theme for Pascal. Affirming dialectically, rather than directly, that the LORD is ordinarily self-occluded, occluded, that is, by (something like) intent and decision and therefore *impénétrable à la vue des hommes*, has an additional benefit. It's a *grande leçon* that might and ought to draw us *à la solitude, loin de la vue des hommes*. This suggests not only, and not even principally, that we should live like hermits, as the solitaries of Port-Royal in part did; it suggests also, and more fundamentally, that reliance upon reasoning to show us the LORD is to be retreated from, too. Deploying the dialectic for theology, whether in pastoral or speculative mode, provides a rhetoric—an attitude toward writing, here, but also toward reasoning—that draws its readers toward what it shows, which is writing's inadequacies for theological purposes. Dialectical devices, which are everywhere in Pascal,[32] are most ful-

---

32. Other instances of dialectical style in Pascal include: the sequence of remarks in *Pensées* 110–22, bundled together within *Pensées* by Pascal under the heading *Contrariétés* (*OC* 2/576–82)—an especially well-developed instance is in *Pensées* 122 (*OC* 2/579–82), on the tension between skepticism and dogmatism; compare the claim that we're given gifts we can't use, in a letter of April 1648 to his sister Gilberte (*OC* 2/8), as well as *Maladies* 7 (*OC* 2/187–88); the treatment of the tension between the delights of the flesh and those of the spirit in *Grace* 7 (*OC* 2/257–58); the analysis of the tension between human greatness and human misery in *Pensées* 113 (*OC* 2/577)—and frequently elsewhere in *Pensées;* the importance of combining apparent contradictions in writing about Christianity in *Pensées* 624 (*OC* 2/794–95); and so on. I've found helpful the comments on Pascalian dialectic in Mesnard, *Pascal*, 39–40; and by Le Guern at *OC* 2/1302–3. Michel Houellebecq, a deeply and self-consciously Pascalian writer, sometimes imagines how Pascal would use dialectic now; see, for an illuminating instance, Houellebecq, *Serotonin*, trans. Shaun Whiteside (New York: Farrar, Straus and Giroux, 2019), 237.

ly evident and thoroughly worked through in *Grace*, because it is there that a systematic-axiomatic style is most inadequate to its task.

A final instance of the dialectic, so well turned that it requires no comment:

> ⇾ We're so necessarily crazy that not to be crazy would be another crazily twisted kind of craziness. (*Pensées* 391, *OC* 2/674)

But perhaps this doesn't quite qualify as natural style: Pascal strikes me here as an *auteur*.

2.5 Aphorism and Irony

And then there's the aphoristic, overlapping with the dialectical in purpose and effect. If an aphorism is a brief, pithy, memorable, suggestive sentence or sentence fragment, ideally not longer than a haiku or an old-style twitter message, then Pascal's work is full of them.[33] Here are some: "True Christianity consists in submission and the use of reason";[34] "I'm not content with what's probable, I tell you; I'm after what's certain";[35] "We're great to the extent that we know ourselves to be miserable";[36] "The Christian life is nothing other than a holy desire";[37] "No dogmatism can overcome our incapacity for proof. No skepticism can overcome our idea of

---

33. On the significance of the aphoristic in Pascal, see Lucien Goldmann, *Le Dieu caché: Étude sur la vision tragique dans les "Pensées" de Pascal et dans le théâtre de Racine* (Paris: Gallimard, 1955), passim; Jean Mesnard, *La culture du XVIIe siècle: enquêtes et syntheses* (Paris: Presses Universitaires de France, 1992), 363–70; Hui, *Aphorism*, ch. 5. Mesnard appears to me to have the better of his argument with Goldmann about the aphoristic in *Pensées*. Most who write about this topic focus, naturally enough, upon *Pensées*; but it's important to see that aphorisms are to be found in most of Pascal's works, and therefore that arguments about the peculiar composition- and editing-history of *Pensées* can't resolve questions about aphorisms as a matter of rhetorical attitude in Pascal's entire body of work.

34. *Pensées* 156 (*OC* 2/601).
35. *Provincials* 5 (*OC* 1/631).
36. *Pensées* 105 (*OC* 2/574).
37. *Grace* 1 (*OC* 2/219).

truth";[38] "Let's conceive that we infinitely surpass ourselves and that we're inconceivable to ourselves without faith's help";[39] "All our unhappiness comes from one thing: that we don't know how to stay quietly in our rooms";[40] "I expect no grace except from your mercy";[41] "There's no shame except in having none";[42] "What are we in nature? Nothing compared to infinity, everything compared to nothing, a midpoint between nothing and everything, infinitely far from comprehending the extremes."[43]

It's not easy to assess the significance of the aphorism for Pascal, however. One cause of that difficulty is that a large portion of his work remained not only unpublished but unfinished at the time of his death, and that the incidence of aphorisms in that portion is higher than in the polished-and-published portion. This is especially true of *Pensées*, in which there are very many sentences and sentence fragments that look like aphorisms but are probably best thought of as notes to himself that likely wouldn't have survived in the form we now have them had he completed and polished the broadly apologetical work to which the fragments belong. Some of these fragments, for example the two-word "zeal, light,"[44] are so brief, so compressed, that it seems to me more natural to think of them as Pascal's mnemonic notes intended to identify themes that he would have expanded in a more developed version of the work. They might or might not have survived in aphoristic form had the work been developed. But whatever the truth about that difficulty, there's no doubt that Pascal's work as we have it contains a high incidence of aphorisms.

This fits well with the dialectical features of his work. Some of

38. *Pensées* 385 (*OC* 2/673).
39. *Pensées* 122 (*OC* 2/581).
40. *Pensées* 126 (*OC* 2/583).
41. *Maladies* 6 (*OC* 2/187).
42. *Pensées* 398 (*OC* 2/686).
43. *Pensées* 185 (*OC* 2/610).
44. *Pensées* 510 (*OC* 2/764).

the aphorisms themselves have dialectical-paradoxical form, saying things like *we are p and not-p*, or, *we can get p only by seeing that we can't get p.* The more closely they approach that form, the more they participate in the feature of Pascal's dialectical prose just discussed: they show, pithily, a feature of language (and of writing, therefore), which is that for some purposes—in some orders, he would more likely say—the best that language can do is point beyond itself by bringing readers to a halt. Halted by "Let's conceive that we infinitely surpass ourselves and that we're inconceivable to ourselves without faith's help"[45]—and it isn't possible to engage the sentence without halting—readers may see that they're being strenuously manipulated. They're being asked to form a concept (*concevons donc…*) whose principal content, which is themselves, is inconceivable; the conceptual content of what they're moved to, in so far as the aphorism has any, is their own self-transcendence (*l'homme passe infiniment l'homme*), which, in turn, is what their inconceivability consists in. Pascal doesn't leave it there, though. With the puzzlement of the first part of the aphorism in mind, readers arrive at its last words, which are *sans le secours de la foi* / without the help of faith. The aphorism prescribes the use of reason to show reason's limits, and then opens readers' horizons by indicating where reason's lacks can be met: by grace, that is (assuming that faith comes only by grace, which is clear enough elsewhere in Pascal). This kind of aphorism, and there are many of them in Pascal, is an ice-pick into the soft tissue of reason's pretensions, and, then, a suture to the bleeding head-wound.

Writing in this style, with this rhetorical attitude, has as its principal opposite number an axiomatic-deductive style such as is found to some degree in Descartes, and supremely in Spinoza's *Ethica* (I mention these two because they're Pascal's approximate contemporaries: Pascal had read—and met—Descartes, but so far

45. *Pensées* 122 (*OC* 2/581).

as I can tell is innocent of textual or personal acquaintance with Spinoza). That style aims at transparency and necessity and ease of flow and completeness: the propositions of the system flow by evident entailment from its axioms, which are themselves transparent to reason's gaze or in some other way basic; and the system that's arrived at is complete in its sphere, or at least aspires to be. Pascal allows this style in its place, as we've seen—that place being, ideal-typically, the mathematical. But in theology, and in the theological parts of anthropology (the nontheological parts, for Pascal, yield only puzzlement and pain),[46] the axiomatic-systematic has no place, while the dialectical aphorism has a significant one. Here too, then, a Pascalian rhetorical attitude is linked with, or is, perhaps better, an aspect of his understanding of the LORD and of our relation to the LORD. The tensions evident on the surface of the dialectical aphorism are resolved not by saying what the truth is, but by turning the reader's gaze toward the place where the truth lies.

But not all Pascal's aphorisms are dialectical in this way. Not all of them have the kind of surface tension I've just discussed. Some are simply surprising, such as: "All our unhappiness comes from one thing: that we don't know how to stay quietly in a room."[47] Readers are, as with the dialectical aphorisms, brought to a halt and pushed into questioning mode. How can that be? What is it about knowing how to stay put that runs counter to unhappiness? What is it to *demeurer en repos dans une chambre*, and what is it to do the other thing? What has doing the other thing—going out into the world?—to do with unhappiness? And, for most readers, probably, the first response to the aphorism is likely not only that it can't possibly be right, but also that it's sufficiently far from being right that it doesn't seem like a mistake so much as an utterance

46. On these themes, see chapter 4, §§4.1–4.2, below.
47. *Pensées* 126 (*OC* 2/583).

from another world. If it were a mistake in, let's say, the theoretical understanding of unhappiness, one that attributed a little too much of that to bad decisions and not quite enough to malign fate, we'd know where we were. But it doesn't seem like that. Staying or not staying in your room seems, at first blush, to have about as much to do with happiness as brushing your teeth regularly seems to have to do with speaking Japanese. This kind of puzzlement, akin to that produced by a koan, turns readers' thoughts back to happiness: what kind of thing is that, if it can have to do in this way with *demeurer en repos dans une chambre*? And because the answer to that question is far from obvious, indeed, almost completely opaque, a long pause is a likely, and a reasonable, response to the aphorism.[48] Bringing thought to a halting pause of this kind is an effect that the aphorisms of bafflement share with the dialectical ones.

This bringing of thought to a halt in puzzlement—the very opposite of knowing how to go on with some activity; what you get from a good Pascalian dialectical aphorism is that you don't know how to go on with this line of thought, whatever it is—can also be called ironic. That word, though, is one with divergent and conflicted meanings in English. There's a relatively minimalist literary-conceit sense, according to which ironic writing states the opposite of what it means, as when Jonathan Swift makes a modest proposal that, in fact, is neither modest nor a proposal. There's the fairly standard Christian-scholastic sense (of *ironia* if not of irony), rooted in pre-Christian rhetorical theory, according to which irony is a kind of dissimulation, an offense against truth, that is, with special reference to self-denigration; the opposite of

48. I've been writing about this aphorism from *pensée* 126 as though it occurred all alone. In fact, in *Pensées* as we have it, it doesn't: many of the questions I've suggested as prompted by the aphorism are discursively taken up by Pascal in the rest of the *pensée*, which is a long one, four pages (*OC* 2/583–87) in Le Guern's edition, on the topic of *divertissement*, and is among the relatively highly polished parts of the *Pensées*. For more on diversion, see chapter 4, §4.2, below.

irony in this sense is boasting. And then there's a more developed theoretical sense of irony and the ironic, according to which ironic experience is related to our practical identities by interrupting them, and ironical discourse is aimed at producing just such an interruption.[49] An ironical interruption of, for instance, the practical identity being-a-Christian or being-an-American, takes the form: as things are, I have no idea how to go on with this.

For Catholic (and some other) Christians, the clearest case of irony in this sense is to hand in the liturgy of the Mass. Consider, to take just one example, the *non sum dignus* said after the climax of the consecration of the elements. This is an ironic moment. Something of great importance has just happened, and I, its participant, am now about to be incorporated into it. But I am constitutively and definitionally incapable of deploying concepts adequate to what has just happened; and, still more important, I am constitutively and definitionally incapable of receiving the gift that is being given in the events now in train. That's just what the *non sum dignus* says: saying it disrupts, beyond comprehension or repair, the form of activity to which it belongs and leaves me on my knees with no idea how to go on.[50] And this moment is the heart of the Christian life here below: the identification of an aspiration that can neither be adequately understood nor acted upon in such a way as to realize it in any other way than by confessing those states of affairs.

Ironic experience, produced by ironic prose, whether dialectical or aphoristical, is both uncanny (we don't know what to make of it) and erotic (it calls us, with longing, to something whose

49. Lear's *Irony* argues, powerfully and lucidly, this understanding of irony, and presents ironic experience as an essential constituent of human flourishing. I draw gratefully upon it here and in what immediately follows. See Jonathan Lear, *A Case for Irony* (Cambridge, Mass.: Harvard University Press, 2014).

50. These formulations are lineally related to those in Pickstock's *After Writing*, on the stammer as intrinsic to the liturgy. See Catherine Pickstock, *After Writing: On the Liturgical Consummation of Philosophy* (Oxford: Blackwell, 1998).

shape we cannot see—*Sehnsucht* seems a better word than any English I can think of for this unrealizable longing, but *Fernweh* is also suggestive); and it breaks apart whichever practical identity it pertains to, showing the repertoire of that identity to be essentially inadequate to its own aspirations. That truth is fundamental to Pascal's understanding of human existence in both its pagan and Christian forms (the Jewish form is a special case), and irony, in the sense distinguished, is a good, perhaps the best, way to show it. Thought's irony-produced pause reflects and is articulated with the opacity and inadequacy of the repertoires of our most deep-going practical identities.

*

Pascal advocates *style naturel* or plain style, and largely follows his own recommendation. This does have the effect, as he claims, of making the act of reading him seem like being addressed directly by someone thinking about something, and wanting to have you think about it too. He shows his work, not just his conclusions, and he does so, often, in a more-or-less conversational style. This is, to me, engaging, though his distinction between persons and authors, in favor of the former and against the latter, is overdrawn. He is no less an author, according to his own understanding of that term, than those whose style he doesn't like. He performs as much as they do. It's just that his performance is in a different register. When I read him, though it's true that I find myself addressed by him, directly, and though it's true that I am invigorated by that address and responsive to it, I would rather think of that address and my response to it as a property of the words on the page rather than one of the man who composed them. Pascal, too often, tends in the other direction.

He also advocates and practices, again more or less, a dialectical attitude toward writing, in which differences are accentuated for the purpose of clarifying them, and for the purpose of instantiating in prose a position about the limitations of thought. All this

I applaud without reservation. Thought about anything proceeds better if differences are accentuated than it does if they're smoothed over. The bones of a position are made clear by dialectics, and the skull beneath the skin is, for the purposes of thought, much preferable to the cosmeticized integument. There are dangers in dialectic, too, the most prominent among which is the reduction of the opposed positions to caricatures of any actually held. Pascal sometimes does this. But the game is worth the candle. If, for instance, you want to see into the structure of Christian-theological debates about grace, it's hard to imagine anything better to read than Pascal's *Grace* or *Provincials*. That is true whether or not the positions he takes are right. Dialectical prose, when well done, clarifies thought even when the conclusions of the one who offers it are erroneous.

There are, too, the delights of clarity and of wit. Pascal's prose coruscates sometimes, and is, even when it doesn't, almost always transparently clear. Reading prose such as that, whether in French or in a translation, provides rare pleasures, and I'm not alone in thinking so. I've taught Pascal, usually *Pensées* and *Provincials*, to anglophone undergraduates and graduate students, perhaps a dozen times in the last several decades, in courses on Christian thought and the like; and it's ordinarily the case that those whose eyes have glazed over and whose shoulders have sagged when faced with the heavy earth-moving machinery of the scholastics sit up straighter and start to pay attention when we come to Pascal. That's in part because of these features of his prose.

Pascal, like Augustine in this, is very aware of his capacities as a writer, and as a thinker, and is not ashamed to let you know of them. He thinks himself superior to his opponents in wit, in argument, in rhetoric, and in orthodoxy, and he says so. It's a question of taste whether this is attractive. I find it so. When Pascal, in his discussion of the significance of his experiments about atmospheric pressure and the vacuum, lets you know that he's confident that he can defeat Aristotle and all his followers,[51] or when he makes it abundantly clear again and again in the *Provincials* that his opponents are not only wrong but fools, whereas he, by contrast, is neither, you may be delighted or repelled, but you'll almost certainly respond to distinctiveness.

And Pascal understands his literary work to have attempted and achieved something new. On this he is no less self-regarding than on those other matters, and, to me, no less delightful (I think also accurate):

> ≫ No one should say that I've said nothing new. The arrangement of material is new. When we play tennis, everyone does it with the same ball, but some do it better. I'd like it as much to be told that I've used old words. As if the same thoughts didn't make a different discourse by being arranged differently, just as the same words make different thoughts by their different arrangement. (*Pensées* 590, *OC* 2/786)

51. As he does in *Vacuum* (*OC* 1/531).

3

ORDER

"Order" (*ordre*), as Pascal uses it, is a taxonomic term. It's used to indicate the parts of some whole as they're related (ordered) one to another.[1] The whole may be a text, in which case its parts are topic-centered sections (sentences, paragraphs, chapters), ordered to one another sequentially and logically. Or, the whole may be the cosmos, everything there is, in which case its parts are the kinds of things taken conjointly to constitute it (as, for example, the material and the immaterial; or the living and the nonliving; or the human and the nonhuman; or the temporal and the nontemporal; and so on), and their order is the relation, often, though not necessarily, hierarchical, these parts ("orders") bear one to another. Or, the whole may be the set of all living creatures, in which case its parts are their kinds, plants, mammals, reptiles, and so on, and their order, the relations those parts bear to one another—in standard-issue Linnaean taxonomy, "order" is a sortal that collects

---

1. On order and orders in Pascal, I've benefited from: Descotes, *Argumentation*, 47–103; and Roland Meynet, "'Les trois ordres' de Pascal selon la rhétorique biblique," *Gregorianum* 94, no. 1 (2013): 79–96.

living creatures of a particular kind together.[2] Or, the whole may be a liturgical act, as in the order of the Mass, where "order" indicates the sequence of the particular acts that together make up the entire celebration. Or, the whole may be human social life, in which case the parts may be political, religious, familial, economic, and so on, with some specification as to their relation one to another. The idea of order, in these and other senses, does a good deal of work for Pascal.

3.1 Intellectual and Political Order

In a letter of June 1652 to Christine, queen of Sweden,[3] Pascal wrote:

> ≫ What's really led me to this [offering of the calculating machine to you] is the joining in your sacred person of two things that seem to me equally to be admired and respected, namely sovereign authority and solid knowledge. I have a particular veneration for those raised to the highest degree, whether of power or understanding. The latter, if I'm not deceived, just as well as the former, may be considered sovereigns. The same degrees are found among intellectuals as among social classes; the power of monarchs over their subjects is, it seems to me, only an image of the power of minds over those minds inferior to them, over which they exercise the right of persuasion, which is, for them, what the right to command is in political government. This second empire even seems to me of a higher order, as minds are of a higher order than bodies, and similarly more equitable, because it can be distributed and preserved only by merit, while

2. A Linnaean order is a classification between a family and a class—as in the *ordo cetaceae*, which belongs to the family of mammals and has whales, dolphins, and porpoises as its principal classes. Mammals in turn, moving upward in the classification system, belong to the phylum of *chordata*, the kingdom of *animalia*, and the domain of *archaea*. That's according to the Linnean system as modified in the twentieth and twenty-first centuries. In its first form, the Linnean system postdates Pascal by more than a century; he would have liked it.

3. Christine (1626–1689) was queen of Sweden from 1632 to 1654.

the other can be so by birth or chance. (Letter of 1652 to Christine of Sweden, *OC* 1/350)[4]

Pascal designed and oversaw the manufacture of a mechanical calculating machine, the pascaline, at the beginning of the 1650s (some of these machines survive), and the ostensible purpose of this letter was to dedicate and offer it to Christine. Of interest in this passage is the clear distinction he makes between two orders: that of mind (*esprit*), to which belongs *science solide* and whose proper power or right (*droit*) is persuasion; and that of *autorité souveraine*, to which belongs *gouvernement politique* and whose *droit* is command.

Each of these has degrees, which is to say an internal hierarchical order. Those who have the most knowledge and concomitant capacity to persuade are at the top of the hierarchy of mind, which is to say the intellectual order; and those who have the most authority in the political sphere (monarchs, that is) and concomitant capacity to command are at the top of the hierarchy of authority, which is to say the political order. Christine, Pascal writes, with some hyperbole, probably (though Christine did, it seems, have scientific and mathematical interests), is sovereign in both spheres (she's a mathematician-queen), and that's why he's offering the calculating machine to her.

Further, the two orders are related one to another hierarchically, as well as having an internal hierarchical order: the intellectual order ranks higher because it's entered and structured *par la mérite* only (you can rule in mathematics only by being a good mathematician), while the political order is entered by birth or hazard (you can become a monarch by being born to one, or by political hazard). Pascal doesn't here say why this difference makes the intellectual order superior to the political one, but it's clear from

4. A similar distinction between the political and the intellectual order is in play throughout *Discourses* (*OC* 2/194–99).

what he writes about order elsewhere that it's because the intellectual order's internal hierarchy is given by the activity proper to it: those better at doing mathematics are ranked above those worse; while the activity proper to the political sphere doesn't produce the internal hierarchy of that order: those best at ruling aren't necessarily those born to it or established in it by chance.

These orders are kinds of human activity, involving thinking and ruling respectively. The only kind of overlap possible between the mathematical order and the political is that particular persons may occupy them both. All of us, in one way or another, find a place in the political order,though not many as monarchs; few of us are mathematicians at all, which means that the number of those who have functions and a place in both orders is just the same as the number of those who have functions and a place in the mathematical order. However, the activities proper to each sphere don't overlap at all: thinking and having solid (mathematical) knowledge and being able to persuade others by argument of mathematical truths has no bearing of any kind on the exercise of political power.[5] The criteria for excellence in the one have no overlap with the criteria for excellence in the other; being good at the one provides no capacity in the other; and rank in the one provides no rank in the other.

It's characteristic of Pascal to draw the lines that separate the orders one from another sharply and brightly in this way: what belongs to one order, he typically writes, doesn't and can't belong to another. In this, his understanding of order and orders is like that evident in Linnaean taxonomy: if you're a member of the animal kingdom, then you aren't and can't be, by definition, a member of the kingdom of plants. Pascal would say the same about, for instance, being a pagan, being a Christian, and being a Jew: in so far as these are properly thought of as orders—in this case of hu-

5. See the discussion of political power in chapter 6, §6.1, below.

man being—then membership is exclusive. There are no Christian pagans or pagan Jews or Jewish Christians.[6] When an order is one of human activity, as in the case under discussion, exclusivity can't work in quite the same way, for it may be that one human person can, at different times, be engaged in each form of activity. But exclusivity remains in that what's proper to one order is insulated from and has nothing to do with what belongs to the other.

3.2 Orders of Being and Orders of Investigation

It's an ordinary intuition that different kinds of topic require different kinds of investigation. If, for example, you'd like to know whether Goldbach's Conjecture (that every even number greater than two can be expressed as the sum of two primes) is true, you won't get far by consulting Hansard. If you want to develop some understanding of how antebellum Christians in the American South used Scripture to justify chattel slavery, considering entailment relations among sets of abstract objects won't help. And if you want to find out whether a vacuum ever occurs, offering exegesis of Aristotle and his commentators isn't the best method. That last is a Pascalian example:

> ➤ Let all the disciples of Aristotle gather everything that's strongest in the writings of their master and his commentators to account for these things [that is, the findings of Pascal's experiments on liquids and atmospheric pressure] by the vacuum-horror, if they can; if not, let them acknowledge that experiments are the true masters it's necessary to follow in physics; that the experiment done in the mountains has overturned the opinion universally held in the world that nature abhors a vacuum, and has opened up this knowledge that can never perish; that nature has no vacuum-horror; that she does nothing to escape it; and that the weight of the mass of the air is the true

6. There are some difficulties here. See chapter 7, below, on the Jews.

cause of all the effects that have until now been attributed to that imaginary cause. (*Vacuum, OC* 1/531)

The backdrop here is two sequences of experiments designed and overseen by Pascal. The first sequence, undertaken at Rouen in 1647,[7] showed that the behaviour of liquids and air placed under pressure by a piston in a glass tube is best interpreted by postulating the existence of a vacuum within the bounded space of the tube. The second sequence, performed in 1648 at or near Clermont, showed the variance in and effects of atmospheric pressure (what Pascal calls *la masse de l'air*) at different elevations.[8] Pascal takes the two sets of experiments to show, first, that atmospheric pressure varies according to elevation above sea level, and that it alone determines the height to which a liquid will rise in a vertically placed liquid-filled tube, one end of which is sealed permanently, the other of which is sealed temporarily and placed in a reservoir of liquid, after which the temporary seal is removed; and, second, that this and associated behaviors of liquids make the conclusion that it's possible to establish a vacuum in a sealed tube massively more plausible than its denial. This second conclusion was the controversial one. The majority opinion at the time was that a vacuum is in principle impossible: anywhere that is anywhere, they thought, has something there, no matter how attenuated. Nature, they thought, exhibits a *horror vacui*, and this was mostly taken to be a truth established by irrefragable authority, Aristotle's and

7. This sequence is recounted in summary form in *Expériences nouvelles touchant la vide/New Experiments Concerning the Vacuum* (*OC* 1/355–65), and in fuller form in *Traité de l'equilibre des liqueurs/Treatise on the Equilibrium of Liquids* (*OC* 1/468–88). Its implications are drawn out in *Preface sur le traité du vide/Preface to the Treatise on the Vacuum* (*OC* 1/452–58), and in the polemical correspondence prompted by these texts, mostly with Étienne Noël (*OC* 1/373–425).

8. This sequence is recounted in summary form in *Récit de la grande expérience de l'equilibre des liqueurs/Account of the Great Experiment on the Equilibrium of Liquids* (*OC* 1/426–37), and more fully in *Traité de la pesanteur de la masse de l'air/Treatise on the Weight of the Mass of the Air* (*OC* 1/489–524).

others', and therefore not capable of refutation by experimental evidence.

Pascal's experimental findings on these matters have their own interest, but of greater concern to me here is the vigor with which he defends the view that there's an appropriate way to investigate how liquids behave under pressure and at different elevations. Those questions have as their object the behavior of material objects extended in timespace. They move, then, within the physical order. Thinking about matters belonging to that order requires attention exactly to the objects in question. One mode of such attention is the experimental: if it's observed that a liquid behaves differently at different elevations, and the question is why that's so, rival answers to that question (vacuum-horror; changes in atmospheric pressure) can be formulated and, ideally, tested. What would you expect liquids to do if one or the other answer is correct, and does their behavior, when tested, support or refute any of the possible answers?

Alternatively: you might think that it's possible to determine whether a vacuum ever occurs by consulting and interpreting Aristotle. Pascal ridicules this. The order of being to which liquids and vacuums belong isn't one appropriately investigated by that method; and in the case at hand, it leads, when it's used, to dramatically false conclusions. Now, Aristotle-exegesis might be a good way of answering the question about the vacuum and the behavior of liquids: if we had independent and reliable reason for thinking that everything Aristotle and his commentators wrote about those matters is necessarily true, then it would be. But, Pascal implies though doesn't quite say, we have no such reason, and so we'd better use the method of investigation appropriate to the question at hand, which is the experimental-hypothetical.[9]

9. For more on that method of investigation, contrasted with appeals to authoritative texts, see *Vacuum* (*OC* 1/452–53, 455); *Sacy* (*OC* 2/96).

The generalizable point is this: there are orders of being and orders of investigation. You'd do well to conform the latter to the former. Using a mode of investigation inappropriate to what you're thinking about will lead to confusion, and usually to wrong answers.

Here's another instance from Pascal of emphasis on the importance of getting your mode of investigation right if you're rightly to think about, and answer, some question:

> ≫ Some bishops, who have resolved to dispossess holders of benefices, and who have no other pretext than this point of fact [that is, about Jansenius], have concluded in their circular letter of March 17 last, "that those who will refuse to subscribe to the fact are to be treated as if they'd refused to subscribe to the doctrine." That, however, is just fine talk—they can't confuse, by all their power, things that are by nature separate. A simple point of fact remains always a simple point of fact, and such a thing can never be ground for depriving people of their benefices. (*Advocate*, OC 1/830)

This comes from a letter in the form of a legal argument purporting to be written by a parliamentary lawyer to one of his friends, and likely composed by Pascal.[10] The occasion for the letter is a decision taken by the Assembly of the French Clergy in 1657 to impose signature of a formulary of submission to Alexander VII's bull *Ad sanctam* of 1656 upon all priests, religious, and teachers of theology in France.[11] That bull had said, among other things, that the five propositions condemned conjointly as heretical (and,

10. The text is *Advocate* (*OC* 1/819–32). Some editors have doubted that Pascal composed this, and others have taken it to be a collaboration between Pascal and Antoine le Maistre. Le Guern provides a thorough discussion of the difficulties (*OC* 1/1285–89), and gives reasons for thinking the text to be mostly or entirely by Pascal. *Pensées* 737 (*OC* 2/869–70) can reasonably be read as a draft of some of the material in *Advocate*.

11. This means that Pascal himself wasn't faced with the decision to sign, though many of his close friends and relatives, including his younger sister Jacqueline, a religious at Port-Royal, were.

variously, said to be rash, false, impious, blasphemous, and scandalous) by Innocent X in an earlier bull, *Cum occasione* of 1653, were drawn (*excerptas*) from Jansenius's book *Augustinus*, and are condemned *in sensu ab eodem Cornelio Iansenio intento*—in just the same sense as that intended by Jansenius.[12] *Ad sanctam* responds in part to the Sorbonne's expulsion of Antoine Arnauld, a friend and collaborator of Pascal's, earlier in 1656. That expulsion, in turn, responds to Arnauld's defense of the view that the five propositions of *Cum occasione*, though justly condemned, do not represent Jansenius's thought, and are not to be found in his *Augustinus*—which is a theme of central importance to Pascal's *Provincials*, and is evident also here, in *Advocate*.

The *point de fait* mentioned in *Advocate*'s quotation from the French bishops' letter is what those bishops, following *Ad sanctam*, take to be the explicit (and perhaps verbatim) presence in Jansenius's *Augustinus* of the five propositions condemned in *Cum occasione*. The *droit* mentioned is the substance of the five condemned propositions. *Ad sanctam* had brought the two very close by saying that the condemned propositions are not only excerpted from Jansenius's book, but are condemned in exactly the sense he meant them. And so the French bishops say that refusing to acknowledge the question of fact entails refusing to acknowledge the matter of doctrine.

These may seem arcane matters, and to most readers now, they are. But for Pascal, the distinction between the question of fact about what Jansenius wrote in the *Augustinus* (and perhaps also about what Jansenius meant by what he wrote), and the question of doctrine about grace (which was, largely, the topic of the propositions condemned in *Cum occasione* and *Ad sanctam*) was a topic of major concern from 1653, when *Cum occasione* was promulgat-

12. For partial texts of *Cum occasione* and *Ad sanctam*, see Denzinger, *Enchiridion symbolorum*, 2001–7, 2010–12.

ed, almost until his death in 1662.[13] That concern was partly directed at an explicitly ecclesiological question: What is the scope of the Church's teaching authority? That I leave aside here.[14] But his discussion of it was also motivated by, and articulated with, his understanding of order, and that's the aspect of relevance here.

The question about what Jansenius wrote belongs, in Pascal's view, in part to the historical order, since it's about something that happened in the past (Jansenius's composition of a literary work), and in part to the order of spatio-temporally extended objects, since it's about the properties of one of those (the printed book in question). If the proper mode of investigating an object is given by the nature of that object—if, to put the matter in terms of orders, the order of being of the object ought to be rightly related to the order of investigation of that object—then the right way to investigate Jansenius's book is by reading it, or otherwise using one's senses to determine its properties. If the question is whether some words—those of the condemned propositions—are found verbatim (same words, same order, no intervening material) in that book, the answer can be arrived at by taking a look.[15]

In *Advocate*, as well as in *Provincials*, Pascal approaches the conclusion that the only way to arrive at an answer to that question is by empirical investigation—by taking a look. That stronger view would, in this case, mean that the only ground upon which anyone could have a defensible view about the point of fact would be to have examined the book and discovered either that none of

13. The distinction is important not only in *Advocate*, but also in *Instruction*, *Nevers*, *Paris*, *Sorbonne*, and much of *Provincials*. See, notably, *Provincials* 1 (*OC* 1/589), *Provincials* 17 (*OC* 1/791), and *Provincials* 18 (*OC* 1/797–815). *Advocate* refers explicitly to *Provincials* 18.

14. For more detail, see chapter 6, §6.2, below, on the ecclesial city.

15. The answer is that none of the condemned propositions is found verbatim in the *Augustinus*. The closest approach is to the first proposition, which is approximated at *Augustinus*, *De gratia Christi salvatoris* 3.13 (volume 3, column 334, of the 1640 edition). But even this is not verbatim. Denzinger (n. 1 to no. 2001), is wrong to indicate this as an exact parallel; "cf." should be provided in that note, as with the other notes connecting the *Augustinus* to the condemned propositions.

the condemned propositions are to be found verbatim there, or that at least one is—and in that case, to show where by citing volume and column numbers (the 1640 edition of Jansenius's book is provided with column rather than page and line numbers). If that stronger view were generalized, the position with respect to orders of being and orders of investigation and knowing would be: for each order of being there is an appropriate order of investigation, and adherence to the norms of that order of investigation is the only means by which knowledge about what belongs to that order of being can properly be had. There are difficulties with that strong view, to which I'll return—and it's not clear that Pascal consistently adheres to it in any case.

The excerpt quoted has other interesting features. One is the strong rhetoric of difference: empirical questions, such as that about Jansenius's book, and doctrinal questions, such as those about grace, have to do with *choses qui sont séparées par leur nature* (things distinct in nature): no overlap and no similarity in their kinds, and therefore (perhaps) also none in the means by which knowledge about them may be had. Separate magisteria.[16] Another is the legal conclusion: errors about matters whose truth can be determined by straightforward empirical investigation can never be ground for drastic ecclesial discipline such as the removal of a benefice, which is to say a clerical living. That legal interest is explicable by the genre and purpose of the letter. In it, Pascal poses as a lawyer, deploying the style and purpose of legal documents, and showing as he does so a considerable literary talent for ventriloquism.[17]

16. A strong statement along these lines is at *Sorbonne* 6 (*OC* 1/958–59).

17. That's assuming, of course, that he is the principal or only author of the letter. As to ventriloquism: it would be interesting to compare, as literary objects, *Advocate* with *Sorbonne*, the former being legal and the latter philosophico-theological. Pascal appears equally accomplished, stylistically, in both genres, and it's probably right to say that neither is his first language. His legal and his theological learning are both second hand, and that fact, perhaps, is consistent with his view, discussed above in chapter 2, on style, that he is, or aspires to be,

Pascal's discussion of the case of the magisterium and Jansenius's book does provide a very clear instance of how the division
of the world into orders works for him. In this case, as often, it
works polemically and heuristically: Pascal discovers a family of
broadly epistemological views that he's sure is mistaken. Instances
of this family of views are: you can determine what's true about the
vacuum by reading Aristotle; you can know what's in Jansenius's
book by attending to what authoritative magisterial texts say about
that matter; being a monarch provides privileged access to mathematical truths. Then, to throw into sharp relief what's wrong with
these instances, he uses the language of orders: the mistake lies in
using methods proper to the investigation of what belongs to one
order of being to investigate things that in fact belong to another
order. In this usage, "order" is a polemical device, and is so used.

3.3 Three Orders: Body, Mind, Love

There is also, in Pascal, a use of *ordre* that approaches, though
never quite arrives at, the systematic. Consider this:

> ≫ The infinite distance between bodies and minds figures the in-
> finitely more infinite distance between minds and love—for love
> is supernatural. All the radiance of greatness is lacklustre for those
> doing intellectual work. The greatness of intellectuals is unseen by
> kings, by the rich, by captains—by all those whose greatness belongs
> to the flesh. Wisdom's greatness, which is nothing if not from God,
> is unseen both by the fleshly and by intellectuals. These are three
> orders different in kind. Great thinkers have their empire, their ra-
> diance, their greatness, their victory, and their lustre,[18] and have no
> need of fleshly greatness, with which they have no rapport. They're
> seen by the mind, not by the eyes. That suffices. Saints have their

---

among *les gens universels* who can write in and make reasonable judgments about any and
every genre.

18. Surely, Pascal, *trop de trois mots hardis*—see *Pensées* 543 (*OC* 2/774–75); and chapter
2 above, on style.

empire, their radiance, their victory, their lustre, and have need neither of fleshly nor of intellectual greatness, with which they have no
rapport because those things neither add nor subtract. They're seen
by God and the angels, and not by bodies or by curious minds. God
suffices them. (*Pensées* 290, *OC* 2/648–49)[19]

There's a threefold division of orders here. In ascending order: the
physical order (Pascal uses *corps*, body, and *chair*, flesh, for this,
indifferently); the intellectual order (the essential term of art here
is *esprit*, mind; there's also *génie*, which has the same roots as "genius," but which I render here as "great thinker"); and the order of
love (*charité*, that is, in Pascal's terms, to which is annexed *sagesse*,
"wisdom"). These orders are *différents de genre*, and saying so makes
this division a clear case of Pascal's refusal to countenance border
crossing with respect to orders: the activities and persons proper to
each order have nothing to do with, are fully insulated from, those
in the other orders. As with Christine, the mathematician-queen,
this isn't to say that a single person can belong to only one of the
orders. It's rather to say that in so far as you're an exemplar of and
active in one, just so far you can't also be an exemplar of and active
in another. There is no border-crossing *rapport* to connect those
active in one order with those active in another; and what those
resident in one order do is invisible to those resident in the other
orders. That's because the organs of vision capable of seeing them
(eyes for those in the physical order, minds for those in the intellectual, and only the LORD and the angels—the archetypes of
wisdom-love—in the order of love) aren't to be found in the other
orders.

   Residents of the physical order, among whom Pascal mentions
kings, the rich, and (military) captains, deploy material resources
to bring about material effects. The rich get and spend; kings rule,
moving persons and material resources around in order to bring

19. Compare *Pensées* 280 (*OC* 2/646–47), and *Pensées* 725 (*OC* 2/864).

about political effects; and captains plan for and engage in battle, which is entirely a matter of the clash of physical objects.

Residents of the intellectual order think, and communicate the results of their thought to others with the purpose of showing intellectual truths to them, in that way, when they doubt or have opposed convictions, persuading them that the truths they've arrived at are indeed truths. Mathematics provides the ideal type, and no doubt the one that Pascal has most clearly in mind given his own capacities. To solve the mathematical problems of the cycloid,[20] and to write works communicating the solution, is a clear case of what *les grands génies* do, and in order to do it they need interact not at all with the physical order.

Residents of the order of love are, among humans, the saints, and, among nonhumans, the LORD and angels. The excerpt quoted above doesn't say what their characteristic activities are, but elsewhere it's clear that what Jesus-Christ did during the time of his incarnation here below provides the paradigm for Pascal.[21] What the saints do participates in what Jesus-Christ did, and shows, more or less imperfectly, what he showed. And what is that? In brief, it is the glory of self-emptying, the radiance (*éclat*) of humility, the *victoire* of *anéantissement*, of bringing oneself to nothing. All that is, simply, invisible to those who act in the physical order, and those who think in the intellectual one. (It's unclear whether Pascal intends blindness to go in the other direction as well, so that what intellectuals and generals do is invisible to the saints; he doesn't discuss that, I suspect, because it's irrelevant to his purposes.)

One of the yields of this way of ordering the cosmos is that it can easily be deployed to provide humans a special place. We, and only we, Pascal likes to say,[22] can and do occupy all three or-

---

20. As he does in *Cycloid* published under the Dettonville name (*OC* 2/319–524).

21. In the remainder of the *pensée* of which part has just been quoted: *Pensées* 290 (*OC* 2/649–50); and *in extenso* at *Jesus-Christ* (*OC* 2/49–81).

22. More on this, in detail, in chapter 4 below.

ders. We are physical, extended in space, and necessarily devoted, therefore, to doing what can be done by moving things around in the spatial order. We are, or can be, intellectual, sometimes, and perhaps always *in potentia*, devoted to doing what can be done via the movement of thought, as Pascal has done in constructing the ordering now under discussion, and as I am doing in writing about it and you in reading what I've written. And, we have at least the possibility of entering the order of love. When we do this, we do it paradigmatically and most perfectly by becoming Christian and living the Christian life with zeal.[23] Other creatures, by contrast, typically occupy, and can occupy, only one of the three orders. Inanimate creatures clearly have their being only in the physical order, and the same might be true of nonhuman animate creatures other than the human, at least if you think of them that they either contingently lack intellectual capacities, or, because of their natures, necessarily must lack them.[24] Unfallen angels, by contrast, might be taken to exist and work only in the order of love, uniquely so among creatures. This might be true if the activity proper to the intellectual order is sequential thought, ordered to and by linear time; angels, on some angelologies, have no need of that (they see what they see directly and atemporally), and so they act out of love, always and only, needing neither thought nor the movement of material objects to do what they do.[25] It would remain to us, then, to live and move and have our beings in all three orders, and to exhibit the strangeness that must belong to any creature so

23. *Zèle* is an important word for Pascal. It occurs half a dozen times in the *Pensées*, and the attitude to the Christian life it denotes provides one of the through-lines in the *Provincials*: Pascal is there concerned largely to combat understandings and recommendations of the Christian life to which zeal is an irrelevance or an obstacle.

24. I don't take this to be the correct view, but I rather think that Pascal did, or would have if it had been presented to him in this way.

25. There are delicate matters in angelology here. I don't take the view of angels suggested here, and while it is coherent with Pascal's delineation of the three orders, and his use of it to discriminate human creatures from all others, there is no evidence of a developed (or even, really, of an undeveloped) angelology in his *oeuvre*.

constituted. Pascal deploys this strangeness in his depiction of the human condition, and in his apologetical arguments for the superiority of Christianity to any other construal of that condition.

3.4 What Reason Can Do

The three-orders division is also implicated with Pascal's analysis of what reason can do. Since the second of the three orders, the intellectual, is that in which mind works, and since there's no spillover from the activities characteristic of one order into those characteristic of another, it seems that reasoning has place neither in the physical order nor in the order of love. And this is, with only minor modifications and reservations, Pascal's position. Thinking (reasoning) has indeed no place in those orders; it can make nothing happen in them. But it is by thinking that we know that limitation, and so it's obvious enough that the separation of the orders doesn't mean that we can't think about the orders to which thought doesn't belong; it's only that when we do think about them we do it from outside, as it were, as spectators and analysts. Thinking about, and understanding, as far as is possible, how the hummingbird's aerodynamics permit it to hover—a state of affairs in the physical order—doesn't bring about any hovering; thinking about, and understanding, as far as is possible, what it is for one person to give sacrificial love to another—a state of affairs in the order of love—doesn't bring about any loving. But such thought isn't nothing: it can show us something about these phenomena, and can show us also what thinking cannot do. Pascal's analyses and depictions of what thought is and can do are tightly articulated with his understanding of the separateness of the orders; and they often, therefore, are at least as concerned to show what reason cannot do as to show what it can. Pascal is an apologist for and servant of reason, certainly (every mathematician must be); but the characteristic form of his depictions of it is to exalt it by showing its limitations.

How, then, does (and should) reason work when it's directed toward the physical order? Part of the answer to this has already been given in the discussion above of how to arrive at the truth about the behavior of liquids under pressure. Reason works on topics such as that by observing closely how in fact liquids do behave under pressure, then by constructing testable hypotheses to explain such behavior, and then by designing and performing experiments to determine which among these hypotheses is correct, or more likely to be correct than its competitors. If all goes well (Pascal is very clear that often it doesn't), then we may come to understand (Pascal's preferred word for this is *connaître*) something we didn't know before. Again, reason brings nothing about; liquids go on doing what they do; reason looks, analyzes, and (sometimes) concludes.

So far, this depiction of reason at work upon the physical order comports well with standard seventeenth-century optimism, still evident today, about what we can come to know about that order. If we can only get our experiments right, we can, and we eventually will, know all there is to be known about that order of things—so runs the hyper-optimistic version of this way of thinking. But that is not Pascal's view. Even with respect to the physical order, he is a strong advocate of reason's limits. One cause of his skepticism in this matter is his strong sense of the size and complexity of the cosmos in which we find ourselves, and of the unsuitability of our intellectual capacities for comprehending it. Here's one way of putting that skepticism, funded in this case by a depiction of the double infinity, of greatness (*grandeur*) and smallness (*petitesse*), which is evident in all things:[26]

» Those who see these truths clearly can wonder at the greatness and power of nature in that double infinity that surrounds us on

---

26. I draw on *Mind* 1.11 (*OC* 2/163) for this vocabulary. Compare *Pensées* 185 (*OC* 2/608–14).

all sides, and learn by that marvellous consideration to know themselves by seeing themselves as placed between an infinity and a nothing of extension, of number, of movement, and of time. By this we
can learn to estimate our worth justly and to make reflections worth
more than all the rest of geometry. (*Mind* 1.21, *OC* 2/170)

We, as thinkers, as thinking reeds (*roseaux pensants*),[27] fragile and
brittle and short-lived, are located in every aspect of our existence
between infinity and nothingness. The excerpt just quoted mentions four such aspects: extension (*étendue*), number (*nombre*),
movement (*mouvement*), and time (*temps*). Those comprise, formally, the manifold of timespace, which is co-extensive with the
material order: it is where all things extended in timespace necessarily are, and their definition and measurement involve their location in it. A good part of *Mind*, the short treatise from which the
excerpt is taken, is devoted to explaining that, if geometry is the
science of measuring and analyzing shapes and solids extended in
space, a science for which number (*nombre* in the excerpt above)
is the principal instrument, then an axiomatic assumption of the
science is that the location for such shapes and solids, namely space
(*étendue* and *mouvement* in the excerpt above), is and must be infinite in extent and infinitely divisible.[28] What goes for space goes
also for time (*temps* in the excerpt above): it too is infinite in extent,
and infinitely divisible. Reason can, for Pascal, know this perfectly
well: with apodictic and demonstrative certainty.[29] But among the
entailments of this certainty is the conclusion that we should be
pessimistic about our capacity, whether individually or collectively,
to arrive at complete understanding (comprehension) of the time-

27. For which phrase see *Pensées* 104 (*OC* 2/574), and *Pensées* 186 (*OC* 2/614–15).
28. See *Mind* 1.8–1.19 (*OC* 2/161–70).
29. That isn't to say that everyone can know these things by reason. Pascal is perfectly
clear in most of his works—it's an explicit theme in *Mind* and in parts of *Pensées*—that most
of us in fact lack the capacity to understand high abstractions such as this, true though they
are, and available to the natural light of reason though they are.

space manifold and its constituents. He is often direct about this limitation, as here: "Reason's last step is to recognize that there's an infinity of things beyond it. It's nothing but feeble if it doesn't go so far as to grasp that."[30] And the things in question belong unquestionably to the material order, which Pascal sometimes also calls the natural order, because the sentences just quoted are immediately followed by: *Que si les choses naturelles la surpassent, que dira-t-on des surnaturelles?*—And if natural things are beyond it, what should we say about the supernatural?[31] It's clear enough, too, that the beyondness spoken of here belongs to the order of knowing as well as to the order of being: it's not just that there are too many things for us to know, it's that we are not constituted, epistemically, so as to be able to know them all in their kinds.

There are further difficulties. Even geometry must make assumptions whose truth it can't demonstrate and must deploy terms it can't define.[32] And when we move to the question of historical or geographic or political or ethical knowledge, matters become more difficult still. Pascal is alive, then, to the power of skeptical challenges to thought about the physical order. You've only to look at the books of the skeptics, he writes, to be easily and perhaps too much persuaded by them.[33] The dogmatists, those who oppose the skeptics, have much less to say: only that we can't, in fact, live as if skepticism were true. What then to do? Pascal, characteristically, waxes dialectically excitable in response to the difficulty, and takes its existence as an opportunity to affirm something of importance about us and our capacities:

>> What kind of chimera are we then? How novel, how monstrous, how disordered, how subject to contradiction, how prodigious?— Judge of everything, imbecilic earthworm, receptacle for truth, cess-

30. *Pensées* 177 (*OC* 2/604–5).
31. *Pensées* 177 (*OC* 2/605).
32. See *Mind* 1.3–1.4 (*OC* 2/157–58).
33. *Pensées* 122 (*OC* 2/580).

pool of uncertainty and error, glory and trash of the universe.—
Who'll disentangle this muddle? It's certainly beyond dogmatism
and skepticism and all human philosophy. We go beyond ourselves.
Let's grant to the skeptics what they've so often said, which is that
truth isn't something we can arrive at or catch. It doesn't live on
earth; it's at home in heaven, where it lies in God's lap; we can understand it only so far as it pleases God to show it to us.... Listen to
God. (*Pensées* 122, *OC* 2/580–81)[34]

The central point, overheatedly if beautifully made, is that thought
about the physical order can't justify itself and can't, particularly,
overcome the aporia provided it by the opposition of skepticism
and dogmatism. We aspire to understand the physical order, and
to some limited extent we do understand it; but that knowledge
is troubled by epistemological questions it generates for itself in
the act of developing its understanding—this is true even of geometry, the best of it[35]—and once these questions arise, we find
ourselves insecure and puzzled. That insecurity shows us that the
skeptics' denial that truth is a proper *gibier*, or quarry, for us—
something we can catch—is correct—at least if "catching" means
chasing it, bringing it to ground, and making it without remainder
ours by killing and eating it. That would be comprehension, complete understanding, beyond doubt: understanding appropriately characterized in that way would be free from epistemological
uncertainties. But we have none of it, and that lack shows us our
own paradoxical nature and situation as aspiring to knowledge we
know we can't have.[36] "No dogmatism can overcome our incapacity for proof (*impuissance de prouver*). No skepticism (*pyrrhonisme*)
can overcome our idea of truth (*idée de la vérité*)."[37]

34. On doubt and its resolution, see also *Pensées* 101 (*OC* 2/573–74).
35. This is an important theme throughout *Mind*.
36. The paradoxically puzzling nature of the human is treated in more detail in chapter
4, below.
37. *Pensées* 385 (*OC* 2/673).

But attending to the LORD—*écoutez Dieu!*—can provide certainty, and not only about the things of the LORD, as in theology, in the etymological sense of that word, but also about the human condition as it finds itself, or, better, is given itself in the physical and intellectual orders. Truths in the order of love, however, about the LORD and the LORD's relations to us, and about the origin and end and meaning of our baffling condition now, aren't available to thought unaided.[38] They're a matter of faith, and that in turn, is a matter of grace, of sheer gift, unmerited.[39] Pascal uses the three-orders division in this connection to insulate the order of love from the other two. Reasoning, the characteristic activity of the second order, can, with respect to the order of love, do no more than prepare us for entry into it by showing us that there is something we need, some resolution of our desires, that nothing in the first two orders can supply us—not the delights and sufferings and puzzling infinities of the physical order, nor the understandings that thinking about those matters yields. On this, Pascal, speaking in the voice of the LORD's wisdom, writes: "It's useless, O men, to look in yourselves for the remedy for your miseries. All your lights can bring you only to the understanding that you can find neither truth nor good in yourselves."[40] Faith, an act of submission, provides more: an entry into the Christian life, and a resolution of otherwise unresolvable intellectual difficulties.

It is possible, however, to attend to what the LORD gives by thinking about it. Pascal does this: he defends, with argument, some construals of what the LORD has given against others, as, paradigmatically, in *Provincials*; he offers an interpretation of the teachings of the Church on grace, with polemical brio and some constructive insight, in *Grace*; he resists some christological and

---

38. For a trenchant statement of this point, see Pascal's debate with Jacques Forton in *Conférences* (*OC* 1/548–50).

39. I treat Pascal's thought on grace in chapter 5, below.

40. *Pensées* 139 (*OC* 2/592).

mariological mistakes, as he sees them, in *Conferences*; he offers interpretations of the meaning and proper use of sickness (in *Maladies*) and of death (in his letter of 1651 about his father's death to his sister and brother-in-law); and he provides a depiction of the life of Jesus, in *Jesus-Christ*. All these involve activities that belong to the intellectual order, and, broadly speaking, take as their topic matters that have to do with the order of love. These acts of thought are, in this respect, like those directed toward the physical order: they take as their topic an order to which they do not belong. The insulation of the orders one from another doesn't go so far as to make the physical order and the order of love incapable of being thought about.

Pascal is, I think, not entirely consistent about the relations between the intellectual order and at least the theological aspects of the order of love. He is consistent, and forceful, that the content of theology—the truths of the faith, let's say—cannot be arrived at by thought alone, but are given by the LORD, and are only then properly topics of thought. But sometimes he limits what thought can do in theology to the strictly exegetical, as here:

> ⟫ There are topics in which we seek to know only what authors have written: history, geography, jurisprudence, languages, and especially theology—in brief, all those whose basis is either a simple matter of fact or an institution, whether divine or human. With respect to these topics, it's necessary to have recourse to their books, because all that can be known about these topics is found there. From this, it's clear that we can have complete understanding of such topics, understanding to which it's not possible to add anything. If it's a question of knowing who the first King of France was, where geographers place the first meridian, which words are used in a dead language, and everything of that kind, what other than books can take us there? And who can add anything new to what they tell us, since we want to learn only what they contain? Authority alone can enlighten us about such things. (*Vacuum*, OC 1/452–53)

Pascal here establishes authority as the only way to arrive at knowledge about *faits simples*: states of affairs in the human sphere—human sphere, because what we want to know about here is what people have said about this or that, even when this-or-that is some feature of the nonhuman world (the first meridian; the LORD). Those are things you can look up; and the only way to know them is to look them up. About theology and authority he goes on, in the same place:

> ↠ Authority has its principal force in theology. That's because there it's inseparable from truth, and we can understand truth only by way of authority—so that to give complete certitude about matters most incomprehensible to reason, it suffices to show them in the sacred books, just as to show the uncertainty of the most plausible things it's only necessary to show that they're not included there. That's because theology's principles are above nature and reason, and because human intellect, too weak to get to them by its own efforts, can arrive at these highest understandings only if it's carried there by an omnipotent and supernatural power. (*Vacuum*, OC 1/453)

Theology is depicted here as the best example of an authority-based act of thought. To think about the LORD and what has to do with the LORD is impossible directly—*la raison n'y peut rien determiner*[41] (reason can determine nothing here)—and that is because:

> ↠ If there is a God, he is infinitely incomprehensible. That's because, being partless and limitless, he has no rapport with us. We're therefore incapable of understanding whether he is or whether he isn't. Since that's so, who dares to undertake to resolve that question? Not us; we have no rapport with him. (*Pensées* 397, OC 2/677)

This is clear enough. The LORD's otherness to us and ours to the LORD is here stated radically and dramatically, as is characteristic

41. *Pensées* 397 (*OC* 2/677).

of Pascal. The LORD is to us, in lack of rapport, much as black holes are to the rest of the cosmos: their only presence is as a kind of absence, and there are then only two ways in which a god so thoroughly hidden can be known. The first is by signs and effects of absence upon what's present: Pascal uses patterns of reasoning like this in his anthropology when he points to features of human existence that make no sense when considered in their own terms, by reason's natural light (a phrase used just before the last excerpt quoted), but that do make sense—or at least more sense—when considered in light of the LORD, the god of Christian confession. And that points to the second way in which a god with whom we have no rapport, and who has no rapport with us, can be known: when that god self-reveals in the incarnation and, thereby and therefore, to the Church. It's that second way that explains Pascal's thought that theology is by definition exegetical. The Church serves as guardian and repository of that self-revelation, and the work of knowing the LORD by thought, the characteristic activity of the second order, must then focus upon what's in that repository, and must explain and order it by way of exegesis. Reasoning *selon les lumières naturelles* can do no more.[42]

And so, with respect to reasoning about the LORD's existence, Pascal writes, continuing from where the preceding excerpt ended:

> ⇢ Who then will blame Christians for being unable to give reasons for what they believe? They say, publicly, that it's foolishness—stupidity—and then you complain that they don't prove it? If they did prove it, they wouldn't be holding to what they say. They remain coherent by lacking proof.—This excuses and removes blame from those who offer Christian belief without reasons. But it doesn't excuse those who accept it.—Let's examine that point and say: God is or isn't. Which side shall we move toward? Reason can determine nothing here. Infinite chaos separates us. (*Pensées* 397, *OC* 2/677)

42. *Pensées* 397 (*OC* 2/677).

If reason is irrelevant to answering questions about the LORD's existence, nature, and relation to us, then what's left to it is exegesis of what's been revealed about these topics. The division of orders is what grounds this pattern of thought, and makes it lucid. There remains the question of how, then, if not by the use of reason, those who don't see what the Church teaches as a repository of truths about the LORD might come to do so.[43]

3.5 Disorder and the Limits of Order

The thought that there are orders of being and thinking and knowing, and that each has its characteristic forms and activities that don't, or shouldn't, trespass the boundaries, permits Pascal a powerful depiction of the nature of disorder:

➤ Tyranny is the desire for universal domination without regard to order. The strong, the beautiful, the clever, and the pious, each rule in their proper sphere and not elsewhere. Sometimes they meet, and the strong and the beautiful stupidly fight for mastery—but their mastery is different in kind. They don't understand one another; their mistake is to want to rule everywhere. No one can do that, not even by force: force does nothing in the kingdom of the wise; its mastery is over external actions. Tyranny—that's wanting to have by one means what's only to be had by another. Our debts to one kind of merit are different from those to another: we owe love to charm, fear to force, belief to knowledge. Those are debts we should pay. It's unjust to refuse them, and unjust to demand different ones. And so it's false and tyrannical to say things such as "I'm beautiful, and so you should fear me"; "I'm strong, and so you should love me"; "I'm ...." It's false and tyrannical in the same way to say "He's weak, and so I don't respect him"; "he's not smart, and so I won't fear him." (*Pensées* 54, *OC* 2/558–59)

43. This topic is treated in chapter 6, §6.2, below, on the ecclesial city.

The four orders mentioned here are those of force (*force*), beauty (*beauté*), cleverness (*bonté d'esprit*), and piety (*piété*). Beauty is the addition: the other three map nicely onto the three just discussed. Tyrants, who can belong to any of the orders, all want the same thing, which is dominion over the inhabitants and activities of all the orders by the exercise of what belongs to only one of them. The pugilist thinks that by his fists he might make himself the cleverest and most beautiful of all; but he can't, because what his fists can do belongs only to the order of force, and can have no purchase on the orders of beauty and intellect. Or, the philosopher thinks that her acuity can make her beautiful, make, too, other beautiful people recognize her as such; but this won't work either—any dominion that acuity offers belongs only to the order of the clever. And so on. When those who have maximal force at their disposal—Ashoka, Alexander, Trump—make others into subjects, those subjects might be tempted to kowtow to them not only as rulers but as excellently handsome and clever, too—not to mention pious. And the rulers might encourage them. But all that, too, would be a confusion: nothing about deploying armies makes you handsome or clever. If Christine of Sweden, to whom Pascal dedicated and offered his calculating machine, was a mathematician-queen, a queenly mathematician, her queenliness had nothing to do with her mathematical skills, nor vice-versa. It's out of order to think so, a mistake about order for which *tyrannie* is a good umbrella word. We should, if our actions comport with order—are well-ordered—believe the knowledgeable, be charmed by the beautiful, and submit to the forceful in fear.

*

Talk of order and orders as Pascal indulges it has considerable additional payoffs. It permits identification and rebuttal of common confusions, for one. You might think, for instance (Pascal sometimes writes as though he thinks), that the properties of some object in the order of being—say, a mathematical object, all of whose properties are possessed necessarily—ought to be reflected in the order of knowing, so that the only right way to come to know some mathematical truth is by constructing or replicating a proof that shows those properties necessarily to be what they are (that 4,988 can be expressed as the product of two primes, say). A judicious deployment of talk of orders can easily show that this is not so. I might ask my calculator, or some human servant, to tell me whether 4,988 can be so expressed, and even which the primes in question are; and I might accept what I'm told on authority, in this case the authority of my calculator, human or mechanical, thus accepting on contingent grounds what's necessary. An inflexible advocate of the conformity of the order of knowing to the order of being would think me mistaken, or at least lacking, in this authority-reliance. But that would itself be an error—almost everything I know in mathematics comes to me from authoritatively testimonial sources of one kind or another, and that has no bearing upon whether I know the truths so arrived at. Talk of orders permits attention to the order to which knowers belong as well as to the orders of what they know, and so permits disjunction between those orders when appropriate. That is a second advantage of talk of order and orders. Other advantages, as noted, include a proper indulgence of the unavoidable taxonomic appetite, together with the gaining of clarity about the regulation of behavior: to treat a dog as you might a rock by breaking it into small pieces with a sledgehammer is as much a confusion about orders of being as is treating a beautiful man as though he were clever.

But there is one strong temptation toward error inherent in taxonomic talk of orders. It's the temptation to over-theorize the *taxa*, the orders postulated, in the direction either of realism or of nominalism—or, as Pascal would rather have it, as the *dogmatistes* or the *pyrrhoniens* might. Realists about orders will think of their *taxa* as being the real ones, the ones that follow the joints of the cosmos; in arriving at them, realists think they've arrived at the true sortals in rather the same way as the man who separates one piece of paper from another where the perforation is thinks he's acted in accord with design. A conviction of this sort leads almost inevitably to boundary-policing questions (does this, whatever it is, belong to the order of love or beauty?), and to questions about definition (can we find and state the conditions conjointly sufficient and severally necessary for something's belonging to this order?). Nominalists, *pyrrhoniens* about the orders, commit themselves, typically, to the view that no *taxon* follows the joints of the cosmos, and in more extreme versions that none could, whether because the cosmos has no joints, or because there's some in-principle reason why they're unavailable to us. Such thinkers find themselves drawn to debates about why those states of affairs obtain, what it is about our cognitive capacities that draws us to *taxa* at all, and what it is about the cosmos that requires the conclusion that it's jointless—or at least that we should think so. Pascal's nonrealist, but not, I think, antirealist, proclivities with respect to the orders are suggested by the fact that, as we've seen, he's happy to write of two, or three, or four orders, as his occasions and (usually polemical) interests demand—without, so far as I can tell, ever getting exercised about questions that would bother a realist, such as, well, how many orders are there *really*? But he also doesn't theorize his tendency to treat order-talk as merely a way of talking, and in that way move it in a nominalist direction. There's no discussion in his work of what it would mean to say, or how we might defend saying, that the cosmos isn't responsive to or reflective of our *taxa*. Those questions seem not to arise for him, just as their realist counterparts don't. Rather, he uses order-talk when it's useful for him to do so, modifies it as occasion demands, and consistently refuses higher-order theoretical questions about the orders. This is all just as it should be, and that it is so about Pascal is made still clearer by considering some texts in which he objects to order-talk and ordering.

Consider the following, in which he considers the *ordre* he might give, or have given had he lived, to the disjointed collection of remarks we call *Pensées*:

> ⇒ Order—I certainly could have given this discourse an order like this: show the vanity of all kinds of conditions, then the vanity of ordinary lives, then the vanity of philosophical lives, whether skeptical or stoical. But the order wouldn't have been kept. I know something about it, and about how few understand it. No human science can keep it. Saint Thomas didn't. Mathematics does, but is useless in its depth. (*Pensées* 588, *OC* 2/785–86)

Human science (*science humaine*) here means something like knowledge about human creatures,[44] and Pascal's point is that attempting a strict hypothetico-deductive order in the exposition of the human condition is hard to keep to and won't be convincing if the attempt is made. Even Thomas Aquinas, who for Pascal is the apostle and archetype of order in exposition (which is not altogether a compliment), doesn't manage to do it. Better, then, perhaps, to offer fragmentary and repeated glimpses of the territory, etched scenes rather than ordered exposition. This amounts to the commendation of the abandonment of ordered exposition of a topic for which it's not fitted, both because of the nature of the topic and because of what Pascal takes himself to know about the capacities for reading and understanding possessed by those who might read what he writes. This is neither a nominalist rejection of the purchase and grip of *taxa*, nor a realist affirmation of the same. It is, rather, an abandonment of those *taxa* when they won't serve, and an enthusiastic use and defense of them when they will.[45]

---

44. See *Pensées* 581 (*OC* 2/783–84), on the difference between *sciences abstraites* and *l'étude de l'homme*, and Pascal's progress from one to the other.

45. See also, on this meta-taxonomic topic, *Pensées* 577–78 (*OC* 2/782–83).

4

ANTHROPOLOGY

Anthropology is, let's say, the study and depiction of the various aspects of human existence: biological, intellectual, social, political, moral, and so on.[1] Christian anthropology is the study and depiction of the same in light of explicit and specifically Christian convictions about the LORD and our relations to the LORD. Pascal is interested in all this. Attention to it is at the heart of his work, and, leaving aside the mathematical and scientific, most of his distinctive contributions are here. He analyzes and depicts the human condition with a distinctively dramatic flair and, so far as the Christian tradition is concerned, with an idiosyncratic focus. We appear, as he shows us to ourselves, as a puzzle: fragile, opaque, often bored, in desperate need of diversion from our inevitable death and suffering, bound by custom and habit, incapable of

---

1. *Anthropologie* isn't a word that Pascal uses; it wasn't in use as a term of art in French theology in the seventeenth century. A great deal of the secondary literature on Pascal treats his anthropology. Carraud's *Invention, Connaissances naturelles*, and "Second Pascalian Anthropology" are excellent places to begin. See Vincent Carraud, "Remarks on the Second Pascalian Anthropology: Thought as Alienation," *Journal of Religion* 85, no. 4 (2005): 539–54; Carraud, *Pascal: Des connaissances naturelles à l'étude de l'homme* (Paris: Vrin, 2007); and Carraud, *L'Invention du moi* (Paris: Presses Universitaires de France, 2010).

coming to agreement about what is good for us, violent, greedy for self-gratification, despairing, miserable, afflicted, out of place in a cosmos infinitely larger and infinitely smaller than we are—and yet also, unlike anything else in the cosmos (so far as we can tell) self-aware, capable of assessing and to some degree understanding the workings of the cosmos, responsive to beauty, thirsty for love, and, most significantly, puzzled by ourselves, by the strange, even monstrous, combination in us, as it seems to us, of subjection at once to physical necessity and unsatisfiable desire, while at the same time striving for something other than that subjection. We can, too, reason our way, if not to the truths that matter, at least to a well-grounded judgment that we cannot so reason and that there are such truths. That combination, too, is a puzzle: Why are we like that? That question, once it is clearly seen, is also, as Pascal presents it, seen as unanswerable, unless by a gift we cannot give ourselves, which is to say by grace.

Pascal's anthropology is in part motivated by apologetical concerns. He wants, while reasoning, as he would say, *selon les lumières naturelles* (according to natural lights),[2] to show to pagans both how they are and how they seem to themselves, and in showing them these things to move them toward adopting the habits and attitudes central to Christian life. To that end, he writes about the features of human existence common to all (death, suffering, boredom, habit, fear, and so on) without using Christian concepts or categories. That part of his anthropology has pagan (that is, neither Christian nor Jewish) humanity as its concern.[3] He is also interested in Christian life—in the habits and attitudes distinctive of that life, and in how the ordinary features of human life

---

2. *Pensées* 397 (*OC* 2/677).

3. *Païen* occurs dozens, perhaps hundreds, of times in Pascal's *oeuvre*. It's a central category: humans are all, as he sees it, pagan or Jewish or Christian, and there's no overlap among these categories. Everyone is born either pagan or Jewish, and anyone can become Christian, by baptism. Becoming Christian overwrites and cancels the other identities. There are difficulties here. I discuss some of them below, in chapter 7, on the Jews.

appear to Christians distinctively. The central themes of Pascal's anthropology, therefore, are often developed contrastively: here's how affliction, for instance, seems to pagans; (sometimes) here's how it seems to Jews; and here's how it seems to Christians. He also develops his themes more or less phenomenologically. That is, he shows, often wittily, how it seems to us to be us, whether we are pagan, Jew, or Christian.

4.1 Affliction

Affliction (*affliction*, *affliger*) isn't a term of art of central importance for Pascal, but he does use it, as when he writes that we hide the present from ourselves by wandering imaginatively in the past and the future because the present afflicts us (*il nous afflige*): it's too painful to remain in and look at;[4] or that we can be afflicted by the death of a spouse or an only son;[5] or, with a typical Pascalian flourish, that we're not afflicted by not having three eyes, but are if we have none.[6] In part because of the violence of its etymology—the Latin *affligere*, from which both the French and the English words come, most often means to be struck violently and painfully by something external to oneself—I use it as the umbrella term here for every variety of unpleasantness in human existence: death, pain, illness, loss, and so on. These are of considerable interest to Pascal, both as they appear to pagans and as they appear to Christians.

Affliction is an ineluctable and frequent feature of human existence. There is death, there are maladies, there is violence, there is pain. These happen to you as to everyone. Often, their occurrence, as well as their memory and anticipation, seems unpleasant, and then there's active affliction, affliction that seems afflictive to those who undergo it: the torturer racks your flesh and it's agonizing;

4. *Pensées* 43 (*OC* 2/556).
5. *Pensées* 468 (*OC* 2/746).
6. *Pensées* 108 (*OC* 2/575).

your child is raped before your eyes and it's a horror; you recall the pain of the beating you got last week and anticipate the one coming to you tonight, blending remembered and anticipated anguish so that its repetition seems inescapable and endless; and so on. But affliction sometimes isn't like that: a razorblade severs your head from your body with such precision that it feels like a cool kiss; you die in dreamless sleep, feeling nothing at all; the surgeon's knife eviscerates you while, anaesthetized, you dream of marshmallows and sunlight; you're whipped bloody while, sexually aroused, the pain delights you. That's passive affliction, affliction that doesn't seem miserable, and sometimes doesn't seem like anything, to those who undergo it, but which is nonetheless affliction in the order of being, a contravention of how things should be and an insult to human existence: a severed head rolls from the guillotine's platform and a life is ended, bloodily; a blood vessel bursts in the brain and the consequent suffusion washes life away; and so on.

Both active and passive affliction are layered by the sense that they're not only yours: if you're as most human creatures are, your affliction is responsive to and increased by seeing and knowing that others are afflicted, too. Solidarity in affliction as often increases its felt intensity as decreases it. Affliction is a feature of Christian life no less than of pagan or Jewish life. Christians die no less frequently and suffer no less horribly than others, and that state of affairs provides something for Christians to think about: it gives us a topic in theological anthropology, discussions of which generally circle around three kinds of question. First, why is there human affliction? Second, why is there Christian affliction? Third, how should Christians think about and respond to their own afflictions and to those of others? All that interests Pascal. His depictions of affliction are frequent, graphic, and intense, and he makes no attempt to minimize or explain away the Christian instances of it. He is concerned, however, to emphasize, often starkly, the contrasts between Christian understandings of and responses to affliction, and those proper to pagans (and, to a lesser extent, those proper to Jews). Such emphasis is part of his apologetic: he wants to show Christianity as being at an advantage in understanding and responding to affliction, and for that purpose he stresses its opacity to and uselessness for non-Christians, and its transfigurability by Christian faith.

There are some things, some states of affairs, which we can't exist and not know of and assent to: *il* [*l'homme*] *ne peut subsister sans les croire.*[7] Among those is the fact that each of us will die. This is as evident to pagans as to Christians and Jews, though it isn't understood and responded to in the same way by each of those groups. Pascal is concerned to show pagans what death is for them, how it should, and typically does, seem to them given their place in the world. That he has this concern indicates that, for him, pagans need reminding, and that when they are forcibly and dramatically reminded they have no choice but to acknowledge the truth of what they're being shown even if they'd rather avert their gaze from it. To say that all of us, pagan, Jew, and Christian, can't not know that we'll die and that it'll be unpleasant isn't, then, for Pascal, to say that we're all constantly aware of those facts, or even that we'll all explicitly acknowledge them when they're presented to us. Rather, it's to say that when we have our noses rubbed in death, by seeing someone die, by feeling intimations of our own mortality, or by looking at literary or painterly depictions of death's particulars, we have only two choices: avert our gaze, or nod our heads, sadly. Depictions of death are important to Pascal's apologetic because of the thought that even when pagans avert their gaze and return to their distractions, something nonetheless happens—the distractions lose some of their glamor because the skulls beneath the skins of those with whom we distract ourselves have become more visible, even if ever so slightly; and it's become somewhat clearer to us what it is that our distractions distract us from. And sometimes, picturing death may have more direct and more tranfigurative effect: it

7. *Pensées* 185 (*OC* 2/608).

may get pagans to see and lament the incomprehensibility of their lives. For these purposes it's important that depictions of death as it is for pagans be direct and dramatic, as many of Pascal's are.

Consider:

>> The last act is bloody no matter how fine the rest of the comedy. At the end they throw earth on your head and that's it. (*Pensées* 154, *OC* 2/600)

And:

>> Imagine a number of people in chains, all condemned to death. Each day, some have their throats cut in full view of the others. Those who remain see their own condition in that of their companions, and, looking at one another with grief and without hope, wait their turn. (*Pensées* 405, *OC* 2/693)

Death, for all, is inescapable. For pagans, it appears also horrible, incomprehensible, final (*et en voilà pour jamais*), and frightening, as in the second excerpt quoted. It yields despair and grief: the pagans, when they think about death, and as the proportion of those they've known whose throats have been cut increases, can do nothing other than look at their co-survivors *avec douleur et sans l'espérance*, knowing that their turn will come.

It isn't easy for those without the LORD to find conceptual resources to moderate this despairing response to death. In a letter following the death of his father in 1651, Pascal writes that without faith in the God of Jesus-Christ, death can appear only as a blankly incomprehensible necessity, a state of affairs natural to us for no reason that we can see. And since that is all, as pagans, we can say about it, we're likely, once again, to understand death to be "horrible, detestable, a horror of nature."[8] Pascal does sometimes acknowledge that understanding death as natural to us and

8. Letter of October 17, 1651, to Gilberte and Florin Périer (*OC* 2/17). See also earlier comments in that letter at *OC* 2/15–16.

as something that extinguishes or deletes us need not lead inevitably to such an intensely negative reaction. It's also possible, if rare and difficult, to understand death's naturalness and inevitability to be goods rather than evils, and to extend that judgment to the conclusion that suicide may sometimes be warranted or required.[9] But to take that position requires an Epictetus or a Seneca or a Marcus Aurelius, and there aren't many of those. Vastly more common among the pagans when faced with the facts of death is some combination of the wail of lament and the aversion of the gaze.

To know that our last act will be bloody, that we are condemned to an unpleasant end beyond which there is nothing and for which we can provide no explanation other than the non-explanation that this is natural to us, is an element, perhaps the most immediately convincing element, in what for Pascal is the most general characteristic of our condition as pagan: misery (*misère*). But our misery isn't limited to the fact of our mortality. It includes, too, ignorance and anxiety.

Consider:

> ⤜ Here's a strange monster, evidently astray. Here it is, fallen away from the place it anxiously looks for. That's what everyone does. (*Pensées* 442, *OC* 2/710)

And:

> ⤜ We don't know where to put ourselves. We're evidently astray; we've fallen away from our proper place without being able to get back. We're anxiously looking for it everywhere, without success, in impenetrable darkness. (*Pensées* 379, *OC* 2/672)

The vocabulary in these two excerpts is the same: there's been a fall away (*tomber*) from some better place; that leads to a condition of being astray (*égarement*), a state of affairs that's evident (*visible*),

9. On these points, see the discussion of Epictetus in *Sacy* (*OC* 2/86–87).

or clear, even to ourselves, and that leads to anxious unrest (*in-quiétude*). We know we're not where we should be, which is an instance of things not being as they should be; this knowledge makes us anxious or unquiet, which is a kind of misery; but we have no way of remedying this anxiety by finding our lost place. Efforts to do that fail. We're in *ténèbres impénétrables*,[10] and we're at least sometimes aware of that state of things. But in this awareness of misery there's always also a tincture of greatness:

> ≫ Our greatness lies in the fact that we know ourselves to be miserable—a tree doesn't know itself to be miserable. It's miserable to know oneself to be miserable, but there's greatness in so knowing. (*Pensées* 105, *OC* 2/574–75)

The greatness in question is like that of a king in exile who has forgotten the country he once ruled, but is at least half aware that he was once a king.[11]

Sometimes, too, Pascal depicts our misery not in terms of our forgetfulness of and anxiety about where we've come from and where we're going, but rather in terms of the kind of cosmos we find ourselves in, together with the limitations of our sensory and cognitive equipment. This is one aspect of the theme of disproportion (*disproportion*): we are not adapted, cognitively and sensorily, to the place we find ourselves in, and Pascal ordinarily connects exposition of that state of affairs with discussion of the two infinities. One infinity is that of largeness: if we contemplate the extent of the cosmos, we see that each of us is a mote, a speck of dust, compared to the size of the planet we find ourselves on; and that our planet is just such a mote compared to the size of the cosmos it finds itself in. We have no imaginative capacity to grasp this infinity: "It's useless to inflate our conceptions beyond imaginable space—we think of

---

10. For more on these themes, see *Pensées* 184 (*OC* 2/607) and *Pensées* 399 (*OC* 2/687–88).
11. See *Pensées* 107 (*OC* 2/575) and *Pensées* 113 (*OC* 2/577).

nothing more than atoms in place of the reality of things."[12] The other is the infinity of smallness: within ourselves, and within the smallest things we can see or imagine, there are smaller things, and these too extend to infinity, beggaring our imaginative capacities.[13] We can, of course, think about these two infinities, and provide formulations of them in the way that Pascal does, just as we can in mathematics when we define and manipulate infinite sets. But we cannot imagine—have a mental picture of—the infinity of largeness or smallness, and much less of the infinitely many particular things (planets, stars, galaxies; microbes, viruses, electrons) found within each. We have a place in these infinities, but it isn't a pleasing or encouraging one. We're astray in a corner of an infinite universe,[14] without mastery or understanding of it, and without the capacity to attain those things. What we can know is real but limited,[15] and Pascal is happy to ridicule those who think they can know more than they can. And so:

> ≫ We should understand what's within our reach. We're something but not everything. What we are obscures from our understanding first principles that come from nothing. And our smallness hides from us the vision of infinity. Our intelligence occupies the same place in the order of intelligible things as our bodies do in nature's physical extent. (*Pensées* 185, *OC* 2/611)[16]

Which is to say, not much of a place at all.

So: we're ill-equipped for and bad at mathematics and physics;

12. *Pensées* 185 (*OC* 2/609). This *pensée* is highly polished, and is in its entirety (*OC* 2/608–14) devoted to this topic.

13. Boeke's *Cosmic View* provides a graphically unrivalled visual representation of Pascal's double infinity. I first saw this book when I was a small boy, perhaps ten years old, and it's remained with me since. When I first read Pascal on the twofold infinity, perhaps five years later, it seemed clear to me that he was writing about what Boeke had shown.

14. I paraphrase *Pensées* 184 (*OC* 2/607–8).

15. Pascal of course thinks that some mathematical knowledge, and some knowledge in physics, is possible. See the discussion in chapter 3, above, on order.

16. Compare *Mind* 1.12–1.21 (*OC* 2/164–70).

we're ill-adapted for observing, imagining, and understanding the world; and when we contemplate the double infinity we see, first and last, that it is beyond us, and this, in our pagan state, is terrifying and baffling. "The eternal silence of these infinite spaces terrifies me," he writes,[17] and that is something we'd much rather not look at, being in that way like death.

But misery produced by an awareness of disproportion isn't in every way like that produced by death. In the latter case, Pascal treats a universal aspect of the human condition: everyone, since the Fall, has always died,[18] and there's always been an awareness of that state of things. But awareness of the extent, and even the fact, of the double infinity is local and dependent upon technology. Without the invention of the telescope and the microscope much of what Pascal writes about the two infinities could not have been written;[19] and although it's not likely that awareness of what these inventions had shown, and of how seventeenth-century science construed the cosmos, was widespread in Pascal's time, its outlines were certainly known to the middle classes, and were commonplaces for the intelligentsia.

If affliction is a central feature, opaque and terrifying, of pagan life, it is equally central, as Pascal depicts it, to Christian life. The Christian difference is that while pagans can do nothing with affliction but deny it, avoid it, or avert their gaze from it, Christians can, and should, Pascal thinks, embrace it and even, sometimes, seek it. One work to which this theme is central is the *Prière pour demander à Dieu le bon usage de maladies*. In it, Pascal addresses

17. *Pensées* 187 (*OC* 2/615).

18. With, from a Jewish and Christian point of view, the usual exceptions: Enoch, Elijah, perhaps Mary, depending upon how the Dormition is understood, and what, from a Catholic point of view, the definition of the dogma of the Assumption is taken to entail.

19. Many premoderns were aware in some degree of the infinity of largeness, of course. But their awareness was not and could not have been calibrated in the way that became possible beginning in the sixteenth century; and the technologies developed in the twentieth century have radically increased our sense of this infinity, and of the inseparability of space and time in which it consists.

the LORD, in part in the person of the Father and in part in that of the Son, on the topic of the work's title.[20] It's often read autobiographically because of Pascal's own illnesses and untimely death, but I won't do that; I take it, instead, as witness to a sensibility toward and set of judgments about affliction saturated with allusions to and echoes of both scriptural and liturgical language.[21]

Pascal acknowledges that the LORD afflicts us; but he traces that affliction not to the LORD's intent to inflict pain upon us, but rather to treat us compassionately and mercifully. All afflictions are results of your mercy, he writes to the LORD, and are to be welcomed as such no matter how difficult that is to do.[22] It's only our corruptions and capacities for misapprehension that make the LORD's favors seem painful; if we can accept them gratefully, they'll heal us. The vigor of health leads us to enjoy the world excessively, and so afflictions are rightly asked for. Pascal asks the LORD to "bring my vigor to nothing and, by bodily weakness or zeal for love, make me incapable of delighting in the world so that I might delight in nothing but you"[23]—beseeching the LORD to bring his vigor to nothing (*anéantissez cette vigueur*) is typical for Pascal: everything about us that turns us away from the LORD needs to be zeroed in this way.

Physical pain need not have positive effects. It can, even for Christians, be a new occasion of sin.[24] But it can be a blessing, and when received in the right spirit appears as a figure and a reminder of the soul's pains. So far as it is that, it will be an occasion for healing because it will provoke a life of *pénitence continuelle* for the soul's distance from and lack of love for the LORD.[25] The vigor of

20. *Maladies* (*OC* 2/183–93).
21. On which see Sellier, *Liturgie*.
22. Summarizing *Maladies* 1 (*OC* 2/183).
23. *Maladies* 2 (*OC* 2/184).
24. *Maladies* 7 (*OC* 2/187).
25. *Maladies* 7–8 (*OC* 2/187–88).

health promotes the seeking of diversions;[26] it exacerbates rest-lessness, whereas the pains of physical suffering keep restlessness in check, and are to be welcomed because of that.[27] And there's an additional reason to seek and welcome affliction: that the LORD was afflicted in the flesh on the cross, that all our afflictions partic-ipate in those, and that we should welcome all such participations. Not only that: there's nothing in our bodies considered in them-selves (*pour lui-même*) that can please the LORD; but our bodies' afflictions are *dignes de votre amour*, worthy, that's to say, of the LORD's love.[28]

Pascal does not, however, implore the LORD for simple, brute suffering, and lots of it—for cancer's agonies, for the immobili-ty of motor neuron diseases, for the quotidian pains of crushed limbs, infected teeth, migraines, and all the other shocks that flesh is heir to. He wants those afflictions, yes; but he wants, or at least begs for, consolations along with them. That combination, affliction-with-consolation, is the distinctive feature of the Chris-tian life here below, he writes, by contrast with the life of the saints in heaven, who lack all affliction and therefore don't need consola-tion, and those of the Jews and pagans, who have afflictions with-out consolation.[29] Consolations, principally the awareness that our afflictions participate in Jesus-Christ's and that they're a nec-essary and agonizing but temporary condition to be brought to an end by the blissful life of the world to come, don't remove the pain of affliction, but do frame it in such a way as to make it bearable. Afflictions so framed and so acknowledged can be received as gifts, with gratitude, as marks of Christian discipleship; receiving them in that way permits them to participate in Jesus-Christ's sufferings in such a way that it's no longer the sufferer alone who suffers, but

26. On diversion see §4.2, below.
27. *Maladies* 9 (*OC* 2/188–89).
28. *Maladies* 10 (*OC* 2/189–90).
29. *Maladies* 11 (*OC* 2/190).

Jesus-Christ who lives and suffers in the sufferer—*ce ne soit plus moi qui vive et qui souffre, mais que ce soit vous qui viviez et qui souffriez en moi.*[30]

Throughout *Maladies*, there's surprise on Pascal's part that most of his fellow Christians don't see affliction in this way. They neither seek nor welcome it, and to the extent that they don't, their lives are like those of pagans.[31] Their attitude toward affliction is a caress offered to the world; and since the world is what afflicted and killed Jesus-Christ, it's a caress offered to a murderer. It's as if, Pascal writes, with characteristic hyperbole, a son were to welcome and delight in and make much of his father's murderer. That would be a sufficiently criminal joy (*une joie aussi criminelle*),[32] and in so characterizing the attitude of many of his fellow Christians to affliction Pascal shows dramatically that he distances what he takes to be properly Christian habits and attitudes with respect to affliction from those of pagans and Jews to these matters, but also from those of most of the baptized, who, in this, have been insufficiently christianized.

The same concerns are evident in Pascal's treatment of death as it ought to appear to Christians. The fullest depiction of this is in a letter from Pascal to his older sister, Gilberte, and her husband, Florin, responding to the death of Pascal's and Gilberte's father, Étienne, on September 17, 1651.[33] That letter contains Pascal's most fully developed thoughts about death as it may and should appear to Christians.

If, for pagans, death is an opaque terror, for Christians it can be understood as a gift. Christianity teaches, first, that death is "an indispensable, inevitable, just, and holy consequence [of the

---

30. *Maladies* 15 (*OC* 2/193), approximately quoting Gal 2:20.

31. For this point, see especially *Maladies* 12 (*OC* 2/191).

32. *Maladies* 12 (*OC* 2/191).

33. The text is at *OC* 2/14–25. The quotations, allusions, and paraphrases from here to the end of §4.1 relate to this letter.

Fall], useful for the good of the Church and the exaltation of God's name and greatness." This is supposed to be consoling: after the Fall it's just and proper that all should die as penalty for sin, and seeing this permits Christians to see death as a sacrifice that turns some of us from being victims of the Devil to being victims of the LORD: Jesus-Christ's death sanctifies ours, and when we see our deaths as participating in his, death can become for us no longer a horror but even lovely, holy, a joy to the faithful. This isn't an easy understanding to arrive at, and Pascal's recommendation to Christians is that we should arrive at it by contemplating Jesus-Christ's death. That death, he writes, was paradigmatically sacrificial, with the death on the cross as its culmination, and the LORD's acceptance of the sacrifice evident in the resurrection and ascension. With that model in mind, we can say that the sacrifice we make to the LORD, constituted while we live the Christian life as a member of Jesus-Christ's body, also finds its culmination in death (*s'accomplit à la mort*), by which means "the soul, truly abandoning every kind of vice and the love of the world, whose contagion infects it throughout this life, achieves its immolation and is received into God's bosom." The language is strong: vice and its concomitants are burned away (*elle achève son immolation*) by death: sickness is purified by fire, and then the soul can be received by the LORD. This life, by being brought to nothing (*anéantir*) in death, provides a fuller life. Such a view provides Christians with hope unavailable to pagans.

Pascal elucidates death further by showing how it does, and should, appear differently to those who've not sinned than to those who have:

>» Horror of death is natural in a state of innocence. Death is truly horrible when it brings a completely pure life to an end. It was appropriate to hate death when it separated a holy soul from a holy body; but it's appropriate to love it when it separates a holy soul from

an impure body. It was appropriate to flee death when it disrupted a peaceful connection between soul and body, but not when it calms an irreconcilable dissension between them. Finally, when death afflicted an innocent body, when it took away the body's freedom to honor God, when it separated from the soul a body submissive to and coöperative with the will, when it brought to an end all the good actions a person can do—then it was appropriate to abhor it. But when it ends an impure life, when it takes away the body's freedom to sin, when it delivers the soul from a very powerful rebel that contradicts everything proper to its salvation—then it's entirely inappropriate to have that attitude toward it. (Letter of 1651 to Florin and Gilberte Périer, *OC* 2/21)

None of us, since Eve and Adam, is in a condition that would make it appropriate to hate and abhor death. Christians, knowing this, should, instead, celebrate it.

As I've written, this is supposed to console—specifically to console Pascal's sister and brother-in-law following Étienne Pascal's death. Had Pascal left it there, with an injunction to celebrate Étienne's deliverance from this body of death, it's hard to see that it would have been consoling. Lament for death on the part of Christians isn't only, and not even principally, for the one who's died; it's as much or more for those who haven't, who've been deprived by death of face-to-face exchange with the one who is dead. Pascal somewhat reluctantly realizes this, and allows that death afflicts the living, and that we respond to it with lament because we're not angels. But the affliction of the death of others can itself serve as an instance of affliction accompanied by consolation, as was the case with sickness and other physical pains. The affliction doesn't cease to afflict; we don't cease to mourn the deaths of others; but we're consoled by knowing what those deaths effect and are for.

And there is a final point that Pascal urges upon his sister and brother-in-law: when a holy or beloved person has died, a gift we can give them, which is also a way of making them live on with us, is *faire les choses qu'ils nous ordonneraient s'ils étaient encore au monde*: do those things they'd want us to do were they still in the world.

*

So much for Pascal on affliction, pagan and Christian. There's much to admire in what he writes about these topics, not least his unblinking attention to the horrors of human life in a fallen world. All that he writes about those is true, and it is salutary because few of us, pagan or Christian, want to or can look at those horrors. Close and repeated reading of Pascal on death and maladies and disproportion and ignorance and frailty and sheerly physical pain alters those who do it: for those so inclined (the wealthy, the protected, the coddled), denial becomes more difficult; and for those whose lives are such that denial is impossible (the poor, the tortured, the raped, the flayed, sufferers from painful and incurable disease), their sense of the shape of things is sharpened and made vivid.

There are, however, some difficulties in what he writes about affliction as it appears, or should appear, to Christians. The fundamental grammar of Christianity with respect to death, to restrict discussion to that paradigmatic instance of affliction, requires two affirmations: that death is an artifact of the Fall, a lamentable horror; and that death is a gift that permits Christians intimate participation in the salvifically sacrificial death of Jesus-Christ. The relative weight given to each of these varies. There are Christians who emphasize the first, for whom lament is the dominant response to death, whether their own or another's; and there are Christians who emphasize the second, and whose first and principal response to death, their own or another's, is to welcome it with open arms. In order to speak and write as a Christian about death, those who celebrate death ought not to forget its lamentability, and those who lament it ought not to forget its beauty.

Pascal gets this right, as his depiction of grief-with-consolation or lament-with-hope shows: that's a way of holding lament and welcome together, with respect to death as well as other afflictions.

But there's another element in the Christian grammar of death that Pascal transgresses, or at least approaches transgression of. Death cannot be placed by Christians, not even since the Fall, without remainder under the rubric of providence. Rather, it's damage (or, if you like—I don't much—punishment) effected by the Fall, which can have felicitous effects. As the Fall was a *felix culpa*, so death, as the principal artifact of the Fall, is damage-with-felicities. Pascal gets very close to categorizing the fact of death generically, and every particular death specifically, as providentially felicitous, and therefore as intended by the LORD as healing punishment. That cannot be right. Death generically remains what it is: damage; and some particular deaths—those of children, dismembered in the womb; those of the victims of Nazi genocide, gassed and incinerated in the ovens; those of the tortured, killed by pain whose intensity is horizonless for them—bring with them, here below, no felicities for those who undergo them, Christian or not. Such deaths are, simply, agonizing damage, and the LORD has nothing, conceptually or causally, to do with them other than, after death, to soothe and welcome those who suffer them. To say that the LORD intends them, or provides worldly felicities by means of them, is an offense against Christianity, and one that Pascal approaches. Can one write of these deaths that they contribute to the exaltation of the LORD's name, and that they are the decree of the LORD's providence, "conceived from eternity to be fulfilled in the fullness of his time in such a year on such a day at such an hour in such a place and in such a way"?[34] Pascal does write this about Christian death in general, and by extension about all death—the difference between Christian and pagan death being not in what

34. Letter to Florin and Gilberte Périer of 1651 (*OC* 2/15–16).

they are but in how they seem; Pascal encourages Christians to see their own deaths, those of their beloveds, and all deaths without remainder, under this rubric. Such a view makes the LORD a torturer and torture a felicity.

Christianity requires this understanding neither of death's affliction in particular, nor of afflictions in general. Pascal, in arriving at it, doesn't apply distinctions he makes copious use of elsewhere. He could have written that the felicities produced by death, whether generically or specifically, are what the LORD providentially intends, and that there are always some of them, whether or not evident to those who die and whether or not evident to those who see their deaths; and that the aspects of particular deaths, or of death in general, that are nonfelicitous, that, simply, tend toward nothing (like sin) are permitted by the LORD and lamented by the LORD as the LORD Jesus-Christ lamented his own death on the cross, and as the Church laments it when the altars are stripped on Good Friday. There's nothing felicitous in torture, and the LORD's death on the cross was torturous; that the LORD's death was salvific does not mean that we celebrate its agonies as agonies; much less does it mean that we attribute them to the LORD. *Mutatis mutandis*, to say that every human death carries felicities with it, and that every Christian death marks a transition from life in a fallen and bloody world to life with the LORD, true as those claims are, does not mean that the pains of death, and the zeroing of life that death essentially is (an essence that is a negative value, a simple lack) are in themselves felicitous, or that they are intended and effected by the LORD. The grammar of affliction, with death as its paradigm, is the same as the grammar of sin. It's lamentable that Pascal didn't see that.

Nevertheless. Reading Pascal on affliction is instructive exactly because he's so clearly and dramatically wrong about it in this significant way. Seeing a wrong view so elegantly and persuasively laid out is a stimulus better than which it's hard to imagine for beginning to think rightly about human affliction in light of Christian conviction.

4.2 Diversion

Misery in the order of being demands a response in the attitudinal and practical orders. If you're actually miserable (mortal, diseased, deluded, insignificant, frustrated, lonely) you may look your condition in the face, see it for what it is, and suffer—be effectively and actively miserable, that is. Then, your life will seem unpleasant to you. But you may also refuse to acknowledge your condition, and show your refusal by looking elsewhere. You may turn to the pleasures of the flesh (food, drink, sex, comfort, intoxicants) or those of the intellect (solving problems, creating systems, writing treatises, contemplating the order of things) or those of power (conquest, domination, the indulgence of ambition, the seeking of admiration), or those of beauty, whether as maker or consumer (cosmetics, art, music, literature). And if you do those things, your life may seem to you, for a while, pleasant: orgasm, wine on the tongue, the admiration of your peers, the new discovery, proving a theorem, making something beautiful, attaining high office— these are pleasurable things, and, while they last, they can seem important, and certainly make the awareness of death and misery recede. Those transported by the beloved's embrace, the beauty of the maple tree, the elegance of the proof, the adulation of the crowd, and so on, are not, at the time, miserable or thinking of their miseries. And all these practices and attitudes are, of course, available to pagans as much as to Christians.

All these, however, can also be understood as diversions (*divertissements*) from attending to the fundamentals of our own death-directed misery, and, thus, as ways of obscuring ourselves from our own gaze.[35] Pascal, as the dialectician he is, is lyrical and

---

35. Carraud, *Philosophie*, 289–347, is helpful on this and connected topics, especially *amour-propre*.

extreme in his depictions of our diversion seeking, even, sometimes, to the point of seeming to claim that we should just stop all
that, stop seeking diversion of any and every kind, and by doing
so learn to see our misery for what it is. If we really are chained to
the floor in a cell with others, sentenced to death like them, daily
subjected to the vision of some of them being bloodily executed
in front of us and knowing that our turn will come soon enough,
isn't it a self-deluding mistake to write books, make love, prosecute
wars, seek office, and, generally, divert ourselves?

And so he writes things like this: "If our condition were really
happy (*heureuse*), we wouldn't need to divert ourselves (*nous diver-
tir*) from thinking about it";[36] and, contrapositively, "Since we haven't been able to cure death, misery, and ignorance, we've decided,
in order to make ourselves happy, not to think about them."[37] Or,
at more length and in more polished and developed fashion:

> ≫ If a king is without diversions and is left to consider and reflect
> upon what he is, his felicity languishes and no longer sustains him.
> He inevitably falls into seeing threats—rebellions that may come,
> and, eventually, death and maladies that will come. And so, if he's
> without what we call diversions he's at once unhappy, and more un-
> happy even than the least among his subjects, who play games and
> divert themselves. That's why gambling, the conversation of women,
> war, and high office, are so sought after. It isn't that they themselves
> bring happiness, nor that anyone thinks that true beatitude comes
> from having the money won by gambling, or the hare hunted. We
> wouldn't want them if they were offered. It isn't that we're looking
> for a soft and peaceful way of being that leaves us to think of our
> unhappy condition; neither do we want the dangers of war or the
> burdens of office. No, it's the disturbance we want: it distracts and
> diverts us. That's why we so like noise and activity, why prison is such

36. *Pensées* 66 (*OC* 2/563).
37. *Pensées* 124 (*OC* 2/583).

a horrible punishment, and why the pleasure of solitude is incomprehensible. So, in the end, the greatest felicity of being a king is that there are always those trying to divert him and find him every kind of pleasure. And that's all we've been able to invent to make ourselves happy. Those who philosophize about these things, and who think the world scarcely reasonable in spending all day running after a hare it wouldn't bother to buy, don't at all understand what we are. The hare doesn't prevent us from seeing death and the miseries that distract from it. But the hunt does. (*Pensées* 126, *OC* 2/584–85)

Several threads are woven together here. The first is that diversion is necessary even for those we might think happiest because they're as wealthy and powerful as it's possible to be. This shows that maximal wealth and power don't, by themselves, and can't, because of the different order to which they belong, address our misery. If they did, then kings wouldn't need diversion. But they do. They, like us, do all they can to avoid looking death and its attendant miseries in the face. And that means they seek diversions, just as we do. If monarchs have any advantage here, it's only that finding diversions is easier for them than for us. It isn't that they've found a condition in which diversion is unnecessary. Matters might be different for Christian kings; but if they were it wouldn't be because they were kings, but because they were Christian.

It's interesting that Pascal doesn't here, or anywhere so far as I can tell, address the condition of those at the other end of the spectrum of wealth and power. Something different would have to be said of them, allowing his terms of analysis. They have no possibility of a soft and peaceful way of being that gives them more time than they want to see their misery. All their time and energy is given to survival, and so they have neither need of nor possibility for diversion. Hunger and pain and violence are always with them, and death before their faces. They, among those chained to the floor and waiting to have their throats cut, have nowhere else to

look but at the executioner and nothing else to feel but the pain
of their bonds. Diversions aren't possible for them. An extension
of Pascal's analysis to them, which means to most of us, in the seventeenth century and now, would show that radical poverty is the
only thing that does or can remove the need for diversion. This
provides the poor an advantage over kings, but it is such a painful
one that almost no one will choose it if offered.

Intertwined with the idea that nothing we can do for ourselves
removes the need for diversion is the thought that diversions are
the best we've been able to do so far as happiness seeking is concerned: *Voilà tout ce que les hommes ont pu inventer pour se rendre
heureux*. If our happiness is placed in our own hands, we invent
gambling and war and seduction and politics and hunting and (to
go beyond the examples Pascal gives) novels and film and pornog-
raphy and multi-player online games, and so on. We are ingenious
in these matters, it's true. Our cuisine can be elaborate and costly
and subtle; our caresses can be staged and ornamented and fanta-
sized; our politics can be theatrically byzantine; our sports gladia-
torial; our shopping all-consuming; and so on. But, for Pascal, no
matter how ingenious and how elaborate our diversions become,
they remain always exactly diversions from something more real
and more agonizing, which is misery. Without our miseries, we'd
have no need of diversions; and without our diversions, we'd not
be able to endure our miseries.

None of this is to say that diversions don't work, or that we
can, here below, do without them. The third thread in the excerpt
under discussion, and the most acutely observed, is that they do
work, and why they do. Hunting hares, to use one of Pascal's examples, isn't about the hare hunted. That's insignificant enough that
we'd probably reject it if it was brought to us on a plate. Neither
is it about the cross-country chase by itself: if we were offered the
chance to walk the fields with dogs on a misty autumn morning
for no purpose other than the walk, we'd probably not do it, and

if we did it wouldn't divert us. No, a good diversion brings two or more relatively uninteresting activities (dead hares, country walks) together and makes a *tracas* of them, a compelling and noisily overpowering spectacle we can't look away from: the walk is now a hunt; the hare now a quarry; and the whole thing now a diversion. Similarly with gambling, which is one of Pascal's deep interests.[38] It's not just about the money you might win. If you were offered the $1,000 you won last night at the tables as a gift, you might accept it, but accepting it wouldn't serve as a diversion; and if you played roulette for hours with no money at stake—well, you probably wouldn't; it would produce *ennui*, and also wouldn't serve as a diversion. Gambling works as a diversion because it brings money and chance together, and makes a *tracas* of them. Similar analyses can easily be applied to courtship, politics, warmaking, and much more. We might say, though it isn't Pascal's language, that anything we're capable of becoming addicted to belongs to the category of *divertissement*; and that there are so many things we're capable of becoming addicted to shows how deep our need is for something to look at that isn't the misery of our own condition.

Diversions, however, aren't always to hand. Sometimes, solitude is forced upon us, or for some other reason our preferred diversions are taken away. We work hard, however, to avoid those diversion-free moments, and Pascal is capable, with perhaps pardonable exaggeration, of tracing most ills and evils, and much of our social and political life, to the depth of our unwillingness to be diversion-free: wars and courtships and politics happen because we're unwilling to stay alone in our rooms.[39] And even when diversions are to hand, they exhaust themselves: that last bloody act

---

38. Pascal discusses gambling as a diversion more fully at *Pensées* 126 (*OC* 2/586), for example. And some of his most creative mathematical work was prompted by a question about probability posed by gamblers. See Pascal's letters to Fermat (*OC* 1/146–62), and *Triangle* (*OC* 1/169–328). See also *Pensées* 647 (*OC* 2/804), where a similar analysis is given to combat.

39. See *Pensées* 126 (*OC* 2/583–87).

always beckons, and sometimes with a directness and clarity that no diversion can easily occlude.

4.3 Custom

Pagan existence is a death-directed opaque misery, oppressed by incomprehensible infinities and alleviated only, and that partially, by obsessively sought diversions. It is also ordered and given form most fundamentally by habit and custom, and in this, as with the unavoidability of death, pagan existence does not differ from Christian existence.[40] Pascal writes that it's a pitiable thing, *une chose pitoyable*, that there are so many Muslims and heretics who are what they are just because their fathers were, in just the same way that trades (locksmith, soldier, and so on) are given by birth and location and imitation. That's why, he gnomically adds, *c'est par là que les sauvages n'ont que faire de Provence*, savages don't care about Provence.[41] They don't because they haven't been given the habit of caring about Provence, in contrast, presumably, to the French, who have. He shouldn't be read to find it pitiable that the custom of the country determines almost everything for us; only that the custom of the country so often leads us astray. Being Muslim is in one way like caring about Provence: local custom gives it to you, or doesn't. But the two are unlike in that being Muslim is something you'd better not be—it is, for Pascal, erroneous at least, and at worst idolatrous and damnable—whereas if you don't care about Provence, you're none the worse for that. What's *pitoyable*, then, isn't the habit-laced and custom-produced nature of these conditions (they can be nothing other), but rather that damaging error is so prevalent. It's a mistake, of course, to think that what local custom provides you is *le meilleur*, the better or best thing, just because it's your local custom. Better to say: this is my way of

---

40. On Pascal on custom and habit, I've benefited from Gérard Ferreyrolles, *Les reines du monde: l'imagination et la coutume chez Pascal* (Paris: Honoré Champion, 1995), 17–119.
41. *Pensées* 182 (*OC* 2/606–7).

life, mode of expression, pattern of conviction, habit of dress. That it is so is neutral as to its truth, desirability, and beauty.

Pascal uses a range of terms for the territory of habit. There's the generic "custom" (*coutume*), meaning local custom, the custom of the country, in whatever sphere—politics, dress, cuisine, language, art, and so on; also "habit" (*habitude*), which covers roughly the same ground. Where you live (*habiter—habitude*) provides you almost all your customs, of which a paradigmatic instance is sartorial (*coutume—costume*, with the Latin *consuetudo* lurking in the background). Those words indicate the fact of habit and something of its range. Pascal also uses terms that indicate the kind of thing habit is. There's its likeness to machines (*machine, automate*), for machines are creatures of habit in the sense that once they're designed and built and given the right input in the right context they always do just the same thing—they are, we might say, habituated to doing just that thing, a state of affairs with which Pascal was familiar by way of his work on the calculating machine, and in designing apparatus for testing the effects of atmospheric pressure on liquids. There's also the habituatedness of nonhuman animals, something in almost every way like our own habituatedness; we engage in political activity, for example, with the same degree of environmentally and genetically (not, of course, Pascal's language) determined habituatedness as starlings do when they flock. Pascal likes the verb *abêtir*—"to animalize, to make or become like an animal"—for this.

Here are Pascal's relatively polished thoughts about the place of habit in the formation of belief:

>> It's important not to misunderstand yourself: you're as much automaton as mind. That's why demonstration isn't the only means by which you're persuaded of something. How few things can be demonstrated! Proofs convince only the mind; it's custom that gives the strongest proofs, and the most firmly believed. That's what in-

clines the automaton, which drags the mind thoughtlessly along with it. Who has demonstrated that tomorrow will come, and that we'll die? And yet, what is there that's more believed? It is, therefore, custom that convinces us, and custom that makes so many Christians, Muslims, pagans, tradespeople, soldiers and so on. And so we must turn to custom once the mind has seen where the truth is, so that we can soak and stain ourselves with a belief that constantly escapes us—it's too demanding to have the proofs always before us. You must acquire beliefs more easily, by habit, which, without violence or art or argument, makes you believe things and inclines all your powers toward them so that your soul falls naturally into them. When you believe something only by the force of conviction and the automaton is inclined to believe the opposite, it's not enough. You must, therefore, make both parts of yourself believe, your mind by reasons that it's enough to have seen once in life, and your automaton by custom and by not allowing it to think otherwise. (*Pensées* 671, *OC* 2/818–19)[42]

We are, cognitively speaking, both automata—habit-formed and habit-motivated—and responsive to reasons and reasoning. How do we come to assent to some claim? What are the means by which we're persuaded of something? They are two. Most common and most effective is custom, or repeated action. That forms the *automate*, and as a result of such formation we assent without thought, and easily, much as we speak our first language without thought, and easily. Much less common and much less effective is demonstration, the giving and receiving of convincing reasons. We may, and sometimes do, come to assent to this or that by way of demonstration, but it is difficult and just too much work (*c'est trop d'affaire*) to do so in the first place, and close to impossible to maintain awareness of the reasons we may once have had for any particular item of belief. It's also the case that we do and must

---

42. Compare: *Pensées* 116–17 (*OC* 2/577–78); *Pensées* 397 (*OC* 2/679); *Pensées* 469 (*OC* 2/746–48). See also the discussion of the wager in §4.5, below.

and should give our assent to many claims for which there are no demonstrative reasons (tomorrow will come; you'll die), or none that anyone knows (every even number can be expressed as the sum of two primes), or none that we know (Napoleon was exiled on Elba). And so we do, because we must (*il faut*), acquire and maintain most of our beliefs by the force of local custom, which is to say of habit; that force provides us beliefs *sans violence, sans art, sans argument*, but, rather, automatically, making *automates* or *machines* of us in much the same way (Pascal doesn't say) as we become speakers of French or English.

Now, in this passage Pascal does imply that where there are reasons for an assent; it would be good for those who make it to have seen and understood those reasons at least once, even if thereafter the automaton kicks in. But it's easy enough to imagine an extension of the position toward the view that there's nothing inferior about assents made without demonstration, even when such demonstrations are available. If you assent to a truth in macro-economics or literary theory without knowing the patterns of argument that show it to be true, or the evidence that supports it, you're still assenting to a truth. You're related to that truth differently than is someone who does know, and can when asked produce, those arguments and that evidence; but it's far from clear that the relation is one of inferior to superior. It is the case that the one who knows the arguments and the evidence knows something more than the one who doesn't. But if what we're interested in is the capacity to live in accord with truths, then the argument- and evidence-knower might be to the one who knows neither as the lexicographer is to the native speaker—that is, a harmless drudge possessed of specialized technical knowledge that's as likely to make her worse as better at speaking the language. Such an extension is in accord with the spirit of Pascal's remark above, and others like it, even if it goes further than he does.

There is a further point about custom and habit that Pascal

makes often and enthusiastically. It is that in cases where something is asked of you and the option is forced (that is, you've no choice but to make the assent/perform the action, or refuse to do so; there's no third possibility), and reason can't decide for you whether you should or shouldn't do what's asked, it's a damaging mistake to attempt to base your decision on reasons or reasoning. There's a clear application of this point to (coming to have) Christian faith, to which I'll turn in a moment. But, for Pascal, it applies to other matters as well, and most notably to obeying, or refusing to obey, the local laws, whatever they happen to be. Local laws (drive on the right; kill those your government tells you to; have at most one spouse) are, for Pascal, paradigmatic instances of *coutume* upon the justice and propriety of which reason has little or no purchase. They should be obeyed because they are laws, he thinks, not because of some standard of justice external to them: "It would therefore be good to obey laws and customs because they are laws,"[43] and not for some other reason. To do otherwise results in revolution or civil war in the name of principles of justice that we've no access to and no substantial agreement about; and that is to introduce violence into the world that otherwise would not have been there.[44] Better not to do that. Better, rather, to respond to a forced option that's a matter of custom insulated from reason by treating it exactly as a matter of custom—which is to say, abiding by it.

The Christian life is as much constituted by custom as the pagan life. And, the habits of the Christian life, like those of the pagan life, ought to be recognizable from outside, by observers. That is in significant part because conversion, which marks the

---

43. *Pensées* 469 (*OC* 2/746). For more on this, see chapter 6, §6.1, on secular cities, below.

44. There are some difficulties here, not least because it's a majority position within the Catholic tradition, with significant doctrinal weight in some of its forms, that there are at least some principles of justice discernible to natural reason, and that local laws should conform to them. I return to these difficulties in chapter 6, §6.1, below.

transition from pagan to Christian life, is a radical event, marked by the pain of violent separation from the habits of an old life and the seductive sweetness of the prospect of a new one.[45] Its radicality uproots old habits and replaces them with new ones. Those new habits are in significant part liturgical—that is, sacramental, but also more broadly devotional. But they are also moral and practical: because Christian life is centered upon the LORD, the habits of the world with respect to such matters as getting and spending, amusement and diversion, love and sex, eating and drinking, are also transfigured in part and abandoned in part by Christians. Pascal is alive to the possibility that Christian liturgical and devotional life can be lived without any re-ordering of habits in these other spheres, and when that happens he blames it mostly on the bad guidance of Jesuitical (and Jesuit) confessors and guides. If your confessor tells you that so long as you devote yourself to the Blessed Virgin and her son you need not abandon or moderate your ambition, avarice, hatred, and violence, then your devotional practice may lose its character as a love-offering of the regenerate to the LORD, and become instead the means of providing you false confidence and false peace.[46] Liturgically habituated action, performed without thought as an automaton or beast would, ought to be zealous and urgent:[47] once touched by the LORD, the Christian is eager to return the touch, and is as hard to restrain from doing so as the lover who has been once kissed and who is eager to return the favor.[48] It's not that the Christian has to decide to be zealous; it's that the touch is so scarifying and so delightful (both at the same time) that zeal is what follows from it as heat from fire.

45. On conversion, and these tropes for it, see §4.4, below.

46. I here draw from Pascal's discussions of *dévotions à la Vierge* in *Provincials* 9 (*OC* 1/673–74).

47. I think once again of starlings flocking: an almost paradigmatic instance of Pascalian zeal in action.

48. *Pensées* 510 (*OC* 2/764). This is among the more gnomic of Pascal's phrases, but it can serve as a suggestive epigraph for the whole of his understanding of the Christian life.

And the zeal informs, or should, both liturgical habit and habits of being in the world.

Pascal's treatment of the Jesuits' approach to and administration of the sacrament of penance is illustrative and representative of his approach to the Christian liturgical and moral life.[49] The Jesuits' goal with respect to this sacrament, Pascal writes, is to make it easier, smoother, and more attractive, and in that way to make it possible for those who would otherwise be likely to avoid it. Jesuits, Pascal claims, permit and sometimes recommend obscuring from your confessor that some among your sins are frequent or habitual, and having one confessor for mortal sins and another for venial ones. Both these permissions are in the interest of removing shame. The Jesuits also, he says, provide absolution without requiring penance, on the ground that penance may be deferred to purgatory—with the goal of removing a fear of penance that might prevent some from confessing at all. They also do not require that penitents avoid proximate occasions of sin, and they manage that by loosening the definition of "proximate" so that it refers only to occasions that prompt very frequent offense, and not, therefore, to those that produce only occasional offense. For example, if you find yourself having occasional sex with someone you're not married to because you live in the same house with that person, that living arrangement need not count as a proximate occasion of sin just because the sex is no more than occasional. Further yet, the Jesuits don't require that penitents be contrite—that they show sorrow for their offenses out of love of the LORD, whom they offend—but only that they show attrition, sorrow for offense out of fear of punishment. All these relaxations (*relâchements*) are, for Pascal, also accommodations: they conform the sacrament to the fears and desires of penitents, not to the form of penitence; and in that way they move toward replacing the sacrament with its

---

49. In what follows I summarize and elaborate upon *Provincials* 10 (*OC* 1/684–96).

simulacrum, and thus obscuring from the baptized the necessity of opening the heart to the LORD, giving themselves fully to the LORD in love for the unmerited touch of grace.

Pascal's attitude to appropriately Christian well-doing and ill-doing outside the sacramental sphere is evident in his ridicule of the Jesuits' apparently endless ingenuity in redescribing what seem on their face to be sinful or criminal actions so that they become permissible or even commendable. For instance (Pascal's imagined Jesuit interlocutor speaks):

> ≫ According to our celebrated Fr. l'Amy,[50] priests and religious are permitted to forestall those who intend to blacken them by defamation by killing them—but always properly directing the intention. Here's what he writes ...: "An ecclesiastic or a religious is permitted to kill a slanderer who threatens to make public his or his community's scandalous crimes when there's no other means of preventing it, as when he's about to spread his slanders unless he's killed at once. In such a case, just as a religious is permitted to kill someone who intends to take his life, so he's also permitted to kill someone who intends to take his honor or that of his community." (*Provincials* 7, *OC* 1/657–58)

[*T*]*oujours en dirigeant bien l'intention*: that's the magic key, *notre grande méthode*,[51] as Pascal represents the Jesuits calling it. By it, what looks like murder—killing someone about to reveal your crimes—can become preservation of your honor or some other kind of self-protection. Under that redescription it's at least permissible, and may even be praiseworthy or required. And the great method is almost infinitely flexible. By means of it, I can rape you or defraud you or lie to you or enslave you by redescribing those acts (giving you what you deserve, redistributing your ill-gotten

---

50. Francesco Amico (1578–1651), an Italian Jesuit moral theologian.
51. *Provincials* 7 (*OC* 1/648).

gains, protecting the safety of the innocent, protecting you from harm) so that they become things I may or should do, adjusting my intent so that the object of my action is now that permissible thing, and then acting upon that redirected intention.

Pascal has a good deal of fun with this magic key. Here's one further example among very many.[52] Suppose I want to lend you money at interest, something forbidden by the Church at the time Pascal was writing. It would be sinful for me to provide you $100 in cash in exchange for a note promising me $100 a year hence together with an additional $10 in interest. That would be exactly to act upon the intention of lending money at interest, which is to say profiting from cash as a medium of exchange. But suppose I give you a quantity of gold in exchange for a note promising me $110 a year hence, and then at once buy back the gold from you for $100 in cash. I still have the gold I began with; you have $100 in cash; and I have a note promising $110 a year hence. The net result is the same as with the original usurious exchange; but it has now been redescribed as selling something expensively, and on credit, and at once buying it back more cheaply, and for cash, which is no longer usury. Pascal likens these methods to magic or alchemy, and presents them in such a way as to encourage his readers to see them so, and to find them ridiculous.[53]

What Pascal objects to here is the same as what he objects to in the case of the sacraments: dilution by redescription. Prescriptions and proscriptions that are on their face straightforward and direct—*don't kill*; *don't lend money at interest*; *if a sin is habitual, confess its frequency*—are evacuated by skilled and subtle specification

52. What follows summarizes *Provincials* 8 (*OC* 1/662–64).

53. The (re)direction of intention isn't the only means that Pascal identifies and ridicules as aimed at the accommodation of the Church to the world, and thus to its corruption. There's also *la doctrine des opinions probables*, which is, roughly, the view that if some authority has endorsed or defended the viability of an action in terms of moral theology, that suffices to make said action defensibly performable. See the discussion at *Provincials* 5–6 (*OC* 1/624–47).

of the intentional objects of particular actions. They may even be
transmuted into their opposites, as when *don't kill* becomes *priests
should kill when about to be slandered*. Pascal presents this evacua-
tion and transmutation of the habits appropriate to the Christian
life as something done to accommodate the world. Christianity so
treated becomes an amusement and a comfort rather than a con-
suming fire. Pascal writes, *Je ne me contente pas du probable ... je
cherche le sûr*—I'm not satisfied with what's probable ... I'm after
what's certain.[54] And certainty about the shape and content of
the Christian life isn't fostered by the dilutions and evacuations
the casuists prefer.

Pascal doesn't, on these difficult matters, offer a theory opposed to the Jesuits' theories about how to discriminate the sinful
from the nonsinful, the mortal from the venial, the confessable
from the not-properly-confessable. He doesn't engage, at the theoretical level, with the question of how to specify the intentional
object of an action, or with that of how to individuate actions one
from another. To engage these questions would be, for him, to enter enemy territory, well guarded and thoroughly fortified, and,
for the purposes of *Provincials*, which is where most of this discussion occurs, it would have been a mistake to go there. He writes
in *Provincials* as a satirist and ironist, and what he needs for those
purposes is scorched earth, not another scholastic theory. It suffices for him to make the Jesuit moral theologians look ridiculous in
the eyes of the ordinary reader, and in that, as it seems to me, he
succeeds admirably.

There is, nonetheless, a method of sorts in play in Pascal's critique of probabilism, and of redirecting the intention. It is that
of the clear case. Pascal outlines some of the more absurd conclusions that the Jesuits' methods lead to—that a religious visiting

---

54. *Provincials* 5 (*OC* 1/631). Pascal writes here about the doctrine of probable opinions rather than that of (re)directing the intention, but both, in their distinctive ways, speak
against certitude about what the Christian life asks and offers.

a brothel in order to have sex with a prostitute may divest himself of his habit;[55] that Jesuits may, under certain circumstances, kill Jansenists;[56] that dueling is sometimes required of priests
and religious[57]—not in order to argue against them but to show
them as clear cases of absurdity. If this is what you get from the
Jesuits' methods, the thought is, then you know something has
gone wrong, and badly so. It's as if you'd followed your satnav into
the middle of a lake when Westminster Cathedral was where you
wanted to get to. The thing you know from that outcome is that
you've followed the wrong route, listened to the wrong guide. You
don't need a rival theory, much less an understanding of what went
wrong with the satnav (sunspots? gremlins?). What you need is a
better guide, and Pascal thinks he can give you one: the unified
voice of Scripture, tradition, the witness of the Fathers, and the
ordinary liturgical practices of the Church. Don't look here, at the
casuistic niceties of the seventeenth century, but do look there. Ad-
verting to the clear case isn't a device only for satirists and ironists;
it's also a good instance of refusing to ascend the ladder of theory
any higher than necessary to make the needed point. A full-blown
theory of intentionality and of action is a good thing to try for if
that's what you're after. But if you'd rather show what the Christian life would be like if the jesuitical accommodation engine is
shunted into a siding, then it's no objection to say that you're not
providing such a theory. Offering it would be a diversion.

And what does the Christian life look like from Pascal's angle
of vision? He shows it to his older sister, Gilberte, in this letter,
written when he was twenty-four:

55. *Provincials* 6 (*OC* 1/637–38).
56. *Provincials* 7 (*OC* 1/658–59).
57. *Provincials* 7 (*OC* 1/658).

» There are those whom God has, by rebirth, gratuitously removed from sin (which is the true nothing because it's opposed to God who is the true being) to give them a place in his Church, which is his true temple. After they have been gratuitously removed from nothing to the point of their creation, receiving in that way a place in the universe, they have a double obligation: to serve him, and to honor him. In so far as they are creatures, they should remain in the creaturely order, without profaning the place they occupy; and in so far as they are Christians, they should ceaselessly aspire to be worthy to take part in the body of Jesus-Christ. But although worldly creatures discharge their obligation by remaining in a limited perfection because worldly perfection is also limited, God's children should not limit their purity or their perfection because they take part in an entirely divine and infinitely perfect body. We see that Jesus-Christ does not limit the command of perfection, and that he proposes to us a model of infinite perfection when he says, *Therefore be perfect as your heavenly Father is perfect*. Christians, even those who profess piety, frequently make the very harmful error of persuading themselves that there's a certain degree of perfection in which they may rest secure and which there's no need to go beyond since there's nothing wrong in stopping there, and they might fall by going higher ...[58] (Letter of 1648 to Gilberte Périer, *OC* 2/9–10)

Pascal emphasizes here the gratuitous (*gratuitement*) way in which the LORD removes the chosen from sin, and sin from the chosen, in order to place them in the Church.[59] He also explicitly connects the regeneration of the baptized with their first creation: in both cases, what we're removed from, taken out of, is nothing (*néant*). Sin, like the absence from which we were called when brought into being out of nothing, as Christian doctrine requires be said, is itself nothing at all. It must be that because it's intrin-

58. The letter hasn't survived completely; it ends with the ellipses.
59. See chapter 5, below, on grace.

sically and by definition opposed to the LORD, who is *le véritable être*, and since it's a commonplace of Christianity to reject all dualisms that postulate real powers independent of and opposed to the LORD, it follows that anything opposed to the LORD, to the extent that it is so opposed, can only be nothing. This in turn entails that anything intrinsically and without remainder opposed to the LORD must be nothing—*néant, nihil*. Pascal embraces this grammatical point with enthusiasm, as all Christians ought. And then, once re-created, we have a double obligation: as creatures to serve the LORD, and as Christians to honor the LORD as participants in Jesus-Christ's body. That second obligation is to perfection. Satisfaction with anything less, with only a certain degree of perfection, with what's safe enough and good enough, is an error both harmful and frequent. It's harmful as an error because it doesn't take seriously the radicality of the gift given: it's a gift that brings the recipient into being and out of sin, and since that's an unstinting gift, given not only to a ready recipient as our gifts are, but also to a recipient brought into being by the gift, as our gifts are not (parenthood is the closest we come to that, and it is not very close), properly constituted gratitude requires that nothing be held back. If perfection is the consummation of gratitude, then having it to *un certain degré* is exactly to hold something back, to keep something to yourself—which is to say to refuse perfection by refusing to acknowledge the gift's radicality. Pascal might have quoted Paul's dictum that we have nothing we haven't received.[60]

The thought that one lives the Christian life as a member of Jesus-Christ's body is present in this letter, as often elsewhere in Pascal's writing.[61] The pagan situation is to be a separated member, dying as any amputated limb would because it lacks the nourishment the body provides. The Christian situation is to be rejoined

60. 1 Cor 4:7.
61. For membership in Jesus-Christ's body, see especially *Pensées* 350–54 (*OC* 2/664–65). I draw on this sequence of thoughts in what follows.

to Jesus, and when that happens Christians find their loves transformed. They now love themselves only for the body in which they take part,[62] because they have no life outside it and everything they do is for it. In the excerpt from the letter to Gilberte given above, I've rendered *faire partie* as "to take part," and that is an apt label for the relation a Christian bears to Jesus-Christ because, according to one of its ranges of meaning, when *x* participates (takes part in) *y*, *x* receives from *y* whatever is properly characteristic of *y* that *x* cannot provide for itself—as does iron participating in fire, blotting-paper in ink, a chameleon in the colors of its immediate environment. To be participant in Jesus-Christ as a member of his body is to be deified—to take part in the LORD. From this, once it's received, comes the perfection of the Christian life. When the finger or the cornea or the kidney is where it should be and is working as it should, there is nothing of themselves they hold back from the body in which they take part; that is their perfection, and it is simply what body parts do when they're functioning as they ought. That proper function looks like zeal (*zèle*)—that, at any rate, is what Pascal often calls it,[63] and his liking for the word always has a polemical edge. He's concerned, in using it, to distance himself from and call into question the Laodiceans, who for him are represented best by the Jesuit moral theologians of his time.

In the letter to Gilberte just excerpted, Pascal uses the language of obligation (*devoir, obligation*). That language is not, perhaps, the best choice for his position, although the semantic range of *devoir* was broad then as now, embracing patterns of action commanded (I must be at work tomorrow), imposed ineluctably by external circumstance (I have to die), given by local custom but

---

62. *Pensées* 352 (*OC* 2/664).

63. On *zèle*, see: *Pensées* 276 (*OC* 2/645); *Pensées* 279 (*OC* 2/646); *Pensées* 298 (*OC* 2/652); *Pensées* 502 (*OC* 2/761); *Pensées* 510 (*OC* 2/764). Pascal's use of the word is often, positively, about the Jews' attitude to the law (see discussion in chapter 7, below), and as a point of contrast between the Church of his time and the early Church as at *Comparison* (*OC* 2/103–7).

in fact unavoidable (I must speak French to him), uncompelled but preferred (you really shouldn't laugh at her). Translating *devoir* as I did, by "should" (they should *se tenir dans l'ordre des créatures*; they should *sans cesse aspirer à se rendre dignes de faire partie du corps de Jésus-Christ*) leaves ambiguous the nature of the obligation. Given the proximity in the letter to the trope of participation in Jesus-Christ's body, the best construal of the obligations of the Christian life is that they are like those under which the members of the body labor (the heart should beat as Christians should aspire to perfection), and not much like, for example, those that bind signatories to a contract (once you've signed, you should pay $100 on the first of the month). The zeal of the Christian for Jesus-Christ or the Jew for the law, then, is like the eagerness with which the eyes of someone moved from gloaming to dawn focus on the detail of objects newly revealed by the rising sun.[64] Here's a conspectus of how that works:

> ≫ Against those who, trusting in God's mercy, remain nonchalant while not doing good works—the two sources of our sins are pride and laziness, and God shows us two of his attributes as their cure: mercy and justice. It's proper to justice to reduce pride, however holy your works may be ...; and it's proper to mercy to fight laziness by inviting you to good works ... and so you're deceived if you take mercy to authorize relaxation. Rather, mercy is the attribute that formally fights laziness. So, instead of saying "if there were no mercy in God we'd have to make all kinds of efforts toward virtue," you should on the contrary say that it's because there's mercy in God that we have to make all kinds of efforts. (*Pensées* 648, *OC* 2/804–5)[65]

Pascal signals here the difference between contrition (compunction for sin out of love for the LORD) and attrition (compunction

---

64. For more on these patterns of thought, see chapter 5, below, on grace.

65. Compare *Pensées* 734 (*OC* 2/867–68).

for sin out of fear of the LORD),[66] and in so doing transfigures the meaning of effort as a keynote of the Christian life. The *toutes sortes d'efforts* that Christians have to make in order to live the Christian life aren't acts of our own; their ideal type is the zealous and eager return of love. Contrition, accordingly, is sorrow for our sins because they've offended the LORD, which is to say because they've created distance between ourselves and the LORD. It's a sorrow motivated by love. Attrition, by contrast, is sorrow for our sins motivated by fear of the sufferings they'll bring to us: it's self-directed, fueled by *amour-propre*, rather than directed toward the LORD. When Pascal writes that mercy doesn't authorize relaxation in living the Christian life—we can do what we like because we're assured of the LORD's mercy—but rather that mercy is the attribute that formally fights laziness, it's to say that the form of relaxation (or *paresse*, laziness) is a turn away from the LORD, and that mercy has the opposed form, which is that of a loving invitation whose answer is a redirection of the gaze back to the LORD, so that *relâchement—nonchalance—paresse* are no longer desirable. If you've relaxed back into your easy chair in order to watch a mindlessly bad film and your beloved walks into the room, your eyes turn to him or her and you embrace. That turn of the eyes, that embrace, these have the form of penitence (and penance); but it's a burden easy to bear for lovers.

4.4 Conversion

Pagan existence and Christian existence are, for Pascal, different in fundamental ways. Even features of human existence that belong to both (habit, the horizon of death, the unavoidability of physical suffering) seem different to pagans than they do to Christians. And since no one is or can be born Christian, while every-

---

66. On contrition and attrition in Pascal: *Provincials* 10 (*OC* 1/684–96); *Pensées* 606 (*OC* 2/790); *Pensées* 653 (*OC* 2/806–7).

one is born either as Jew or as pagan, some account is necessary of how the transition from a pagan mode of existence to a Christian one happens.[67] Pascal frequently addresses this. When he does, he has two concerns. The first is about agency: What is the relation between what the LORD does and what we do in conversion? That is a question about grace.[68] The second concern is instrumental and phenomenological: How might the unconverted be converted, and what does it seem like to the converted to be converted?

Violence is one thread in Pascal's depiction of conversion:

> ≫ Our LORD said that since John the Baptist's coming, which is to say since his own coming into the world, and consequently since his coming to each of the faithful, the kingdom of God suffers violence, and the violent bear it away. Before we're touched [by Jesus], we've nothing but the weight of our concupiscence, which drags us to earth. When God lifts us up, these two opposing forces cause this violence. Only God can overcome it. (Letter of 1656 to Charlotte de Roannez, *OC* 2/28)[69]

Conversion's violence is produced by a tension between concupiscence, which is desire for creatures as if they were intrinsically desirable rather than desirable only and exactly as creatures; and as if having them would satisfy, when in fact it never does because the goods in them, as also they themselves, are transient, and so whatever pleasure and good is to be had from them won't last. Creatures leave us, or we them, and so our felicitous relations with them aren't our sovereign or final good, our *souverain bien*, however temporarily felicitous they may be. Concupiscence, in Pascal's

---

67. There are additional questions in this area, including: what's to be said about the transition from Jewish to Christian existence, or from Christian to Jewish? And, what account is to be offered of the efficacy of baptism for infants, or for others not capable of understanding or acknowledging what's being done? These are not questions in which Pascal shows any interest. See chapter 7 below, on Jews.

68. See chapter 5, below, on grace.

69. Compare *Pensées* 514 (*OC* 2/765–66).

usage, isn't merely a desire for relation with creatures; there can be nothing wrong with that. No, it's a desire for creatures as if they were not creatures; it's intense and passionate and heavy (that metaphor of weight is broadcast in Pascal), and since the Fall works always upon us. When we're touched, as in the excerpt above, by the triune LORD—Pascal writes above about Jesus-Christ, but following the axiom that the LORD's actions upon us are always and indivisibly of all three persons of the Trinity, it's reasonable to interpret the passage in this way—a desire with a different object is proposed and given to us. That desire is for the LORD as our proper and final good, and it's incompatible with concupiscence. The LORD's touch brings tensive conflict, then. The excerpt above mentions the tension between being lifted up and being dragged down: conversion stretches us toward breaking: we're racked or strappado'd by it. We want what we can see or smell or hear or taste or touch as if it's the only thing to want; but we also, when touched, want the Lord as our supreme good. The two loves work on us violently, and we're unable to bring peace to the conflict.

Pascal emphasizes the felt violence of conversion in another way as well: by calling conversion self-annihilation. Here's a characteristically dramatic instance:

> ≫ They imagine that conversion is worshiping God; they picture it as a transaction or a conversation. But real conversion is self-annihilation before that universal being whom we've so often irritated, and who can legitimately destroy us at any time. It is recognition that we can do nothing without him, and that we deserve nothing from him but disgrace. It is recognition that there is an unconquerable opposition between God and us. (*Pensées* 358, *OC* 2/666)

All we are independently of the LORD is, for Pascal, opposed to the LORD. There's nothing of us or in us, therefore, that can enter into exchange (*commerce, conversation*) with the LORD, as some models of conversion suggest. There's certainly nothing in us that deserves or merits anything but destruction or damnation (*perdre—perdition*) from the LORD; that is put more graphically still by saying that we deserve from the LORD not grace, the free gift whereby our salvation is assured, but rather its opposite, disgrace, the opposite of grace: *on n'a rien mérité de lui que sa disgrace.* Self-annihilation, the bringing to nothing of all that we take to be ourselves, its immolation,[70] is painful because, among other things, of the depth of ingression of the habits that, as pagans, we've come to take to constitute ourselves. But, for Pascal, conversion, the transition to Christian existence from pagan existence, requires it. Our sense of ourselves must be burned to the ground, and that is not something we can do by or to ourselves.

There's another corollary of conversion's pain. It is that the inner conversation, our talk with ourselves upon the brightly lighted stage of our inner theater, needs to be stilled, and will be when conversation ends. In the excerpt just given, Pascal denies that conversation is an appropriate metaphor for conversion. One implication of this is that silence before the LORD is preferable to speech—certainly preferable to speech that we use to show to the LORD what we take ourselves to be. That's because what we take ourselves to be (teacher, cobbler, king, sister, seamstress, father, soldier, prostitute, scholar, cook) is given to us by local custom, and then given solidity by the habits of the automaton. Grounding our conversational exchange with the LORD on these habits, communicating ourselves to the LORD as if they are what we are, is an error because they aren't. We are, for the purposes of conversion, nothing but sinners, which is only another way of saying nothing but nothing. The habits that give us our sense of ourselves, that make it seem to us like something to be us, are partly received from other locals,

---

70. For Pascal's use of the metaphor of fire for conversion, see *Pensées* 711 (*OC* 2/851–52). There's a reproduction of the autograph of the text at *OC* 2/1562.

from the customs and conversation, that is, of whichever locale is ours. But they are also in part given form and apparent solidity by our conversations with our selves. As it comes to seem to you that you are a teacher, and so on, you will tell yourself that you are that, as well as listen to others telling it to you. Your self-constituting inner monologues need to be silenced, as well, and will be by conversion.[71] This way of thinking has implications for the Christian life after conversion. A radical way of putting the most important of those implications, never quite approached by Pascal so far as I can tell, is that the Christian life involves a progressive alteration of the sense of who we are by way of a progressive stilling of any voices that say we are somebody. The first-person pronoun recedes toward the horizon. This is certainly an implication of what he writes about the necessity for self-hatred.[72]

Conversion, then, for Pascal, is inseparable from the pain of conflict between desire for—love of—the pagan world, and love of the LORD; and from the pain of bringing to nothing what you've spent time and trouble convincing yourself is something. But pain and violence aren't the whole story about conversion. There's also sweetness, delectation, delight, and joy. As here:

⇥ God changes our hearts by spilling a heavenly sweetness into them that overcomes our flesh's delectations. The result is that we sense our mortality together with our nothingness, on the one hand; and discover, on the other, the glory and eternity of God, so that we come to have a disgust for the deliciousness of sin that separates us from the incorruptible good, and to find our greatest joy in the God who charms us. And so we're drawn unfailingly to that same God, by an entirely voluntary, free, and loving movement, in such a way that it would be pain and punishment to be separated from him. It

---

71. I paraphrase here *Pensées* 91 (*OC* 2/570), and draw upon themes and vocabulary from *Conversion* (*OC* 2/99–102).

72. On this necessity see, e.g., *Pensées* 485 (*OC* 2/755), and *Pensées* 509 (*OC* 2/763–64).

isn't that we can't always distance ourselves, nor that we wouldn't do so if we wanted to. But how could we want to, since the will is always drawn to what pleases it most, and nothing pleases it as much as the unique good that includes in itself all other goods? *It's necessary that we act according to what pleases us more*, as St. Augustine says. (*Provincials* 18, *OC* 1/800–801)

This is the language of seduction rather than that of terror and pain. The LORD's touch here is sweet beyond compare, and so when you receive it you want nothing other than more of the same. You're like the hungry infant at the breast: the sweetness of the milk that flows from the nipple is, you realize when it enters your mouth and belly, exactly what you'd wanted and needed, and you'll continue to focus upon it and it alone until your hunger is satiated. In the case of the *douceur céleste* that the LORD spills (*repandre*) upon us and into us, however, there's no satiation because the LORD is infinitely desirable and infinitely satisfying. Once you've had a taste, you'll always want more, and it's impossible that you could want anything less or anything different. Pascal begins to write, in the excerpt above, about grace and freedom, and is concerned here, as typically, to use and affirm of the movement toward the LORD the language of necessity and inevitability (*infailliblement*; *necesse est*) together with that of freedom (*tout libre, tout volontaire, tout amoureux*), without providing a full justification of how the two languages are to be held together.[73] Neither are the languages of delight and pain fully reconciled, but in that case it's easy enough to see how they might be: delight is present to the extent that the LORD's touch is received and reciprocated; and pain is present to the extent that the self-regarding and self-centered delights of the world are being bloodily excised by that same touch. The proportions of each will vary from case to case, and from time to time in a particular case. As the burning pain of separation recedes and

73. For more on this, see chapter 5, below, on grace.

the wounds it leaves are cicatrized,[74] delight increases (that is the same as increase in holiness) until, eventually, there is only delight.

4.5 Wager

There are barriers to conversion. Of special interest to Pascal among them is the thought that the truth of Christianity needs to be proved by argument before it can be accepted, and before the things that Christians ordinarily do can be done. Pascal is interested in this because of the audience for whom his apologetical work was intended. They, disproportionately and unusually, placed a high value upon reason, and thought it problematic that Christianity's central claims appear not to be capable of argumentative demonstration. Pascal is scathing about this. It belongs to Christianity, he writes, to claim that its claims are not demonstrable in that way, and to claim that faith, minimally an act of trust in thought and life in what the LORD has shown of the LORD's self, is without remainder a gift of the LORD to which the giving and taking of arguments in the space of reason is irrelevant.[75] Briefly, and representatively:

> ≫ Faith is God's gift. Don't think that we're saying that it's a gift of reasoning. The other religions don't say this about their faith. They offer nothing but reason as a way to faith, but it doesn't get you there. (*Pensées* 501, *OC* 2/761)[76]

---

74. The pains of Jesus-Christ in Gethsemane and on Golgotha are the primary analogy for Pascal here. See, among many other places, *Jésus-Christ* 279 (*OC* 2/74). Compare *Pensées* 717 (*OC* 2/855–59).

75. On these themes, see: *Conférences* (*OC* 1/549–50); *Sorbonne* 3 (*OC* 1/955–56); *Pensées* 5 (*OC* 2/545); *Pensées* 397 (*OC* 2/679); *Pensées* 501 (*OC* 2/761). See also chapter 3, above, on order.

76. Compare *Pensées* 5 (*OC* 2/545), *Pensées* 101 (*OC* 2/573–74), *Pensées* 138 (*OC* 2/590–92). I've benefited from David Rabourdin, *Pascal: Foi et conversion* (Paris: Presses Universitaires de France, 2013) on these questions.

Thinking that reason might get you there is an error (I leave aside Pascal's claim that [all?] other religions make that claim) of order: it's to deploy reason in an order to which it doesn't belong. The category of disproportion is relevant again here, as it was earlier in considering the orders; there, the emphasis was on the disproportion between our cognitive capacities and the two infinities within which we find ourselves. Here, the disproportion is between us and the LORD, a disproportion that makes the LORD completely (Pascal is often excitable and extreme about this) inaccessible to us by way of reason, whether that reason is used to establish the LORD's existence, or to delineate the LORD's nature.[77] But reason, having established its own limits and, what is the same, its proper sphere of action, can deploy what's been given to it about the LORD to establish what it's reasonable for us to think and do. That is an exercise within its proper sphere, and Pascal deploys it as an instrument to remove obstacles to faith.[78]

The first move in what Pascal calls *le pari*, the wager, is to state a dichotomy:[79] either the LORD exists or it is not the case that the LORD exists. This is intended as a contradictory pair that doesn't allow for a third option: *p or not-p*. The next move is to say that everyone is already committed to one or other of these options: you're already embarked (*vous êtes embarqué*), like it or not. Why is that? Because you're either worshiping the LORD and otherwise doing what believers do, or you're not. The pattern of your life shows which of the two possibilities you affirm. There's no neutral ground. And since reason has no competence to decide the truth here, each decision is identically related to the demands of reason. The question of what's reasonable in this connection can therefore

77. See the texts cited and discussed in chapter 3, above, on order.

78. I've been helped in thinking about the *pari* by Henri Gouhier, *Blaise Pascal: Commentaires* (Paris: Vrin, 1966), 245–306.

79. The next dozen paragraphs or so paraphrase, translate, gloss, and comment upon *Pensées* 397 (*OC* 2/677–80).

be jettisoned without remainder. How then to decide which direction to set sail in—whether, that is, to continue in the direction you're already going, or to change course?

Pascal's answer to that belongs to game theory. You should assess what the possible gains and losses are in each case, while acknowledging that so far as you know, in the sphere of subjective probability, there's an equal chance: the probability that *god exists* is true is one-half, and the probability that *it is not the case that god exists* is the same. There are then four possibilities: you bet that god exists, and you're right; you bet that god exists and you're wrong; you bet that it is not the case that god exists, and you're right; you bet that it is not the case that god exists, and you're wrong. You might ask what you have to bet in such a game. What stake is at your disposal? The answer is your pattern of life: either you will live as if the LORD is who the LORD is (*ego sum qui sum*, as Scripture says), or you will not. And recall that you've already made this bet: your life already exhibits one pattern or the other. Those are the stakes, then: living a Christian life, which is to say doing what Christians do; or living a pagan life, which is to say doing what pagans do.

Suppose you bet on the truth of *god exists* by conforming your life to the LORD, or at least beginning to do so. If you're right (the first of the four possibilities), then since what properly belongs to living as Christians do is *une éternité de vie et de bonheur*, an eternity of life and happiness, because that's what's promised to the faithful and what the faithful therefore hope for, then your winnings are infinite: endless bliss, just what you've always wanted. But suppose you make the same bet and you turn out to be wrong. Well, then you'll die and be buried and that'll be the end of that. The pattern of your life will have been based on an illusion.

Suppose that you bet on the truth of *it is not the case that god exists* by living as pagans do, and you're right. That's the third alternative. Then you'll live a life of obsessive *amour-propre*, terrified of death and the opacity of life, amusing yourself to death with whatever distractions are available and being frightened and bored when those distractions aren't to hand. You'll live the life depicted earlier in this chapter, that is, and when you die, as in the second alternative, that will be the end of you. The last remaining alternative is that you bet on the truth of *it is not the case that god exists* by living as pagans do, and you're wrong. In fact, it turns out, the LORD is and the promises are. When you die, in this last possibility, you lose what you really want, what we all really want, which is infinite delight in the embrace of the only one who can provide it, the LORD of Abraham and Isaac and Jacob, the LORD who is Jesus. You are, that is, damned.

In the case of the first two possibilities, where you place your bet on *god exists* by ordering your life as if that were so, you have an equal chance of an infinite gain (the bottomless bank account, like Strega Nona's pasta pot) and a finite loss, which is having a life that doesn't conform to reality. In the case of the second two possibilities, where you place your bet on *it is not the case that god exists* by ordering your life as if that were so, you have an equal chance of finite gain, which is having a life that does accord with reality, and infinite loss, which is, one way or another, endless torment.

Leaving aside any other questions (and there are many), Pascal thinks it clear that you should bet that *god exists*. That's the direction in which you should set sail. "Our argument," he writes, "has infinite weight (*une force infinie*) because the stake is finite, the game is one where there's an equal chance of winning and losing, and there's an infinite good to be won (*l'infini à gagner*). That's demonstrative: if we're capable of any truth, this is it." You'd be irrational, that is, a fool, if you didn't embark LORD ward.

The argument is formally correct, as is easy enough to see if you transpose its terms to those of the gaming table. The stake demanded of you (let's call it $100) is one you have in your pocket, as everyone does in Pascal's set-up, and the bet is single and simple: You have to place your stake on either red or black, and one of those must come up. If you bet on black and it comes up you get the bottomless bank account, and if it doesn't come up you lose your stake; if you bet on red and it comes up you double your money, and if it doesn't come up you lose all the money you've ever had, will ever have, or could ever have. That's an approximate equivalent to Pascal's wager, and if you were ever to find yourself at such a table and you didn't bet on black, you'd be a fool. And Pascal thinks that you are, right now, at just such a table, and have already placed your bet—though still with time to shift it from one color to the other.

Formally, there's no problem. If you're a pagan and you're faced with Pascal's wager, you ought to adopt a Christian way of life. You'd be irrational not to. But the argument carries conviction only if its axiomatic assumptions are accepted. First among these is an assumption about the LORD—that the LORD rewards those living as Christians with an infinite good, and punishes those who live as pagans with an infinite evil. In the strongest form of the argument, it's inevitable that those who live as Christians get the reward, while those who don't get the punishment—as inevitable, anyway, as the bank paying those who bet on black when it comes up. But there's no reason for pagans to accept such an understanding of the LORD. A pagan knowledgeable about Christianity might rightly note that some Christians, at least, teach that the LORD has a universal salvific will, and that loss of the infinite and everlasting good of life with the LORD need not follow, even on Christian assumptions. Such pagans might reasonably say, well, on the Christian understanding of the LORD I prefer, I don't need to change my life now. Making the wrong bet now at worst yields purgatory, not damnation.[80] Pascal might respond that even if the loss involved in making the wrong bet isn't infinite, it's still very

---

80. There are good Christian reasons for preferring a view of the LORD like this, and even some that Pascal seems to share. See the discussion in chapter 5, §5.5, below.

large (millennia in purgatory, perhaps), and so you'd still be irrational to bet on black. But then the argument's footing has been changed. There's no need to resolve this disagreement here. That it can occur shows, illuminatingly, that the LORD's universal salvific will is in play in the argument, and that considering the argument can throw that issue into sharp relief is among the benefits of reading Pascal.

The argument might also be challenged by raising questions about the importance of the stake. That stake is the habits of a life. You might say that those habits have greater weight than the argument makes them seem to have. You, as a pagan, might be being asked to give up all, or very many, of the habits—emotional, sexual, gastronomic, sartorial, social, political, professional—that give your life meaning, and that is a weighty matter. It may seem weighty enough to you that you can't imagine being able to do it. As I've already shown, Pascal's emphasis on the radicality and violence of conversion suggests that something of revolutionary significance is done to pagan habits when conversion occurs. In the monetary terms appropriate to the gaming table, $100 that you have in your pocket might not be the best analogy. Better might be a contractually guaranteed promise that one-half of all your future income will be garnished at source and given to the poor, and that your expenditure of the other half will in future be limited to a short list of church-approved categories. That would mean that your style of life would become drastically different. You might reasonably be given pause by this. You'd still be gambling a finite stake for a possible infinite reward, but the stake might begin to seem so weighty that you can't bring yourself to put it on the table. That discussion, also not to be resolved here, raises the question of how deep the difference is between the habits of a Christian life and those of a pagan life, and it is another of the benefits of reading Pascal on the wager to have this question forced upon you. Pascal has his own views about it, as we shall see.

Pascal's imagined interlocutor in this discussion of the wager objects that he isn't free simply to believe in the truths of Christianity: "I'm such that I'm not able to believe (*que je ne puis croire*)." This is reasonable: we can't ordinarily make ourselves give assent to some claim. When faced with a claim, we find ourselves responding to it in the way that we do—with assent, with doubt, with rejection, with puzzlement, with ridicule, and so on—and that response can't be changed by fiat. But it wasn't Pascal's point to say that it could. His recommended response to the wager isn't that you should, if you see the wager's reasonableness, at once become a believer. It's that you should begin to do something different in the interest of establishing new habits. At more length:

>> You'd like to arrive at faith and you don't know the way. You'd like to be cured of infidelity, and you ask for the remedies. Learn from those who were bound as you are and who now bet everything. These are the people who know the way you'd like to follow and have been cured of the evil you'd like to be cured of. Begin as they did, which was by acting as if they believed, taking holy water, having masses said, and so on. Doing exactly that will make you believe naturally, like an animal—But that's what I'm afraid of.—Why? What do you have to lose? (*Pensées* 397, *OC* 2/679–80)

You're not being asked to believe by an act of will. You're being asked to undertake what believers—Christians—do, by imitation. The examples Pascal provides are liturgical: holy water, Mass, and so on. The "and so on" is important: it indicates the entirety of the liturgical life. Pascal recommends, therefore, that you should commence that life. If you do it regularly, you'll come to believe *naturellement* (naturally, inevitably, as speaking English produces in you exactly the habituated capacity to speak English), and "like an animal" (*abêtir*), which is to say unreflectively, as the hummingbird hovers and the snake slithers. Christian liturgical habits, on this view, make a believer of you over time; the same account could be offered of other patterns of action characteristic of the Christian life, such as the works of mercy. They are the customs of the Christian country, and doing them makes you into an inhabitant.

This treatment of the wager and what comes after shows the depth of the formal parallels between Pascal's first (pagan) anthropology, and his second (Christian) anthropology.[81] Both have custom and habit at their heart, and each set of customs is alike in lacking for most of us most of the time demonstrations of their reasonability independent of their practice. There is, for Pascal, no reason to think that a condition necessary for entering upon or continuing in one life or another, pagan or Christian, is having to hand or on the lips arguments whose conclusion is, "this is the right/good/true/beautiful life," or the habits that constitute this life have fewer disadvantages and more advantages than their competitors." No. Rather, *vous êtes embarqué.* You can gain clarity about what kind of life yours is, and what its characteristic marks are; and you may even, with arguments like the wager, be able, in exceptional circumstances to show why a change from one life to another is rational or desirable—but even when you can do that, the argument won't be, as the wager isn't, about the substantive merits or virtues of one set of habits over another. Rather, it'll be a procedural or hypothetical argument, a game-theoretic conditional that's neutral as to the truth—as the wager is to the question of which way the dice will in fact fall. Pascal, in this way of approaching matters of justification, runs counter to much in the Catholic tradition, and especially to some natural-law-centered kinds of Thomism. He is best understood as espousing skepticism about the possibility of there being standards of justification for modes of life independent of their practice,[82] while at the same

81. On this, Daniel Garber, *What Happens after Pascal's Wager: Living Faith and Rational Belief* (Milwaukee, Wisc.: Marquette University Press, 2009).

82. This view is dominant in present-day anglophone epistemology, which takes no doxastic (belief-forming) practice to be capable of justifying its own reliability without assuming it and deploying the assumption.

time being quite clear that the habits that make a Christian life are in accord with the order of things, while those that make a pagan life are not.

One misunderstanding of the wager needs to be noted and rejected. It's the view that the establishment of the habits that make a Christian life is just the same thing as having faith. That reading is in such tension with other themes in Pascal that it's hard to defend. I have in mind Pascal's view that faith is without remainder the LORD's gift, and therefore not something that can be produced *ex opere operato*, by anything we do. That understanding of faith is an element in Pascal's depiction of grace, as shorthand for the relation between divine and human agency. The wager is not, then, best read as a claim about the efficacy of what human creatures alone can do, as is evident from Pascal's view that not all those who live a Christian life are in fact to be understood as Christians.

> ⋙ There aren't many true Christians. I say the same about faith: there are many who believe out of superstition, and many who don't because they don't like constraint. Few are in between. I don't include in this those whose conduct is truly pious, or those who believe out of the heart's feeling. (*Pensées* 168, *OC* 2/603)

Le sentiment de la coeur, which is what Pascal wants faith to spring from, is nothing but the LORD's gift. Those who have it need not be, and in Pascal's view are not, the same as those with habits appropriate to the Christian life, even if it's not possible for us to discriminate the one from the other.

*

Jansenist understandings of the Christian life are often represented as unremittingly grim: life is affliction; it ends in death, which is usually painful; worldly attachments are problematic because they're death-shadowed; desire for them and delight in them should be at best moderate, and punished with fear and guilt when, as is almost inevitable, they become immoderate. There are elements of such a picture in Pascal, and those elements may well have been accentuated by some Jansenists. But there's a fundamental difference. Pascal doesn't encourage a teeth-gritting bootstrap out of desire for the world; rather, he shows what it's like to be so in love with and delighted by the LORD that worldly delights assume their proper place. He does, of course, with polemical and satirical vigor, castigate those who make of the Christian life an ornament to the norms and mores of seventeenth-century French bourgeois life. And he does show the deep incompatibility of much in those norms and mores with Christianity. But he does that in order to turn the gaze away from the world and toward the LORD, not to recommend an agonized struggle with the world's temptations. He does sometimes over-theorize his rhetorical positions, especially when he writes about the providential nature of all affliction, as discussed in §4.1; but for the most part he's a poet of delight rather than of suffering.

Pascal's anthropology, it's worth emphasizing again, is a mixture of the universal—here's what all human creatures are like—and the very particular—here's what the seventeenth-century French bourgeois are like. A significant portion of his diagnosis of the human condition does, however, presuppose a social class that isn't pressed by life-threatening material needs, and that has some leisure. That wasn't most people in Pascal's Paris, just as it isn't most people in the twenty-first century. His depiction of *ennui* and the restless need for *divertissement* as means of avoiding contemplation of our parlous condition resonates with our bourgeois (to whom I belong), to the extent that it does, for the same reasons as it resonated with his: we have time and leisure, we don't know what to do with it, and we would very much rather not contemplate our mortality or our sin. But for those whose main concerns are whether they'll get through today without being killed, or this week without dying of starvation, the resonance will be less. That is a criticism of Pascal's anthropology only to the extent that it presents itself as more universal than it is, which sometimes it does. It is, rather, an observation about that anthropology: like the *pari*, Pascal's analysis of affliction and diversion works most effectively upon those whose lives have in them space for consideration and action not immediately directed toward survival.

The strongest element of Pascal's anthropology is his depiction of custom and habit. He is entirely right to show them as fundamental to the lives of all human creatures, pagan, Jew, and Christian alike. We are as he depicts us: in large part like machines and nonhuman animals: creatures who do and must habituate themselves so that almost all of what we do neither requires nor uses self-awareness. Among the interesting implications of such a view, not drawn out by Pascal, is that the phenomenology of the inner theater—of what it seems like to us to be us—may itself be an artifact of the Fall, and no necessary part of the Christian life here below, or of the life of glory. Interest in our inner lives and effort to develop them may be just one more *divertissement*. A Pascalianism for our time would take up that theme.

5

GRACE

"Grace" (*charis, gratia, grâce*) is central to the Christian lexicon, and to Pascal's when he writes theology. In the fundamental grammar of Christianity, "grace" designates as gift the relation the LORD bears to all that is not the LORD. It's by grace that there is anything at all other than the LORD: that grace is the gift of being *ex nihilo*. It's by grace that the created order as a whole continues to be, as is also true of each particular creature. Without grace, there would have been nothing, and were grace to be withdrawn there would at once be nothing. The LORD's graceful gift brings its recipient into being, and that shows with gorgeous clarity some of its fundamental features: the gift isn't given because of the merits of its recipients, which is to say that it is not a reward; it is neither anticipated nor worked for by its recipients; it cannot be refused; and it asks nothing in return. Grace, therefore, is a pure gift, and in all the respects just mentioned unlike the gifts that we give, which, typically, do respond to and are conditional upon the merits of recipients; which are, often, anticipated as reward by recipients; which can be refused, and often are; and which do, ordinarily, expect a return. Gift-giving, for us, establishes a broadly contractual relation between giver and recipient; the LORD's grace does not, at least in its ideal type as the gift of being.

The graceful gift of being isn't the only gift, however. There are, according to Christianity's grammar, more particular gifts: Abraham is called by grace to be the father of Israel; David is made king by grace; Ruth is called into Israel and made the mother of Obed by grace; Gabriel announces particular graces to Mary (*ave Maria, gratia plena* ...); and so on. These particular graces seem in some ways unlike the grace of creation. Perhaps they are given in response to the merits of their recipients; it seems that they can be refused; maybe they do ask something in return; and they are certainly not given to all. These particular gifts seem, on their face, to presuppose recipients apart from the giver, with their own freedom, agency, and power of decision. What account is to be given of the relation between human freedom and the LORD's graces? That is one of the fundamental questions about grace, and it exercises Pascal. Another is: What account is to be given of the particularity of the LORD's gifts? Why Abraham and not some other wandering Aramean? Why Mary and not some other Jewish woman? Why you and not me? Why me and not you? Why not everyone? This isn't a problem that arises about the gift of being, which is, by definition, given to all creatures. But it is a problem about grace as it works in a world already in being, and it too exercises Pascal. He takes characteristically extreme, dialectically sharpened, positions on all these questions, and in doing so maps the conceptual territory with abundant clarity.

5.1 The Five Propositions

Accounting for grace was especially important to and difficult for Pascal because of magisterial interventions on the topic in the 1650s. These lie in the background of much of what he writes about grace, and are sometimes foregrounded. It's important to have them before us.

In a bull of May 13, 1653, *Cum occasione*, Innocent X identified five propositions on the nature and workings of grace as heretical (and, variously, as rash, impious, false, blasphemous, scandalous, disgraceful, and so on). They were:

> ≫ (1) Some of God's precepts are impossible for the just who want and try [to keep them] with the strength they now have; they also lack the grace that would make them possible (2) There's no resisting interior grace in the state of fallen nature. (3) Freedom from necessity for people in a state of fallen nature isn't required for desert or its opposite; freedom from coercion suffices. (4) The semi-Pelagians admitted the necessity of a prevenient interior grace for every act, even for the beginning of faith; but they were heretical in wanting that grace to be such that human will can resist it or submit to it. (5) It's semi-Pelagian to say that Christ died or shed blood for everyone without exception. (Denzinger §§2001–5)

These propositions were, in addition to being heretical, attributed in passing by Innocent to Cornelius Jansenius's work *Augustinus*, which had been published in 1640, and which was of foundational importance for Pascal, as also for his theological mentors, Saint-Cyran, Arnauld, and Nicole. They took Jansenius's reading of Augustine on grace, predestination, election, and associated matters to be both correct as an interpretation of Augustine and orthodox on the substance of the questions. So did Pascal. This was so in spite of the fact that in 1643, a decade before Innocent's ruling in *Cum occasione*, Urban VII had, in the bull *In eminenti ecclesiae*, condemned and prohibited Jansenius's work because it contravened Paul V's 1611 prohibition (re-affirmed by Urban in 1625 and 1641) of the publication of treatises concerned with auxiliary graces—with disputes, that's to say, about whether there are particular graces needed for this or that human action, and if so, which they are and how they should be named—unless by prior authorization of the Holy Sée.

Paul V's prohibition had been, or at least could be read as, purely procedural. That is, it didn't identify any particular views on grace as problematic, but, rather, identified an entire theological topic and placed it under a moratorium.[1] And if so read, it didn't have any particular significance for the substantive questions in play, and thus didn't place Pascal under any particular magisterial pressure. But Innocent's condemnation of 1653 was different: that was indubitably substantive, and it did identify the heretical opinions it rejected as being argued for by Jansenius in the *Augustinus*. That did place Pascal under pressure. And the pressure was intensified in 1656, when Alexander VII promulgated the bull *Ad sanctam*, in which, among other things, he wrote that the five propositions of *Cum occasione* were drawn (*excerptas*) from the *Augustinus*, and were condemned *in sensu ab eodem Cornelio Iansenio intento*—in just the same sense as that intended by Jansenius.[2]

As is typical for a document of this kind, it's not easy to say with precision what positive claims about grace are implied by *Cum occasione*'s identification of the five propositions as heretical. That's mostly because the bull proceeds by negation: it identifies five things—more exactly, five Latin sentences—you can't affirm if you don't want to be heretical. One way to understand this is to read the document as affirming the contradictory of each of the five propositions it identifies as heretical. So, in the case of (1), that would yield: *It's not the case that some of God's precepts are impossible for the just who want and try [to keep them] with the strength they now have; they also lack the grace that would make them possible.* That sentence isn't easy to gloss—or, rather, the possible glosses are

---

1. There's a long backstory here about the grace controversies of the late sixteenth and early seventeenth centuries, and Pascal's treatment of grace is only one node in a vast seventeenth-century French Catholic literature on the topic. As Gouhier nicely puts it: "le problème religieux qui domine le siècle est celui-là même pour lequel Port-Royal a combattu: celui de la grâce" (Henri Gouhier, *Blaise Pascal: Conversion et apologétique* [Paris: Vrin, 1986], 8).

2. Denzinger, 2012. For more on the ecclesiological implications of Pascal's response to this pressure, see chapter 6, §6.2, below, on the ecclesial city.

very many. The negation with which it begins might be compatible with denying only one of the two qualities (*want with the strength they now have*; *try with the strength they now have*) predicated of the just; or it might require denying both of them. And, it might be compatible with affirming *some of God's precepts are impossible for the just who want and try [to keep them] with the strength they now have*, so long as *they also lack the grace that would make them possible* is denied—or vice-versa. Or, in the case of (3)'s denial, *It's not the case that freedom from necessity for people in a state of fallen nature isn't required for desert or its opposite; freedom from coercion suffices*, the relation between freedom from necessity and freedom from coercion could be construed in a number of ways. One could, for example, say that freedom from coercion doesn't suffice, while freedom from necessity isn't required; or that freedom from necessity is required and that freedom from coercion doesn't suffice; or one could affirm that freedom from necessity isn't required and that freedom from coercion suffices—but only for people not *in statu naturae lapsae*. And so on. Many different, and some incompatible, positive understandings of grace's workings are compatible with denials of the five propositions, and so it is always a mistake to identify just one positive construal of grace's workings as what's required (entailed) by *Cum occasione*'s identification of the five propositions as heretical. Rather, deflationarily, *Cum occasione* (and *Ad sanctam*) go no further than identifying some (Latin) sentences as heretical to affirm.

However, it isn't difficult to discern the various topics the five propositions are about—the areas, that is, into which they move thought. Most prominent and fundamental is the relation between what the LORD does and what we do; or, differently put, between grace and human action. (1) is about what we need from the LORD in order for it to be possible for us to keep the commandments, while (2) and (4) are about our capacity to resist grace. More specifically, the denial of (1) moves in the direction of ruling out strong claims about the impossibility of keeping the commandments without particular aid, while the denials of (2) and (4) worry at, and about, strong claims as to grace's irresistibility.

The five propositions, whether denied or affirmed, also assume that grace comes in kinds that may be variously named. They mention interior grace (*gratia interior*), and prevenient interior grace (*gratia interior praeveniens*). Among the issues that had divided, for example, Jesuits and Dominicans in the *de auxiliis* controversies was that of the kinds of grace and the appropriate names for those kinds. Dividing grace into kinds is one way of approaching the question about human and divine agency: some human actions may be taken to require particular (named) graces.

The question of determinism, and by implication predestination, is also present in the five propositions. (3) makes a distinction between freedom from necessity (*libertas a necessitate*) and freedom from coercion (*libertas a coactione*). Innocent may be read to affirm that both freedoms are necessary in order for desert to be possible. The verb is *merere*, and the thought is that in order for it to be possible for your actions to be deserving or otherwise (*ad merendum et demerendum*), they must be free—neither necessitated in any way, nor, particularly, subject to coercion (*coactio*) by another. This topic, too, belongs to the question about the relation between divine and human agency. If what you do isn't free because it's necessitated or coerced by the LORD, then desert can't be in play, for desert, deserving or meriting this or that because of what you've done, requires freedom. Only if you could have done otherwise, Innocent's denial of proposition (3) suggests (but doesn't quite say), can you deserve anything.

The denial of (5) raises a different question: that of the scope of Jesus-Christ's salvific work. *Cum occasione* may be read to affirm that Jesus-Christ dies for all, and that, therefore, salvation is offered to all, contra some strong claims as to the predestination of some to damnation. I suppose it should also be said that (5)'s denial

could also be read more simply, to deny the propriety of categorizing a view as semi-Pelagian.

Innocent's formulations in *Cum occasione* provide the backdrop for much of Pascal's discussion of grace, and that in two
ways. First, there's the question about Jansenius's *Augustinus*: did
Jansenius in that book defend the propositions Innocent rejects?
Alexander, in *Ad sanctam*, is explicit and precise in saying that he
did. Pascal devotes considerable energy to this question. Second,
there's the question of substance: what, given *Cum occasione* and
Ad sanctam, is to be said about grace? How can a theory of grace
properly responsive to Augustine, as the premodern theologian
of weight for Pascal, and to Trent, and to the magisterial developments of the seventeenth century, be enunciated? Pascal writes
about these topics not as an historical theologian, and not even as
a systematician; no, he writes about them as a dialectician, an aco-
lyte of high abstraction in which the possible positions can be laid
out in something close to their pure propositional form. A signal
benefit of reading him on this topic isn't that he's right (though in
large part, he is), but that he brings clarity about the conceptual
territory on which discussion of these matters must move.

5.2 Pascal's Language for Grace

Pascal's lexicon for discussion of these matters is important to
get straight. He doesn't, of course, make up the words and phrases I'm about to discuss; they all have roots in the tradition, some
of which he shows awareness of. His use of them is also in some
respects idiosyncratic. In what follows I largely eschew mention
of the sources Pascal draws on and analysis of how he treats those
sources. Instead, I set out Pascal's developed position as I understand it.

First, there's *pouvoir prochain*, "proximate power." This is something you can have or lack. If you have it with respect to some action, then two things are true of you: first, you're so constituted as to

have the capacity to do it; second, there's nothing standing in your way of doing it. If you're chained but otherwise unhurt, you've the capacity to walk across the room but not the proximate power to do so—that's because of the chains, which provide an external obstacle. If the chains are removed, then you've not only the capacity, but now also the proximate power.[3] Proximate power, then, is unhindered capacity; it can, for Pascal, never be separated from grace. All the proximate powers, unhindered capacities, you have are given to you, which is to say graced. Anyone who defends the thought that we, since the Fall, have ungraced proximate powers, moves outside the sphere of orthodox Christianity. Proximate power implies grace, and that, for Pascal, is true of all human actions, from the most trivial (breathing, digesting, walking across the room) to the most demanding (observing the commandments, praying).[4]

Second, there's *secours efficace* (effective help), which overlaps with *grâce suffisante* (sufficient grace), *grâce efficace* (efficacious grace), *secours actuel* (actual—operative—help), and *secours spécial* (particular help). These are all ways of talking about the LORD's gift of the proximate power to do something-or-other. Pascal uses them interchangeably for that purpose, as we'll see in a moment, but the last, *secours spécial*, adds a connotation: that the help in question isn't *commun à tous*, common to or shared by all.[5] Instead, it's given only to some, and only sometimes.[6] As to *grâce suffisante*: this doesn't suffice for the doing of the action for which it's given; it suffices, rather, for the removal of obstacles to such doing, for, that is, possession of the proximate power, the *pouvoir prochain*, to do it.[7]

The equivalences under discussion here show, too, that at least

3. *Grace* 5 (*OC* 2/240–42).
4. *Grace* 8 (*OC* 2/264–75).
5. See, among many examples, *Grace* 1 (*OC* 2/213–16), *Grace* 10 (*OC* 2/285).
6. See, among many examples, *Grace* 2 (*OC* 2/222), *Grace* 4 (*OC* 2/240). Compare the parable given at *Provincials* 2 (*OC* 1/602–3).
7. For *grâce suffisante* in Eve's and Adam's cases, see *Grace* 11 (*OC* 2/287): it gave them the power to do what was right, but didn't necessitate their doing it.

most of the time *secours* (help) and *grâce* (grace) are exchangeable for Pascal. That's so, anyway, in his technical discussions; it isn't so when he becomes lyrical or gnomic about *grâce*; then, he writes things about grace that he doesn't, and I think wouldn't, write about help. For example: "Even grace is only a figure of glory, for it's not the last end. It has been figured by the Law and itself figures glory; and so it is itself the figure and the principle or cause of glory."[8] And: "I thank you, my God, for the good impulses you give me, and even for the impulse you give me to give you thanks."[9] It's difficult to imagine Pascal writing in that way about *secours*, which is a more mundane word. Nonetheless, the two remain largely exchangeable in technical analyses of grace.

Third, there's the LORD's *volonté absolue*, or absolute will (desire, intention, purpose), unconditioned by anything external to the LORD. Pascal distinguishes this from the LORD's *volonté conditionelle*, or conditioned will, which responds to contingent and particular events, such as the Fall and everything that flows from it.[10] This distinction is important for Pascal, because much of his analysis of grace depends upon drawing sharp distinctions among the situation of human creatures with respect to grace before the Fall, after it, and in heaven[11]—and within the second category, among the situations of pagans, Jews, and Christians. Pascal needs the distinction between absolute and conditional will in order to make sense of how things go with respect to grace in these different situations. There's a strong tendency on Pascal's part to make *volonté absolue* irresistible, which is to say that if the LORD has it with respect to you (your salvation, your election, your damnation), then what the LORD wills happens inevitably, irresistibly,

8. *Pensées* 258 (*OC* 2/638).

9. *Maladies* 6 (*OC* 2/187).

10. The distinction is made in *Grace* 7 (*OC* 2/259–60), and discussed in what immediately follows at *OC* 2/259–64. The same topics are treated in more detail in *Grace* 11 (*OC* 2/287–93), and *Grace* 15 (*OC* 2/308–16).

11. See *Grace* 8 (*OC* 2/272–73).

necessarily. By contrast, *volonté conditionelle* doesn't ensure the outcome of its object: the LORD had conditional will for Eve's and Adam's salvation, and for any who might, prior to the Fall, avoid sin; but that didn't prevent the Fall.[12]

Fourth, there's the at least occasional equivalence between *par charité* (by love) and *par grâce* (by grace).[13] To act in, or by, the LORD's love—responsively to the gift of that love—is, sometimes, the same as to act by, or in, or under, the LORD's grace—responsively to that gift. Grace is always a gift of love; and the gift of love is always graceful.

With those terms of art and the distinctions they mark in mind, we can now turn to Pascal's particular analyses.

5.3 Keeping the Commandments

First, there's Pascal's discussion of what it means to say that observance of the commandments is possible for the just, which was the concern of the first of the five propositions. Pascal affirms this, at least because he takes it to be among the teachings of the Council of Trent, as well as to have had its denial anathematized by Innocent. But he takes the proposition *les commandements sont possibles aux justes* (the commandments are possible for the just) to be equivocal, which is to say reasonably construable in at least two ways. The first is to say that the just, meaning, in this discussion, those who have been justified (made just) in and by the baptismal gift of grace, always have the proximate power to do what the commandments require. More exactly: "The just, considered in any moment of their justification, have always the proximate power to fulfil the commandments in the immediately following moment."[14] That is, once just (baptized), you have, ipso facto, the capacity to do what the commandments require, and there are no

12. Explicitly in *Grace* 11 (*OC* 2/287–88).
13. See *Grace* 1 (*OC* 2/211–20).
14. *Grace* 1 (*OC* 2/211).

obstacles preventing you from doing so. The second construal is to say that "the just, acting as just and by a movement of love, can fulfil the commandments in the action they do by love."[15]

Pascal takes the first interpretation to be Pelagian, which is to say both heretical and false, because it attributes to us the capacity, unaided, to do what's right. And he takes the second construal to be Augustinian, which is to say both orthodox and true, because it makes clear that anything we do that is right must be responsive to and entwined with the LORD's love (and, therefore, grace). There is no sphere of human action separated from that love and the response for which it calls: that is Pascal's fundamental intuition, and he deploys it here to show how it's possible to affirm that we can do what the commandments require. We can do so when, and to the extent that, we're in love, which is to say always and necessarily with the lover's presence and help. In summary:

> ⇒ [T]the Council establishes that the just not only lack actual perseverance without particular help, but that they don't even have the power to persevere without particular help. And that is nothing other than to say that all the just who lack that particular power lack the power to fulfil the commandments in the immediately following moment—for to persevere is nothing other than to fulfil the commandments in the immediately following moments. (*Grace* 1, *OC* 2/213)

Prescinding from the question of what the Council of Trent does or doesn't say, it's clear that Pascal affirms *the commandments are possible for the just*, but denies that the just have proximate power to do what the commandments require just because they're just; they can do that only with particular help, which is to say a (kind of) grace additional to that which brought them into being and justified them. Without particular help, they have the capacity to

15. *Grace* 1 (*OC* 2/211).

do what the commandments ask, but not the power. They're like those in chains who'd like to walk, or those whose eyes are open in a dark place: someone other than they (the LORD) must unchain them, or provide light. Pascal's concern here, as always, is to rule out the idea that there's anything about us, anything of ours, that permits us to act without the LORD's help.[16]

Pascal understands his way of affirming the proposition to hold a middle position between two erroneous extremes. One the one hand there are those (Manicheans, Lutherans, Calvinists)[17] who deny absolutely that it's possible to keep the commandments. For them, any attempt to do so here below is always sin-inflected. Pascal denies this: when we're in love, when we act with *secours spécial*, we can and do fulfil the commandments without sin. On the other hand, there are those (Pelagians, Jovinians, semi-Pelagians, Molinists) who affirm that it's always possible for us to keep the commandments, with or without special help, with or without the fire of love that is always preveniently given. As here:

> ⇒ Suppose that God never refuses the just who've not sinned again in the moment following their justification the grace to pray; then it's evident that one can say of all the just that they have the power to pray because God always gives them the grace proximately sufficient for future prayer. Consequently, by the promises of the Gospel, they will always obtain the effects of their prayer. Therefore, the power to persevere in prayer contains the power to persevere in justice; all the just have the power to persevere in justice without special help, but by way of nothing other than the help common to all the just— which is in direct contradiction to the Council. And it isn't possible to pretend to escape this by saying that it's morally impossible that

16. Almost the whole of *Grace* 1–2 (*OC* 2/211–33) is given over to analysis and defense of this way of taking *les commandements sont possibles aux justes*.

17. These are doxographic categories for Pascal. He has no interest in seriously engaging texts or representatives of any of these traditions, and is happy, for instance, to take Lutherans and Calvinists to be defending the same territory.

the just persevere without sinning venially and so lose the power [to persevere], and consequently that they don't persevere without special help. That muddle is useless because the Council anathematizes not only those who say that the just persevere in justice without special help, but also those who say that the just have the power to persevere in justice without special help. And so the Council has also anathematized that latter proposition. (*Grace* 10, *OC* 2/286–87)

Again, this is couched in terms of what the Council of Trent says. Leaving that aside, Pascal here denies two positions: first, that justification is the same as perseverance—that once you've been justified by baptism, you'll then inevitably reap the rewards (*il obtiendra toujours l'effet*). That position would make the community of the just the same as the community of the saved, a position that Pascal takes to be clearly wrong. Second, that it's only venial (minor, light) sins that prevent the just persevering, and that because these are practically unavoidable (*moralement impossible*) the just who commit them need the special help of pardon for them. This view, Pascal thinks, is a *défaite*, a muddled undoing, of the correct position (also that of the Council), because it retains for the just the proximate power to persevere, allowing that power to be checked or stained or damaged in only minor ways. Pascal's position is that justification carries with it only a removal of sin and damage to that point, leaving those who've been transfigured in that way still unable, by themselves, to do anything other than look for and, when it's given, respond to the LORD's gift;[18] he denies that justification remakes the just in such a way that, without any further need for or response to the prevenient gift of love, they can do what's necessary. For Pascal, the just are like toddlers snatched from the mortal danger of traffic on a busy road by a loving parent; they're momentarily safe, and they respond with love and relief to the parent's graceful grip; but, being toddlers, they're still incapa-

---

18. For more on this, see §5.4, below, on noncompetition.

ble of crossing the road safely without the parent's *secours spécial*; their hand still needs to be held, and they lack, in Pascal's terms, both the capacity and the power to cross the road safely.[19]

5.4 Delectation and Noncompetition

Pascal's anthropology makes delectation and delight of central importance to us since the Fall. Our wills are *liée par la delectation*,[20] bound by delectation, whether we're justified or not, baptized or not, lovers of the LORD or not. We're always slaves to delight, and we act in accord with our particular forms of enslavement, whether to the LORD or to the world. Pascal likes the Augustinian tag, *quod amplius delectat, secundum id operemur necesse est*,[21] which is to say that we necessarily act in accord with what delights us most. We can be delighted by the LORD even after the Fall; but our tendency now, and in this we are unlike Eve and Adam before the Fall, is to delight in the world alone (theirs was to delight equally in both the world and the LORD: they were balanced on a razor's edge, while we are not). That tendency is so deeply rooted and so powerful that we are *maintenant hors d'état de se porter à Dieu*,[22] quite incapable of getting ourselves to the LORD. When the LORD helps us, graces us, then we can begin to take delight in the LORD.[23]

But how, more exactly, is this shown to work in Pascal's writing? If the problem of theorizing grace is in large part the problem of theorizing the relation between what we do and what the LORD does, then how does Pascal do that? We've seen already that we do no good things independently of the LORD; we have neither the capacity nor the power for such actions, and, further, the very

---

19. An approximate gloss on the parable at *Provincials* 2 (*OC* 1/602–3).
20. *Grace* 8 (*OC* 2/274).
21. *Grace* 8 (*OC* 2/273); *Provincials* 18 (*OC* 1/801).
22. *Grace* 8 (*OC* 2/273). In what follows, I paraphrase and extend *Grace* 8 (*OC* 2/271–75).
23. For more on conversion, see chapter 4, §4.4, above.

idea that there might be such actions makes no sense, because they would have to occur in a place sequestered from the LORD's presence—and there are no such places.

Pascal gropes toward a depiction of how what we do when we act well relates to what the LORD does. Consider this, from a letter to his sister Gilberte:

> ≫ It's not that we can't recall and retain a letter of St. Paul's as easily as a book of Virgil's; but the understanding we acquire is nothing but a work of memory, as also is its continuation. By contrast, in order to understand that secret language which is strange to those strange to heaven, it's necessary that the selfsame grace, which alone can give the first understanding, continues it and makes it always present by ceaselessly retracing it in the hearts of the faithful to make it always live there, as God constantly renews beatitude for the blessed, which is both a result and a continuation of grace—and as the Church holds that the Father continually produces the Son and maintains the eternity of his essence by an uninterrupted and endless outpouring of his substance. And so the continuation in justice of the faithful is nothing other than the infusion of grace, and not a single grace that lasts for ever; it's this that perfectly shows us our perpetual dependence on God's mercy, since if he interrupts its flow even a little, drought necessarily follows. (Letter of 1648 to Gilberte Périer, *OC* 2/11–12)

Once you've understood some item of secular literature, the first thought here is, that's enough: it's up to the ordinary working of your memory to retain it and re-present it when necessary—as I can recite to you at call the multiplication tables or some speeches from *Macbeth* and *Hamlet* once they're firmly lodged, as they were for me by the age of eleven or so. But it's different with beatitude, the life of and under and in grace. There we need an infusion, an inflow, that doesn't stop. The likeness given is from trinitarian theology (that topic is rare in Pascal): the relation between the Father and the Son isn't best characterized as a single gift, once given; no, it's an outpouring uninterrupted as well as endless, and without it the relation between Son and Father would cease, because the relationship just is that outpouring. Just so with *la dépendance perpetuelle où nous sommes de la miséricorde de Dieu (our perpetual dependence on God's mercy)*: while that relation continues, there are green fields and fertility; should it cease, there's only *sécheresse*, dryness or drought, baked red rock where nothing grows.

That image moves the needle a little. Here's something more explicit and a little more theoretical:

> ↠ The only way to reconcile the apparent contradictions that attribute our good actions now to God and now to ourselves is to recognize that, as St. Augustine says, *our actions are ours because of the free will that produces them, and also God's because of the grace that makes our free will produce them.* And, as he says elsewhere: God makes us do what pleases him by making us want what we're able to not want: *God makes it so that they want what they're able to not want.* (*Provincials* 18, *OC* 1/802)

Pascal here, with Augustine's help, begins to dissolve the distinction between the LORD's actions and ours. Dividing good actions up in that way—*tantôt à Dieu et tantôt à nous*—is what produces the difficulties, and so a way must be found of saying that our good actions are, at once and indiscriminably, the LORD's and ours. Our freedom is found in the fact that we're able to not want (*nous pourrions ne vouloir pas* in French, or, how much more briefly, *nolle potuissent*, in Latin) what the Lord wants for us; but that is a negative freedom, one that the LORD's grace gives us the possibility of not wanting—not wanting what we shouldn't want, in other words, or, more exactly, not wanting sin, removing a lack by an absence. When we cease to want sin, however, what we and the LORD want is the same; and our not wanting sin is what grace effects in us. It, grace, removes a negative, and effects a positive inseparable from what the LORD wants and does.

Again, in language saturated with Scripture and some elements from the tradition, both Augustinian and Thomist:

>> [G]race is given to merit glory and glory is given because merited by grace; but the gift of glory and of grace together and in common have no other cause than divine will. So, if we consider the Christian life, which is nothing other than holy desire according to St. Augustine, we find that God comes before us and that we come before God; that God gives without being asked and that God gives what is asked; that God operates without our coöperation and that we coöperate with God; that glory is a grace and a recompense; that God departs first and that we depart first; that God can't save us without us and that there's nothing we can do or undertake but only God who has mercy. (*Grace* 1, *OC* 2/219)

This passage is largely a series of antitheses, some so extreme as to be prima facie contradictions: *et que Dieu prévient l'homme et que l'homme prévient Dieu*, in which prevenience—coming first, coming before—is predicated of both the LORD and us; or *et que Dieu quitte le premier, et que l'homme quitte le premier*, in which the same is said of departing—giving up. Coöperation is denied and affirmed as a category proper to explain the relation between what we do when we act well, on the one hand, and what the LORD does, on the other. *Gloire*, the proper end of the Christian life when understood as our participation in the LORD-who-is-glory, is both *une grâce et une récompense*, where grace is precisely not a reward for merit (a recompense), and anything that is such can, by definition, not be grace, which is given freely, unmerited, and not as fulfilment of a contract. These paradoxes are given by Pascal in this passage as ways of interpreting the Christian life when that is understood as a matter of *saint désir*, holy desire: we are, recall, for Pascal, creatures bound to and by delectation. Should these antitheses, these prima facie contradictions, be dismissed as nonsense, as Pascal's failure to provide an account of the relations between what we do and what the LORD does when we're acting well?

No. An ordinary way of dealing with affirmation or denial of a matched pair of contradictory predicates of some subject is to say that there's some problem with the subject term. If, as we should, we deny both baldness and nonbaldness to the present king of France, it's because there is no present king of France and so we ought to deny both predicates of him: it isn't the case that the present king of France is bald; and it isn't the case that he isn't; and that's because there's no present king of France. Suppose the subject-term of the excerpt under discussion to be *good human action apart from the* LORD (Pascal's preferred instances of good human action in these discussions are doing what the commandments require, and praying). Suppose, further, that this phrase, like *present King of France*, picks out nothing: there is no good human action apart from the LORD. Then, pairs of predicates such as *comes before the* LORD's *action* and *comes after the* LORD's *action*; *is a reward* and *isn't a reward*; *is necessary for salvation* and *isn't necessary for salvation* may properly both be denied, or, what is the same, both be affirmed. Doing this kind of thing, as Pascal does in this excerpt, presses the reader to ask: what's wrong with the subject term? The right answer for Pascal, as for me and as for orthodox Catholic theology, is that the subject term is empty: there are no such actions, no good human actions independent of the LORD's gift, and so all the debates about kinds and quantities of grace(s) aimed at rightly ordering the balance between good human action and the LORD's action are misguided and can never be resolved.[24] The thing to say when difficulties of this kind are raised is that divine and human agency are noncompetitive. It's not that when you have more of one you have less of the other; there's no zero-sum. No, rather it's that talking about the one—human freedom, let's

24. Paul V's requirement that there be a moratorium on debates *de auxiliis* is a magisterial ruling concordant with this Pascalian view.

say—is a way of also talking about the other—the LORD's graceful prevenience, for instance. As here:

>> She [the Church] maintains in her unshakeability the power of grace against those who deny it and the freedom of the will against those who destroy it. She makes known to the one that grace doesn't ruin freedom but on the contrary liberates it; and to the other that the coöperation of the will takes nothing from the efficacy of grace, because it [coöperation] is itself an effect of grace. (*Grace* 2, *OC* 2/232)[25]

This excerpt shows Pascal as grammarian. The Church affirms, first, that there is grace and that it is a power; and then, second, that we humans have *la liberté de la volonté*, and that it does something. To deny either is to place yourself outside the sphere of orthodox Christian talk, which is a place Pascal wants not to go. But the Church does not teach how best to bring these affirmations together. That is a theoretical question, a task for those with talent and time for such things—like Pascal. And Pascal's speculative resolution of it is to say that each affirmation—of grace and of free will—must be made in light of the other; the meaning of free will is part of the meaning of grace, as the meaning of grace is given, in part, by the meaning of free will. Grace's efficacy (*secours spécial*, *grâce efficace*, and so on) is, in part, that it makes the will free; and freedom's efficacy is, in part, that it coöperates with grace. Theoretical treatments of these two terms that try to analyze them independently of one another, according to the zero-sum, stand about as much chance of success as analysis of white's strategy in a game of chess that makes no mention of black's. White has no strategy independent of black's moves, and vice-versa. Attempts to carve out space for white-as-agent independently of black-as-agent have

25. Compare *Grace* 12 (*OC* 2/294) and *Grace* 7 (*OC* 2/257), which latter applies this perspective and its associated conceptual machinery to the question of predestination.

about as much chance of success as attempts to carve out space for human agency independent of the LORD's.

I've pressed Pascal a little further than he explicitly goes on the topic of the positive relations between divine and human agency. But not much. He is quite clear and quite explicit, indeed repetitively so, in affirming that there is no space at all for us to give an account of our doing anything whatever that is good without the categories of coöperation and participation being used. Not to use these categories, for Pascal, ends in depicting a god who is not the LORD and creatures who are not creatures; if there were, ever, in any possible world, a *pouvoir prochain* to do good independently of the LORD, that would mean creatures had powers belonging to them in the same way, which is to say independently of what the LORD has given and continues to give them, powers the LORD might then reward or punish them for having. In Pascal's doxography, positions like that are Manichean or Molinist, and sometimes also Thomist; they lie at the root of Jesuit moral theology as he understands it, and are doomed to conceptual failure, typically by denying grace in favor of some concept of nature construed independently of creaturehood. All that, which is explicit in Pascal, brings him within spitting distance of understanding divine and human agency as noncompetitive with one another, in the way I've set that out in the last few paragraphs. And this puts him on the side of the angels: it's the right grammatical move.

There's one more element of Pascal's thought that does some work here. I mean the noun *néant*, nothing, and the verb *anéantir*, to ruin (something) by bringing it to nothing. His principal use of these words is anthropological. Nothing is what we came from, and, in order to receive the LORD's grace, which remakes us as members of Jesus-Christ's body, we must bring our fallen selves to nothing, ruin them by nothing-ing them, and refrain from *amour-propre*, which is the embrace of ourselves as if we were something. There's also a mathematical use, related to Pascal's analysis of orders:[26] the physical order is, inter alia, the sphere of measurement, where everything is located somewhere between nothing (nowhere) and infinity. The connection here to the question about freedom and grace is obvious enough; if everything we are and everything good we do is graceful gift, which means that there's no competition between our good acts and what the LORD does, then the sphere in which we act by and for ourselves can only be the sphere of nothing. The goal (purpose, object, aim) of action in that sphere is nothing, and acts performed there come to nothing. To look at acts such as that, and at where they take those who do them, is to look at nothing. All of which may be taken as a gloss on the idea of sin: if free acts are those done independently of the LORD (not, as we've seen, Pascal's understanding of what freedom is), then they are, all of them, purely sinful. And if, as Pascal prefers, free acts are those done in coöperative participation with the LORD's graceful gift, then sinful acts are those enslaved to nothing.[27]

In one of the more gnomic observations in *Pensées*, with a characteristic interest in a quotidian act, Pascal writes:

» In writing what I think, my thought sometimes escapes me. But that brings my weakness to mind, which I'm always forgetting, and that teaches me more than my forgotten thought, for I care only to understand my nothingness. (*Pensées* 555, *OC* 2/778)

26. See chapter 3, above, on order.
27. On the transition from nothing to something in Pascal, see my discussion of the letter of 1648 to Gilberte (*OC* 2/7–10) in chapter 4, §4.3, above. On the infinity-nothingness dialectic see, usefully, João Cortese Figueiredo Nobre, "Infinity between Mathematics and Apologetics: Pascal's Notion of Infinite Distance," *Synthese* 192, no. 8 (2015): 2379–93; and see the depictions of the self's nothingness in *Pensées* 33 (*OC* 2/550), *Pensées* 358 (*OC* 2/666), *Pensées* 403 (*OC* 2/692), *Pensées* 758 (*OC* 2/892–94).

Forgetfulness serves as a typical, perhaps even a paradigmatic, instance of what results when we don't coöperate with the LORD: a simple lack. Seeing that lack for what it is permits a recognition—a *connaissance*—of what, without the LORD, we are: *néant*.

5.5 Predestination

It's clear to Pascal that grace (*secours spécial, grâce suffisante, grâce efficace*) permitting perseverance in the Christian life and eventual salvation is not given to all.[28] He also affirms, with clarity and force—and frequently—that this means that not all are saved; that the reasons for the salvation and damnation of particular persons remain obscure to us in practice and in principle because the predestination of some to salvation and others to damnation rests upon the LORD's inscrutable (to us, as we now are) will, and has nothing to do with their merits, evident or otherwise (to us); and that we are prospectively entirely incapable of discriminating the saved from the damned (retrospectively it's different: the Church identifies saints for us).

Consider, as illustrative and typical, the following passage from *Grace*:

> ⇒ God is obliged to give graces only to those who ask for them, and not to those who do not. And because you can't ask for grace to pray without having it, it's evident that God is not obliged to give grace to pray to anyone, because no one can persevere in asking for it who doesn't continue to have it. But because God is engaged by his promises to give to the children of the promise, even to those who never ask it, he is engaged to give exactly to them grace to pray for grace to live well; but because the obligation follows only from the promise, he should do this only for those to whom he has promised—which is to say, only to the predestined. (*Grace* 6, *OC* 2/255)

28. For an especially clear statement, see *Provincials* 1 (*OC* 1/596).

The business about grace and agency is familiar by now: to get grace, you must ask; but the capacity to ask is already a gift. It's all grace, and your asking is an act of noncompetitive coöperation with the LORD's gift. What's added here is that the LORD promises, and is then obliged (*s'est obligé*) or engaged (*s'est engagé*) by the promises made. This is the language of election: the LORD is bound in this way to Israel, but also, by extension, to those among the baptized to whom the promise is made. The languages of promise and obligation are here applied exchangeably to the LORD: *l'obligation n'est qu'en suite de la promesse.* And then a third term is introduced: the predestined (*prédestinés*). They are the ones to whom the LORD has freely promised and therefore freely obliged himself to.

Such people are not everyone, as we read in a passage closely following the one just discussed:

>> It's established that many are damned and many saved. It's further established that the saved wanted to be saved, and that God also wanted them to be. For if God hadn't wanted them to be, they wouldn't have been; and if they hadn't themselves wanted to be, they wouldn't have been. The one who made us without us can't save us without us. It's also true that the damned very well wanted to do the sins that have merited their damnation, and that God very well wanted to condemn them. It's therefore clear that God's will and ours concur in the salvation and damnation of those who are saved and those who are damned. There's no question about all this. If, therefore, we ask why people are saved or damned, we can in one sense say that God wants it, and in another that it's because we do. (*Grace* 7, OC 2/257)

Again, the standard Pascalian position on grace and agency: concurrence (*concours*) of the LORD's will and ours, understood under the rubric of noncompetition. Contribution to salvation and damnation is shared, therefore, in the way already described. But why exactly is it certain (*il n'y a point de question en toutes ces choses*) that, in fact, there are some (many) whose sinful will concurs with the LORD's in their own damnation? Pascal's account to this point can be taken as an account of how it would be were there any damned: there'd be those who, damaged already by being born as Eve's and Adam's descendants, then sin by turning from the LORD toward nothing, a sin permitted them and concurred in, therefore, by the LORD, who in permitting them this does not give them the *grâce efficace* or *pouvoir prochain* that would allow them to renounce, with the double negation of removing a lack, their own nothing-seeking sinfulness, and thereby to participate fully in the LORD's graceful gift, which would, with due and proper perseverance, bring them to salvation, but whose lack issues finally in their damnation.[29] But that account doesn't show why we should say that, in fact, there are some in that condition—why, that is, we should shift the account from the subjunctive to the indicative.

Pascal asks the question directly: Is the fact (as he takes it to be) that there are some who are saved and some who are damned due to the LORD's will or to ours?[30] Answers to this question, he writes, fall into three families.

The first is Calvinist, and according to it the LORD's *volonté absolue* is that some are saved and some damned, and that, therefore, some are created with damnation, and others with salvation, as their unavoidable ends, without respect to what they, or anyone else, has done, might do, or will do. On this view, the LORD not only permits but directly causes the damnation of some: their damnation is what they are for, the LORD's purpose in creating them. Pascal considers this an opinion both *épouvantable* (ap-

---

29. It's noteworthy that Pascal's own lexical and conceptual devices could, and perhaps should, have led him to entertain the possibility that damnation is extinction. He doesn't, however.

30. As, for example, in *Grace* 7 (*OC* 2/259).

palling) and *abominable*,[31] because it makes the LORD directly responsible for evil, and because it makes impossible any talk of human freedom, which, he has already established, belongs non-negotiably to Christian discussion of these matters.

The second kind of answer Pascal calls Molinist. This family of views, he writes, abandons any talk of the LORD's absolute will for the salvation or damnation of anyone. The LORD has only a *volonté conditionelle* in those matters, which is to say that the LORD wills responsively to what we do, or to what we would do had we the chance (the LORD's omniscience, Pascal's Molinists hold,[32] provides knowledge of that, as of all counterfactuals). If we make good use of the LORD's grace (or would, had we the chance), then the LORD provides us salvation; and if we make bad use of the LORD's grace (or would, had we the chance), then the LORD provides us damnation. Such views as these make each of us *maître de son salut*, master of our salvation (and damnation); those outcomes proceed from what we choose to do; and the LORD is constrained to respond accordingly. Pascal takes this kind of view to be responsive to and contradictory of Calvinist views. Those make everything dependent on the LORD; these make everything dependent on us.[33]

There is a third answer, and Pascal calls it Augustinian. This family of views begins by distinguishing the condition of human creatures before the Fall from their condition after it. Before the Fall:

> ≫ God created the first human, and in him the entirety of human nature—just, sound, strong—without concupiscence—with free will equally capable of good and evil—desirous of beatitude and unable not to desire it. God was unable to create anyone with abso-

31. *Grace* 7 (*OC* 2/260).

32. I emphasize again that I make no claims here about any actual Molinists. Pascal's Molinists are, at best, possible ones.

33. For Pascal on the Molinists, see *Grace* 7 (*OC* 2/260), which is what I summarize and gloss here; compare *Grace* 15 (*OC* 2/308).

lute will to damn them—God did not create anyone with absolute will to save them—God did create them with conditional will to save them all, in general, if they observed his precepts. If they didn't, then, following his own pleasure and disposing of them as a master, he saved some and damned some. Innocent human creatures coming from God's hands could not, even though strong and sound and just, observe the commandments without God's grace. And God could not justly impose precepts upon Adam and innocent humans without giving them the grace needed to fulfil them. If humans at their creation had not had sufficient grace necessary for fulfilling the precepts, they wouldn't, by transgressing them, have sinned. God gave Adam sufficient grace, which is to say that to which nothing else was necessary in order to fulfil the precepts and live in justice. By this means, Adam could persevere, or not, according to his pleasure—his free will could, as master of this sufficient grace, render it empty or efficacious, according to his pleasure. God allowed and permitted Adam's free will to make good or bad use of that grace. If Adam had persevered by means of that grace, he would have merited glory, which is to say eternal confirmation in grace with no danger, ever, of sin—as the good angels have merited this by the merit of the same grace. And each of his descendants would have been born justified and with sufficient grace the same as his by means of which they could have persevered, or not, according to their pleasure—and so merited eternal glory, or not, like Adam. (*Grace* 11, *OC* 2/287–88)[34]

Before the Fall we were all as the Molinists take us all still to be: recipients of the LORD's conditional will for our salvation, and, therefore, also of *grâce suffisante* to coöperate with the LORD in doing what's right, and to persevere in that coöperation. It's important to note in the excerpt just translated that Pascal takes care to distinguish what the LORD cannot do, which is create anyone with an absolute will for their damnation (*Dieu n'a pu créer …*),

---

34. Compare *Grace* 7 (*OC* 2/261–62).

from what the LORD didn't do but could have, which is create anyone with an absolute will for their salvation (*Dieu n'a pas créer* …). Doing the former would make the LORD not the LORD; doing the latter wouldn't, even though, for Pascal, the LORD did not do this either. Eve and Adam made their choice, and so they did not do what they could have done, which is persevere in grace. The LORD permits them this freedom—a freedom, recall, for nothing, a freedom that has nothing as its content, goal, and culmination—and they are, therefore, damned.

After the Fall, according to the Augustinian family of views Pascal expounds and defends, we, all of us, inherit damage: we are ineluctably concupiscent, bound by sin's delectability. None of us has, at birth, *grâce suffisante* or *secours spécial*; we are all worthy of damnation, a *massa damnata*. It remains the case that we weren't created for damnation: the LORD has no absolute will for us to end there, but only a conditional one, conditioned, that is, by the state of affairs that obtains since the Fall. But, by contrast—and this is the central thing that distinguishes, for Pascal, the state of things after the Fall from before—the LORD does, now, have an absolute will for the salvation of some. They are the elect (*élu*), chosen inscrutably; and because the LORD's absolute will suffices to bring about what it intends, differing in this from the LORD's conditional will, those elected, the recipients of the promise, necessarily persevere and come, at last, *infailliblement*, to salvation.[35] This doesn't mean that the noncompetitive view of human and divine agency is abandoned: in coming to salvation, the elect join their will to the LORD's in the way described. The difference between them and Adam lies not there, but in the inevitability of their salvation. Here's a summary statement:

35. Here I summarize and gloss *Grace* 11 (*OC* 2/288–90).

> ⤞ God, by absolute and irrevocable will, wanted to save his elect by a purely gratuitous act of goodness; he has given up the rest to their bad desires to which he might, with justice, have given up everyone. (*Grace* 11, *OC* 2/289)

And:

> ⤞ God by his mercy gives to the just full and complete power to accomplish the precepts when it pleases him; and by a just but hidden judgment he doesn't give it always. (*Grace* 4, *OC* 2/240)

The LORD, after the Fall, is related asymmetrically to the elect and the nonelect. For the elect the LORD has an absolute will for their salvation, which is an inscrutable act of mercy; and for the non-elect the LORD has a conditional, which is to say responsive, will for their damnation, which is an ordinary act of justice.

So far with Pascal: that complex position—conditional will for salvation before the Fall, combined with grace sufficient for coöperation, and with humans sufficiently flexible to turn toward good or evil; absolute will for salvation of the elect after the Fall, combined with humans inflexibly evil-oriented unless elected.

A further point, already mentioned, needs emphasis. None of us, post lapsum, whether ourselves elect or not, is able prospectively to discriminate the elect from the nonelect; and, inextricable from that point, the baptized, who seem to be and in some sense really are receivers of a *secours spécial*, are not all elect—and, though Pascal doesn't emphasize this, there are some among the unbaptized who are elect. There are, as he likes to say, three kinds of people: those who are abandoned to their sin without ever receiving remedial graces; those who receive such graces in baptism, but who don't persevere; and the elect, who receive such graces, typically but not necessarily in baptism, and who persevere.[36] The distinc-

---

36. *Grace* 7 (*OC* 2/262).

tion between the elect and the nonelect is, therefore, for Pascal, one with theoretical import only. It prescribes how this aspect of the theology of grace should be elucidated; but it does nothing else. It has no import for the Christian life in any other way. It can't, for instance, specify one set of actions as appropriate for the elect and another as appropriate for the nonelect; it can't prescribe that the elect should be treated in one way and the nonelect in another; and, it remains neutral—has no effect upon—how the prescriptions and proscriptions proper to teaching or preaching about the Christian life should be put, nor upon the prosecution of the apologetical enterprise.[37] Here's Pascal's way of putting this:

> ⇒ [E]veryone in the world is obliged to believe, though with a belief mixed with fear unaccompanied with certainty, that they're of the small number of the elect that Jesus-Christ wants to save; and not to judge anyone else among those who live on earth, however wicked and impious they may be, so long as there remains a moment of life, not to be among the number of the predestined—in this way leaving to God's impenetrable secret the discrimination of the elect from the rejected. It is this that obliges them to do what contributes to their salvation. (*Grace* 7, *OC* 2/262)[38]

If you don't and can't know whether you or anyone else is among the elect, it's still open to you to make some working assumptions about that. Pascal recommends two: first, assume that you are, and act as if that were so; second, don't assume that anyone else isn't, and act as if that were so. It's those two assumptions that oblige you to live a Christian life with the passion of a beloved who delights in the lover's presence; and it's those two assumptions that make sense of recommending the Christian life to pagans, as Pas-

37. For more on these things, see the discussion of the place of reason in chapter 3, §3.4, above; and of the wager and other apologetical enterprises in chapter 4, §4.5, above.

38. Le Guern laconically and accurately comments: "Cette remarque concilie le projet de construire une apologie avec la conception augustinienne de la prédication" (*OC* 2/1228).

cal does, and criticizing misconstruals and misrepresentations of that life, as he also does.

*

Pascal's developed position on grace has, then, the following central commitments, here stated in skeletal fashion: (1) Nothing good is possible without grace; that includes good human actions. (2) Good human actions occur only when we are given the grace to do them, and when, moved by delight, we coöperate with that grace. (3) Any zero-sum account of the relation between God's agency and ours fails, which entails that such a relation must be noncompetitive. (4) We can do nothing by ourselves, and the doing of that nothing is sin; with sin the LORD has nothing to do. (5) Since the Fall, every human creature is born damaged, which is to say both mortal and sin-bedazzled.[39] (6) The LORD creates no human creature for damnation; if damnation occurs, it is because our damaged and sin-bedazzled condition reaches its proper term. (7) The LORD, since the Fall, has chosen—elected—some for salvation, and that election is irresistible; the rest the LORD leaves in their damaged and bedazzled state, which issues, eventually, in their damnation.

Each of these points is worth a large volume or two to itself; much more if the history of Christian speculation and argument about them were to be presented and analyzed. I limit myself here to an equally skeletal endorsement of part of what Pascal gives us, and a critique of part.

I endorse without reservation points (1) through (6). These points, though not necessarily in that language, are essential to the grammar of Christianity. Rejection of any one of them leads to insoluble problems, and Pascal is in my judgment very good at indicating those problems. That's especially true with respect to points (2) and (3): rejection of those, which requires attempts to

---

39. Save Mary, in whom Pascal shows little interest.

balance the relations between divine and human agency according to the zero-sum, inevitably fail, and Pascal is virtuosic in showing how and why. He's good, also, on the nature of sin in (4), though I wish that he'd been more attentive to the systematic possibilities here, and more consistent in drawing the connections between sin and nothing. Points (5) and (6) I take to be beyond reasonable objection.

Point (7), however, is a different matter. It's possible to affirm (1) through (6), without reservation, without arriving at (7), which is neither entailed nor even suggested by (1) through (6). Here's how, using Pascal's language, it might go differently. The Fall, let's agree, does what Pascal says it does: we're all damaged and sin-bedazzled; left to ourselves, we turn, inevitably and with a dying fall, toward nothing, of which turning our mortality is a sign and a correlate. But the LORD's response to this state of affairs, which is to give them up to their corruption and sin-bedazzlement, and in that way to give up on their salvation, need not be what Pascal says it is. Nothing in his depiction of that state of affairs, or his grammar of grace, leads there. The problem lies in the idea of irresistibility of the LORD's *volonté absolue* so construed, and in a correspondingly bad interpretation of the idea of election.[40]

As to the first, irresistibility: Pascal's distinction between the conditional and the absolute will of the LORD is tied to a distinction between what's resistible and what's not. He needs that distinction only because he's committed to the idea that not all are, or can be, saved, and that the saved are so in virtue of an irresistible act of election that isn't given to all. Were he not committed to that idea, and if he'd abandoned the sharp distinction between the

---

40. Recall, in the discussion of the five propositions in §5.1, above, that one of them had to do with this matter: *Interiori gratiae in statu naturae lapsae numquam resistitur* (there's no resisting interior grace in the state of nature). Pascal's position may end in affirming at least a version of that proposition, though much depends on how *in statu naturae lapsae* is read. It's possible, too, that he affirms the fifth proposition in some of its possible readings.

LORD's conditional and absolute will and replaced it with an understanding of the LORD's will that stressed its constancy, then he could have written that, since the incarnation, the baptized are, by baptism, placed in the condition of Eve and Adam before the Fall: that is, the LORD's constant will is for the salvation of all of them, as it was for the salvation of Eve and Adam and their progeny. And since the baptized's inherited damage is now healed by baptism and their sin-bedazzlement now checked by baptism, though neither indefectibly, they can, as Eve and Adam could, choose life or choose death, look to the LORD or look to the *néant* the Devil offers. And when, as always happens, there is forgetfulness, the look away, the reprise of sin, there is a sacramental economy (the sacraments of penance and of extreme unction) that makes possible the re-establishment of the sinner in the pre-lapsarian Adamic position. The offer never stops being made, and can be rejected for a time; but it can never be finally rejected while those to whom it's made continue in being. While that's the case, an affirmative response to grace is always possible. For a time, perhaps a very long time, defection is possible: there can be an alternation between returning the LORD's embrace and turning away from it. That alternation is part of the Christian life, and is sacramentally marked. But there comes a time when defection is no longer possible, when we enter into glory, as Pascal has it; then, there is only the embrace and its return, and that is salvation. Non-competition remains the structure of things—the LORD, to use the Augustinian tag much quoted by Pascal, doesn't save us without us; but the LORD never despairs, gives up hope, of the salvation of the most determined of sinners among the baptized—as is reflected in the liturgical prayer of the Church. That line of thought, very much not Pascal's, leaves open the question of whether all the baptized are saved. For him, that is a closed question.

As to the second, election: a parallel line of thought can be developed here. Pascal's view is that the election of the saved is, in form, like the election of Israel: mysterious, irrevocable, irre-sistible, and for some only, not for all. If you're a Jew, on this view, there's nothing you can do about it; you're a member of the chosen people by birth, like it or not, and it's intrinsic to the idea of a chosen people that there are people unchosen. Abraham, perhaps, could have said no; but once he's said yes, the promise is made and the promise is irrevocable. Just so, on Pascal's view, for *les élus*: mysteriously, irrevocably, and irresistibly, they are the saved, not for any merit on their part, not with any possibility of resistance on their part, and they are, by definition, some among many. But it could go differently. It could be that the LORD's election of Israel is an anticipation, a type, of the LORD's universal election: as the Jews are a light to the Gentiles, all of whom will come to Zion at the end of all things, so, now, since Jesus-Christ, the Church is a light to the world, all of which will come to Jesus-Christ at the end of all things. Coming-to-Zion and coming-to-Jesus-Christ complement one another: both are promises, and promises are not revoked; but these two are compatible promises, even if the texture of their compatibility isn't yet evident.[41] The LORD, then, makes the promise made once to Israel now to all (that is a feature of the LORD's constant will for the salvation of all), and establishes the Church as the rainbow-sign of that promise, the ordinary means (there are always and necessarily extraordinary ones) by which damage is healed and the dark-adapted eye is made accustomed to the light. What the incarnation shows that the LORD wants, in constancy, is that everyone should be saved.[42] Election isn't, now, for some; it is for all, but the promises made to Abraham are not thereby nullified, for those promises contained within them pre-cisely an affirmation of their significance for all.

41. For more on this, see chapter 7, below, on the Jews.
42. A recent and full-throated defense of universalism, with only negative reference to Pascal, is David Bentley Hart, *That All Shall Be Saved: Heaven, Hell, and Universal Salvation* (New Haven, Conn.: Yale University Press, 2019).

6

POLITICS

Since Augustine, it has been a commonplace of western Christianity that the political world is double, constituted by two cities, each with its own laws, mores, habits, purposes, marks, methods, and goals. One of these cities is ours: a human creation and a human possession, made by us for our own purposes; it's the human city. The other is the LORD's, given by the LORD to the chosen for the LORD's own purposes; it's the *civitas Dei*, as Augustine calls it, or the LORD's city. A city, according to this usage, is a polity: a set of habitable institutions, practices, structures, and norms by means of which and under the aegis of which human creatures have a life together.

Cities have citizens, and the formal purpose of a city is to make it possible for its citizens to have a common life. The index of a city's success is the degree to which the common life it establishes for its citizens permits their individual flourishing within a context shared by them all, which is to say in terms of goods common to them all. The individual flourishing of citizens happens, when and to the extent that it does, in symbiosis with the common good of the city, just as that common good is symbiotic with the individual flourishings for which it provides the ambit and context. The city's common good is additional to and emergent from the sum of the goods of its citizens; it provides their context, and they its condition; neither is reducible to the other.

According to Christianity's grammar, neither city, during the time between the Fall and the general resurrection, can be found pure and unadulterated anywhere here below. In the case of the human city, that's because its purity would mean its annihilation. That follows, anyway, if we define the good of the human city as exclusively its own: any attempt to instantiate a good capable of possession without remainder by human creatures can yield, by definition, nothing. There are and can be no such goods, for were there any they would have to be in every respect independent of the LORD, and that would make them null. The LORD's city, too, though for different reasons, can't be found pure and unadulterated here below. Were it so, some polity in the fallen and devastated world would be identical with heaven, for heaven is another word for the LORD's city. It's a city in which all human political action participates fully in the LORD's purposes, a city, that is, in which every political act accords—noncompetitively coöperates—with the LORD's political will. That political order is real: it's the communion of saints. But human creatures can, here below, participate in it only in part and proleptically. It is not available without admixture.

According to this way of setting up the difference between the two cities, they are antitheses, dialectically opposed. The laws and norms and marks and purposes of the one oppose those of the other, and the degree to which the one is present and evident is the degree to which the other is absent and occluded. If the one is warlike, the other is peaceful; if the one makes slaves, the other liberates them; if the one underwrites abject poverty for some among its citizens and spectacular wealth for others, then the other guarantees that all citizens' material needs are met; if the one treats power as the central political good, then the other so treats love. And so on.

This isn't the only way to understand the relation between the two cities. It's possible, and some Christian political theologians have so recommended, to relate the two cities hierarchically, depicting some political goods (justice, perhaps) as common to both the human city and the LORD's city, and then reserving others (mercy, maybe) as proper to the LORD's city. On models of that sort, the LORD's city supervenes upon and perfects the human city. Models such as that are structural kin to understandings of the relation between our agency and the LORD's according to the zero-sum.[1] They suffer from most of the same drawbacks. The antithetical model is more congruent with a correctly ordered understanding of sin and grace, and of the relations between the LORD and creatures.

Here's a representative statement by Pascal on this matter:

>> After all, Fathers [Pascal addresses his Jesuit interlocutors], whom do you want to be taken for—the Gospel's children or its enemies? You've got to be of one party or the other. There's no middle course. Whoever's not with Jesus-Christ is against him. Everyone belongs to one of these two kinds. Two peoples and two worlds are spread throughout the earth according to St. Augustine: the world of God's children, who together make a body of which Jesus-Christ is head and king; and the world in enmity with God, of which the Devil is head and king. That's why Jesus-Christ is called king and god of the world: he has subjects and worshipers everywhere. The Devil is also called in Scripture prince of the world and god of this age: he has agents and slaves everywhere. Jesus-Christ has placed laws that please his eternal wisdom in the church that is his empire, while the Devil has placed laws he wanted to have there in the world that is his kingdom; Jesus-Christ honors suffering and the Devil its absence;

---

1. For further discussion, see chapter 5, above, on grace.

Jesus-Christ says to those who are slapped that they should turn
the other cheek, while the Devil says to those about to be slapped
that they should kill those who want to do them such an injury;
Jesus-Christ declares happy those who share his disgrace, while the
Devil declares unhappy those who are disgraced; Jesus-Christ says,
"Woe to you when people speak well of you," while the Devil says,
"Woe to those whom the world doesn't esteem." (*Provincials* 14, *OC*
1/746)

This is as antithetical as possible. There are only two kinds of people and you have to belong to one or other (*ces deux genres d'hommes partagent tous les hommes*). The laws—both kinds of people
have them, Pascal explicitly says—that order the lives of the Devil's children are in particulars and purpose opposed to, which is to
say in every sense incompatible with, those that order the lives of
Jesus-Christ's children, and in the series of antitheses with which
the excerpt concludes Pascal provides instances. He doesn't here
write of cities; but elsewhere he often does, and his depiction here
of both kinds of people as living in law-governed communities
makes that language appropriate. The LORD's laws and the Devil's
both make cities. It doesn't suit Pascal's polemical purposes in the
Provincials, from which the excerpt just quoted is taken, to write
that both kinds of people are to be found in every actual polity,
ecclesial as well as secular; and that none of us is in a position to
tell who belongs to which city. But he is abundantly clear on both
points elsewhere.[2]

If the two cities are understood antithetically, then some
among the tasks of Christian political theology are clear. First, to
discriminate the characteristics of the human city from those of
the LORD's with as much precision and detail as can be mustered.
Second, to guard against the error of identifying any actual polity
here below with the LORD's city—this error is tempting, which is

2. See the discussion in chapter 5 above, on grace.

why it needs to be guarded against; it's especially tempting when it comes to the Church, the community of the baptized here below, and so special vigilance is needed to prevent it in that case. Third, to clarify the nature and limits of the authority possessed by particular polities, secular and ecclesial, over their Christian citizens. Pascal shows interest, though not to the same degree, in each of these tasks, and is, typically, dialectical and polemical about all of them, to the usual clarifying effect.

But that is not an exhaustive account of what political theologians need to do. If, as is obvious, there are many polities here below, and if none of them is identical with either the LORD's city or the human city, then the political theologian will need to offer an account of how the particular cities (including the Church) that together constitute the political aspects of the fallen world are individuated one from another; of how their respective claims to allegiance ought to be balanced and adjudicated; and of what it is to obey their laws. Pascal is concerned, with differing degrees of emphasis and explicitness, with all these questions, too.

6.1 Secular Cities

One way of individuating the particular cities that together make up the political world here below is by the bodies of law that order their common life. Those laws ordinarily include specification of who's subject to them and who isn't, which is to say of who's a citizen and who isn't, and they ordinarily do that by specifying how a particular person becomes, and ceases to be, a citizen.[3] For example, I am a citizen in this sense of three cities. One is ecclesial: I became a citizen of the Church by baptism in 1977, which is the ordinary means of entrance into the ecclesial city; and then

3. This is, of course, too simple. Noncitizens are taken by particular cities to be subject to their laws in various ways, too. But it remains true that citizens are more fully subject to their city's laws than noncitizens are, and so it will do, to a first approximation, to say that those subject to a city's laws are its citizens.

in 1996 that citizenship was extended and further specified by reception into the Catholic Church, of which I remain a citizen.[4] Minimally (and politically) that means I'm subject to its laws. And then, in virtue of being born on English soil to English parents, I became, at birth (or perhaps, more precisely, when my birth was registered), a citizen of the United Kingdom, and by extension (for the moment) also of the European Union. I remain a citizen of those cities, even though I was naturalized in 1994, with due pomp and ceremony, as a citizen of the United States. Of that city, too, I remain a citizen. It is possible, at either my wish or that of the city, for me to cease to be a citizen of the United Kingdom or of the United States, and the laws of those cities specify at least some of the conditions that need to obtain for that to happen.

This example shows some of the differences between citizenship here below and citizenship in the LORD's or the human city. Those latter two are mutually exclusive, whereas earthly citizenships are not. I may, finally, be among the elect, as Pascal would have it, which is, for him, the same as my being a citizen of the LORD's city; but whether or not that is the case, it has no effect upon whether I'm a citizen of the Church (or of the United States or the United Kingdom) now. The same is true if I turn out finally to belong to the human city. Those citizenships are determined eschatologically, while the three in my example are present realities, without obvious connection with the finalities. That's among the reasons why I can have multiple citizenships here below, and among the reasons why citizenship in the Church doesn't rule out other citizenships. It's still the case, however, that multiple citizenships may, and perhaps typically do, create tensions. If the laws of one city require something of me that the laws of another ban, there'll be such a problem: perhaps the laws of the United States

---

4. Arguably, citizenship in the Church is unlike other citizenships in that exit isn't possible. I can't erase my baptism, and neither can anyone else. Excommunication is possible according to the canon law of the Catholic Church, but that is a different matter.

of America require me to obey them whenever there's a conflict of that sort;[5] or perhaps the canon law of the Catholic Church requires me to disobey the laws of a secular sovereign state when they conflict with the prescriptions or proscriptions of canon law.

Particular polities here below are all alike in having citizens and laws that bind and order the collective life of those citizens. They are not all alike in other ways, and for Pascal's purposes it's important to discriminate the ecclesial city, the Church, from all others. That's not because the ecclesial city is identical with the LORD's city; rather it's because its sovereign is Jesus-Christ, and citizenship in it is understood to be membership in his body.[6] Other polities—France, England, Spain—have earthly sovereigns, and are all alike in that. For convenience, we can call these secular cities (that isn't Pascal's language), and the Church the ecclesial city. Here I'm concerned with Pascal's thought about citizenship in secular cities (he was a citizen of the France of Louis XIII and Louis XIV) as it is in itself, and as it relates to citizenship in the ecclesial city.

Pascal's first move is to locate the laws of secular cities within the orders of being.[7] They belong, he writes, to the physical sphere, which means to the sphere in which force is dominant. Consider:

> ⇒ Justice—force. It's just that what's just should be followed; it's necessary that what's more forceful should be followed. Justice without force is powerless; force without justice is tyrannical. Justice without force is opposed because there are always the wicked. Force without justice is accused. We should, therefore, put justice and force together and thus make it so that what's just is forceful or that what's forceful is just. Justice is disputable; force is very recognizable

5. That might be one implication of the explicit renunciation of allegiance to all foreign powers required in the oath of allegiance said at the naturalization ceremony.

6. For more on this see chapter 4, §4.3, above, on custom and associated topics.

7. For more on this see chapter 3, §3.1, above.

and not subject to dispute. And so we can't make justice forceful because force opposes justice, calling it unjust and itself just. And since we can't make justice forceful, we've made force just. (*Pensées* 94, *OC* 2/571–72)

Suppose that the subject of this remark is the laws of France as a secular state. Why should they be obeyed by French citizens? Ideally because they're just. But laws, in order to be obeyed, also need sanction, typically the threat of punishment—*la force*, that's to say. So, the laws need to be both just and enforced. But justice is *sujette à dispute*: no one can be sure of what justice is, and therefore no one can be sure whether some law or body of laws is just. Force, by contrast, isn't disputable: the executioner's sword and the soldier's musket can be seen by all, and what they do, or may do, is also evident. Justice therefore dissolves into force so far as the laws are concerned: what's evident and indisputable is self-guaranteeing. Force says that it is itself just—*que c'était elle qui était juste*—at least if justice means the reason why the laws should be obeyed.

But, you might object, doesn't this dialectic rest upon the thought that there's no certainty about what's just—about the content of justice? If there were certainty, or at least widespread agreement—as widespread, perhaps, as that about what the guillotine's blade is and does—about the laws' justice, then couldn't we say that justice would provide a reason for obeying the laws? Pascal agrees with the conditional, but doesn't affirm its antecedent:

≫ There are, no doubt, natural laws, but this beautiful corrupted reason of ours has corrupted everything. Nothing's more ours than what we call ours by art. It's by senators' laws and peoples' votes that crimes are committed. Once we labored under vices, now under laws. From this confusion comes the fact that some say the essence of justice is the legislator's authority, others that it's the convenience of the sovereign, others that it's present custom—which is the most certain. There's nothing whose intrinsic justice can be arrived at by reason alone; everything changes in time. Custom produces all equity for the sole reason that it's accepted. That's the mystical basis of its authority. Whoever tries to reduce justice to its first principle brings it to nothing. Nothing is so faulty as laws that correct faults. Those who obey laws because they're just obey the justice they imagine, not the essence of the laws; that's entirely self-contained—it's law and nothing more. (Pensées 56 (*OC* 2/560)[8]

Pascal here allows that there are natural laws (*lois naturelles*), but not that we know what they are (*rien suivant la seule raison n'est juste de soi*). Our rational capacities are too corrupt for such knowledge. Instead, we should acknowledge that the laws of secular cities are matters of art: we make them, and once they're made, they bring crimes into being, because crimes are, definitionally, offenses against the law, which means that without laws there are and can be no crimes. Evidence for the appropriateness of this understanding of the laws is that people differ as to what makes them just. Lacking agreement about this, Pascal's claim is, what we have is the fact that according to local custom these are the laws: they should be obeyed because of that, in something like the same way that we agree to abide by local sartorial or gastronomic customs, or local conventions about which side of the road to drive on.[9] There's nothing external or additional to the fact that these are our laws that can be appealed to for their justification. The claim that laws should be obeyed, then, is a comment on the meaning of *loi*. But still more: attempts to justify, or call into question, particular local laws leads, often and perhaps typically, to conflict about them, the active form of which is civil war. This Pascal understands as the worst of political evils—*le plus grande des maux est les guerres*

---

8. And see the connected series of thoughts of which this forms a part, *Pensées* 54–63 (*OC* 2/558–63). See also *Pensées* 469 (*OC* 2/746–48), on the relation between custom and obedience to the laws.

9. For further discussion of custom and habit, see chapter 4, §4.3, above.

civiles.[10] If irreducible and unresolvable disagreement about the laws' justice is typically violent, then it's preferable to renounce the pattern of thought that attempts to assess the laws' justice by extra-legal appeals.

This pattern of skeptical thought fits well with the thought that the political sphere belongs to the physical order. What counts there is *la force*, not reasoning. And established custom has a force of its own. Attempts to justify that force rationally are then like attempts to establish mathematical truths by the force of arms: it can't be done, and trying it leads to bloodshed.

Pascal applies the same view of the place of the political order to his analysis of social rank.[11] Imagine, he asks, a castaway seized upon by the locals and made their king. He knows he isn't king, that the kingdom he's been given isn't his. He may, nevertheless, over time learn to behave externally as if he were the monarch of that place; but unless he's self-forgetful, he'll know, and recall inwardly, his *condition naturelle*, which is as a person in no way different from his subjects except that they've decided to call him king. Rank in general is like this, Pascal thinks: it's conventional, and the product of *une infinité des hasards*.[12] Aristocrats and kings aren't what they are by natural law or intrinsic merit, but by chance and force and human institution. Forgetfulness of that is what permits the violence with which those who take themselves to be great behave toward those they take to be less great.

In more detail:

>> There are two kinds of greatness in the world: established and natural. The former depends on the will of those who've judged it reasonable to honor certain conditions and to attach particular kinds of respect to them. Dignitaries and the nobility are like this.

10. *Pensées* 87 (*OC* 2/569).

11. In what follows I depend largely upon *Discourses* (*OC* 2/194–99). These contain Pascal's most extended writing on social rank.

12. *Discourses* 1 (*OC* 2/195).

In one country nobles are honored, and in another commoners; here the first-born, there the younger. Why? Because it's pleased people to do so. The thing was indifferent before it was established; afterward it became just because it's unjust to disturb it. Natural greatness, however, is independent of human fantasy. It consists in real qualities of soul or body that make this or that one more worthy of esteem. Examples are knowledge, intelligence, virtue, health, and strength. We owe something to both these kinds of greatness, but what we owe is different because they're of different kinds. To established greatness we owe established forms of respect, such as external ceremonies that may also be accompanied, and with reason, by interior recognition of the justice of this order; but these don't lead us to think there's some real quality in those we honor in this way. We have to speak to kings on our knees; we have to stand in the chambers of princes. It's stupid and base to refuse them these requirements. But we owe natural respect, which is esteem, only to natural greatness, just as, by contrast, we owe contempt and aversion to qualities opposed to these natural greatnesses. I don't need to esteem you because you're a duke, but I do need to salute you. If you're a duke and an honest man, I give what's appropriate to each of these qualities. I refuse neither the ceremonies appropriate to your quality of being a duke, nor the esteem appropriate to that of being honest. And if you're a duke without being honest, I should still do what's appropriate: for in giving you the external respect that people have attached to your birth, I ought not lack the inward contempt your baseness merits. (*Discourses* 2, *OC* 2/196–97)

So understanding the social ranks recognized in secular cities is concordant with understanding their laws as conventional. Inhabitants of secular cities, including Christians, should obey local laws and should honor those judged locally worthy of public respect. They should do those things, however, not because they think the local laws just or the local worthies estimable, but because the local laws are laws and the local worthies are worthy. All that belongs to the physical order in which force and custom dominate, as they should.

Pascal approaches the same set of questions from a different angle in a letter to Florin and Gilberte Périer from perhaps 1657.[13] This letter deals with the question of how Christians should engage in controversy (*fronde*), political and otherwise. If you're a Christian, Pascal writes, you can be sure, first, that the LORD has permitted (and perhaps directly wills) your opponents to hold and act on the view they have, just as the LORD has permitted (and perhaps directly wills) you to hold and act on the view you have. You can be more sure of this than that you are correct about the topic under dispute, especially when the dispute is about arcane or complex matters. The skepticism that Pascal exhibits here about our capacity to know whether we're right about disputed questions is cognate with his skepticism about our capacity to assess the justice of some law. Unfortunately, as he sees it, we typically become attached to the truthfulness of our political opinions, and attempt to establish that truth by vanquishing our opponents because of what he calls, in the letter, *esprit propre*,[14] which he elsewhere, and more commonly, calls *amour-propre*. That is, our engagement in controversy is typically informed by a self-centered judgment that we can, by ourselves, win the battle and that, if we do, it is to our credit as it is to our discredit if we do not. Pascal finds judgments and patterns of thought of this kind confused. It isn't up to us to establish the truth by winning our controversial battles:

> ⇒ We act as if we had a mission to make truth triumph rather than to fight for it. The desire to vanquish is so natural that when it takes

13. The letter is at *OC* 2/39–41. The use made of this letter by Auerbach in "Political Theory" is illuminating. See Erich Auerbach, "On the Political Theory of Pascal," in *Blaise Pascal*, ed. Harold Bloom (New York: Chelsea House, 1989), 17–35. See also my "The Quietus of Political Interest," *Common Knowledge* 15, no. 1 (2009): 7–22.

14. At *OC* 2/39–40.

cover under the desire to make truth triumph we often take the one
for the other and think we're seeking God's glory when we're seeking
our own. It seems to me that the way in which we endure obstruc-
tions is the most certain indication of this: for if we want nothing
other than God's order, it's doubtless the case that we hope as much
for the triumph of God's justice as for the triumph of his mercy, and
that, unless we are negligent, we'll be indifferent whether the truth
is known or fought against, because in the former case God's mercy
triumphs, and in the latter God's justice. (Letter of 1657 (?) to Florin
and Gilberte Périer, *OC* 2/40)

Pascal here distinguishes between two desires, or *missions*. One is
to win; the other is to fight. We confuse these easily, mostly because
it's hard for us, because of *amour-propre*, to enter into controversy
without thinking that we'll be damaged if we don't win. Fighting
(*combattre*) seems to most of us most of the time to entail a desire
to win. But the two can be analytically separated, and they need to
be if Christian political controversy is to be performed. The desire
to win serves ourselves; the desire to fight serves the LORD. Our
controversies should involve only the second, and this means that
we should have an *égalité d'esprit* (not an *esprit propre*) with respect
to the outcome of our engagements. We should care to engage in
the service of what we take to be true or just; but victory is up to
the LORD, and whatever the outcome, the LORD will be served.

Given these assumptions, the purpose of advocating or oppos-
ing this or that local law isn't victory but rather tranquil support
of the proposals that seem to you to accord with the LORD's will,
together with a similar opposition to those that do not so seem.
Victory-seeking, that *désir ... si naturel*, doesn't sit well with the
double skepticism Pascal advocates: skepticism, that is, about
whether what seems to you to be true is in fact so, coupled with
skepticism about whether in advocating what you advocate you're
inspired by the LORD or by *amour-propre*. What does sit well with

this double skepticism is an advocacy that can't be discouraged by the prospect of defeat, and which is without concern about the effects of victory. This is because, first, the defeat of the preferred proposal, should it be defeated, is itself permitted by the LORD, a fact of which you can be more sure than that the victory of the preferred proposal is what the LORD wants; and, second, because the enactment of the preferred proposal is not the central point of advocating it: the point is, rather, to persist in advocacy of what seems true and (or) right. Pascal doesn't explicitly address in this letter skepticism about our ability to know what the effects of victory will be, but such skepticism is entirely concordant with what he does advocate. And he does add a third kind of skepticism, in a remarkable throwaway comment:

» I'm unable to prevent myself [from abandoning indifference], so angry am I against those who absolutely insist that we should assent to the truth when they've demonstrated it, something that Jesus-Christ didn't do in his created humanity. It's a mockery, and it seems to me to treat ...[15] (Letter of 1657 [?] to Florin and Gilberte Périer, *OC* 2/41)

Pascal here confesses his own subjection to the advocate's anger (*colère*), which is exactly what he criticized earlier in the letter. What provokes this anger is the claim to transparent self-evidence in controversy, to the possession of arguments in support of a preferred proposal, whether political or otherwise, that should, because of their persuasive power, at once convince all those faced with them. Pascal hates (the word is not too strong) those who demand instant assent to what they claim upon the basis of demonstration (*que l'on croie la vérité lorsqu'ils la démontrent*). This is a mockery: it isn't what Jesus-Christ did in advocating what he advocated, and it is not, thinks Pascal, what we should do either.

15. This is where the letter's surviving fragment ends.

What he means by this, as is abundantly evident elsewhere in his work, is that Jesus-Christ taught, performed miracles, died, and was resurrected; this complex pattern of action does not amount to an argumentative demonstration of the truth of any set of claims, and does not convict those who reject what it presents of blindness to what is self-evident. When it persuades, which it often doesn't, it moves those persuaded to that peculiar form of imitation that Christians call discipleship, and it does so by the transformative power of its presence. We, though we are not Jesus-Christ, should, thinks Pascal, take the same line when we engage in controversial advocacy.

There is in this point a deep skepticism about both the persuasive and the truth-conducive capacities of argument that attempts demonstration. Such argument, whether about political or theological proposals, rarely persuades, and when it does it generally ought not. This means neither that argument is always unpersuasive, nor that it ought never persuade. As is evident from distinctions drawn elsewhere in Pascal's work, he thinks that in the sphere of mathematics, for example, demonstrative arguments both can and should persuade, because the matters treated in that sphere are exactly those reason is designed and equipped to treat. The same is, by implication, true of arguments about reason's own limitations: these are more like mathematical arguments than arguments about matters of substance in politics or theology. In matters of theology beyond the elementary, and politics beyond the local, reason cannot offer demonstrative arguments—not, anyway, if "demonstrative" includes the thought that these arguments should, or, worse, do, convince all, or even most, comers. If, then, on Pascal's view, you become convinced that (for example) the pope can legitimately propound doctrine on matters of faith and morals but not on matters of textual exegesis, or that monarchy is preferable to republicanism, or that democratic polities are preferable to those ordered by Islamic law, it will rarely and perhaps never be the case that you have arrived at your view as a result of being persuaded by argument; and even when you have been so persuaded, your conviction about the matter ought to be inconstant and shallow because, if you are clear-sighted, you will know that whatever the argument that brought you to this view, it is sufficiently complex, opaque, and subject to challenge that you cannot be sure you have ever understood it, that you understand it now, or that you will continue to understand it in the future. You can always be more sure that your grasp of the arguments which have brought you to conviction on matters of this degree of complexity is imperfect than you can that the arguments are valid and their conclusions true.

*

Much in what Pascal has to say about the political order is correct and admirable. The laws of secular cities are matters of local convention, and ought in principle to be obeyed just because they are local laws. Those given high social rank for qualities provided them by some admixture of chance and convention ought be given the marks of respect judged locally appropriate to that rank. Even in the United States of America, we honor judges and senators and presidents principally because of the office they hold, not because we take them to be morally or intellectually estimable. They may be those things too; but when they are that's not why we give them the titles and the respect we do (or should). We honor them because they've done whatever was necessary to get elected or appointed to the offices they hold, and those necessities typically have little to do with merits of what Pascal would call the estimable kind. Being elected to Congress or as President is neutral with respect to moral or intellectual estimability; so, in large part, is being appointed to a federal judgeship. That doesn't make those who hold such offices any the less worthy of respect exactly as office-holders. To think otherwise is confused, and Pascal is salutary in showing that to be so.

Pascal's distinction between advocacy of a political position with the hope of success in getting it established, and advocacy of a political position with no interest other than advocacy, is also at least suggestive. It's a kind of quietism—quietism, we mght say, with respect to outcome—but not one that places advocacy *simpliciter* under the ban. A systematic quietist, if that isn't an oxymoron, in matters of politics, would rest content with whatever the local political order happens to be. That isn't Pascal. He's happy to advocate changes in the local laws, but not because he thinks advocates need to know what will happen if their advocacy is successful, and not because he thinks they need to be interested in whether their advocacy will be successful. Rather, advocates of this law over that, this policy over that, this procedure over that, perform their advocacy because it seems to them a proper act of service to the LORD to do it—or, to use language that Pascal doesn't use in these contexts, because so acting is beautiful and in pursuit of beauty. Advocacy of those kinds has one great strength: those who practice it can't be discouraged, by the prospect of its failure or in any other way.

There are, however, drawbacks to Pascal's position on the laws and norms that govern secular cities. One especially pressing upon those, Christian and pagan, who think it easy enough to discriminate worse from better in the sphere of law, is exactly Pascal's skepticism about the confidence we should have in our capacity to offer convincing arguments to those who don't share our discriminations, so that they will come to do so. Isn't it, you might say, easy to both see and show that laws permitting slavery, or abortion, or the ownership and use of automatic weapons, or the exclusion of women from education, and so on, are worse than those that ban such things? And isn't it, you might continue, easy to both see and show that secular cities ordered as democracies are better ordered than those whose order is given by Sharia, or by the Communist Party? Advocates of the existence and knowability of natural law within the Christian tradition are likely to think things like this, as are pagans with a high estimate of political reasoning's powers. Disagreements of this kind with Pascal, though, tend toward resolution in Pascal's favor. He can argue, unimpeachably, that such positions are refutable empirically: it isn't the case that arguments whose conclusion is the preferability of some political proposal over its competitors carry the conviction they ought according to such views, and that provides a disabling disadvantage for their advocates under which Pascal and his epigones on these matters (among whom I include myself) don't labor because we don't expect our arguments to yield conviction in this way, and therefore don't offer them with that expectation in mind. Recall that Pascal does take some laws to be preferable to others, and advocacy of them to be possible and sometimes called for. But he does not take such advocacy to be in the service of winning arguments or getting laws passed; instead, it's in the LORD's service, from which those results may or may not flow—but in any case should not be expected.

A lacuna in Pascal's remarks about politics is address to the question of the proper response of Christians to a real or perceived incompatibility between what the laws of their secular city ask of them, on the one hand, and what those of the Church, the ecclesial city, ask of them, on the other. He insists that local laws should be obeyed because they're laws, and that it's a mistake to look elsewhere (to justice, to righteousness) to support such obedience. But he also insists that both the laws and the purposes of secular cities are typically opposed to those of the Church. That is because of the intimacy between secular cities and the Devil, and the intimacy of the ecclesial city with the LORD. How should the baptized respond to this situation? We have to go beyond what Pascal writes to begin to answer this. A modified and extended Pascalianism on this question might look like this: If you're zealous for the LORD, your will and vision bound by delight in the LORD,[16] then when

16. On such bondage, see chapter 5, §5.4, above.

your secular city demands actions of you noncompossible with your LORD-directed delights, you'll find yourself able to do them no more than lovers find themselves able to do what harms or brings their beloveds into contempt. If the secular city—your local sovereign state—punishes you for not acceding to its demands, you'll suffer the affliction with delight.[17] The degree of your zeal (the extent of your holiness) tracks the thoughtlessness with which you'll do what your citizenship in the ecclesial city asks. Pascal's consideration of affliction suggests that he would happily embrace the category of martyrdom as the correct one to label what happens when a Christian does not, for the love of Jesus-Christ and as a member of his body, do what some secular city improperly asks. But Pascal has no conceptual resources for advocacy of civil disobedience or revolution on rational grounds independent of intoxication by love for the LORD: the laws of the secular city are to be obeyed in the ordinary course of things just because they are laws.

6.2 The Ecclesial City

The Church, in Pascal's preferred metaphor, is the body of Jesus-Christ, and Christians, therefore, his limbs. This is not a description of the elect, those bound ineluctably for salvation; it is, rather, about the baptized, only some of whom are among the elect. It's not possible without confusion to exchange *les élus* for *l'Église* when reading Pascal. When he writes about the elect, he is ordinarily explicit in doing so; when he writes in passing of the Church, he ordinarily means the baptized here below, together with the laws, institutional forms, and practices that together are the outflow and evidence of the relation the baptized bear to the LORD. Jesus-Christ's body here below (it also has heavenly members, who are the angels and the saints, and purgatorial ones, who are those who will be heavenly members but aren't, in the temporal

17. On affliction, see chapter 4, §4.1, above.

order, yet in that condition) is on this understanding a city in the sense already given to that word. When Pascal writes that there's pleasure in being on a storm-battered ship (*un vaisseau battu de l'orage*) when you're certain it's not going to sink,[18] or that "the only religion that's against nature, common sense, and our pleasures is the only one that's always existed,"[19] it's the ecclesial city he's writing about. Sometimes, his more lyrical writing about the Church can begin to slip the bounds of this restriction to the baptized, as here:

> ≫ The Church looks at the children promised her at all times as if they were present; bringing them all together in her womb, she looks for rules to order the conduct of those to come in imitation of those now gone, and prepares the means of their salvation with as much love as she gives to those she presently feeds by way of a clairvoyance co-extensive with the loving-kindness she brings them. (*Grace 2, OC* 2/225–26)

But even here, the reference is to the baptized, and their life in the Church—the rules to order this conduct (*les règles de la conduite*), that is. It's just that those rules, given as food to the Church's *enfants* in the present, are in part derived from the behavior of those now dead, and are aimed, too, at those not yet baptized.

When Pascal is explicit about it—he usually isn't—it's clear that he understands the Church to be co-extensive with the Catholic Church, and its members, therefore, to be those in full communion with the Bishop of Rome. For example, in a letter to Charlotte de Roannez, whose deeper conversion he's seeking and guiding:

---

18. *Pensées* 627 (*OC* 2/798).
19. *Pensées* §267 (*OC* 2/643). Pascal very often—hundreds of times in the *oeuvre*—uses *notre religion* or *la religion chrétienne* as a synonym for the ecclesial city.

➤ [I]t's the Church that merits, together with Jesus-Christ who is inseparable from her, the conversion of everyone not in the truth—and then it's the converts who help the mother who birthed them. I praise with all my heart the small zeal for union with the Pope that I see in your letter. The body doesn't go on living without the head, just as the head doesn't without the body. Whoever separates from one or the other is no longer of the body, and no longer belongs to Jesus-Christ. I doubt that there's anyone in the Church more attached to this unity of the body than those you call ours [that is, the Port-Royalists]. We know that all virtues, martyrdoms, austerities, and good works are useless outside the Church and communion with the head of the Church, who is the Pope. I will never separate myself from this communion, or at least I pray God to give me that grace; without it I'd be lost forever. I'm making you a kind of profession of faith, and I don't know why. (Letter of 1656 (?) to Charlotte de Roannez, *OC* 2/34)[20]

Pascal is here explicit that Jesus-Christ's body here below has the Pope as its (earthly, temporal) head, and that those who separate from that body, so headed, *n'est plus de corps, et n'appartient plus à Jésus-Christ*. Pascal intends, he writes, always to be joined to that body; and that should he not receive the grace to do that, *je serais perdu pour jamais*. The implications of this view aren't all concordant with the doctrine and practice of the Catholic Church since the Second Vatican Council;[21] neither, if pressed, do they harmonize exactly with Pascal's definition of how the LORD's *volonté absolue* should be understood.[22] But what he writes here is representative of the ease and naturalness with which he identifies the Church that provides rules for the conduct of the Christian

20. For a similar assertion of Pascal's (or de Montalte's) intention to remain in full communion with the Catholic Church, see *Provincials* 17 (*OC* 1/781).

21. Since Vatican II (and by implication long before), the Church has recognized baptisms in the triune name performed by those not in full communion with the bishop of Rome.

22. For Pascal's understanding of *volonté absolue* and election, see chapter 5, §5.5, above.

life with the Catholic Church. It's that body he thinks of when he thinks of the Church as a political body—as the ecclesial city.

Among the things the Church does when it acts politically is to exercise authority under the rubric of discipline. Pascal shows interest in this aspect of the life of the ecclesial city from the 1640s on, and several episodes show, from different angles, his involvement in it. For example: Early in 1647, Pascal and two of his friends, Raoul Hallé des Monflaines and Adrian Auzoult, met twice with Jacques Forton, sometime Abbé de Saint-Ange, an ex-Capuchin who was by then a secular priest. They discussed theological topics.[23] The three friends appear to have been intrigued by Forton, whose theological views had by then received considerable public discussion and seemed to them repellent, scarcely Christian but sufficiently prominent to be worth a rebuttal. By the end of their discussions, and perhaps before, the three were convinced that Forton ought not work as a priest in Rouen, which is what he was at that time seeking to do. The three submitted a document, signed by each, initially to Jean-Pierre Camus, bishop of Belley, and then to François de Harlay, archbishop of Rouen, in an attempt to prevent Forton from being given an appointment, on the principal ground that his theological opinions were heterodox. Harlay investigated, and ruled that Forton's responses to his questions, which were almost entirely prompted by the document Pascal and his friends had submitted, ought not prevent his appointment in Rouen. Forton nevertheless withdrew from consideration, which was the outcome Pascal and his friends wanted. The episode shows Pascal's willingness, indeed eagerness, to intervene in an ecclesial political question: as a young man (he was twenty-five at the time of the discussion) he thought it important to see that those exercising priestly responsibilities were, by his standards, at

23. A record of what they said is in *Conferences* (*OC* 1/547–65). On this text, see my brief comments in chapter 1, above, on Pascal's life and works; and Le Guern's discussion at *OC* 1/1111–13.

least broadly orthodox—and he was prepared to manipulate the machinery of episcopal power to see that this happened. The episode shows that Pascal recognized the validity and importance of episcopal authority, as well as the importance of having the pastoral and teaching offices of the diocesan priesthood exercised by those possessed of an orthodox (by his standards) understanding of Catholic doctrine. All that shows a deep concern for the proper ordering of the ecclesial city.[24]

A second episode: In *Advocate*, Pascal, adopting the voice and method of a lawyer, responds to the initial decision of 1657 on the part of the French bishops to require signature of a formulary of submission to Alexander VII's *Ad sanctam* (that decision wasn't finally enforced until 1661, after many vicissitudes) with an argument about the proper limits of papal power.[25] There are two major lines of thought in this text. The first has to do with the balance between centralized Roman authority, and the authority of a local—in this case French—church. Pascal's lawyerly voice claims that the decision of the French bishops to bow to Rome in this way, by demanding a signature, is to shift the balance too far in the Roman direction, and to be an abuse of the rights of all French people, not just ecclesiastics—to be, in fact, the basis of a new inquisition on French soil.[26] Pascal often writes in this way; his polemic in the *Provincial Letters* against the laxism of Jesuit moral theology and penitential practice often, and none too subtly, makes the point that the Jesuit authorities aren't French but are, rather, a pack of foreign-sounding Spaniards and Italians and Germans.[27] The second point, interwoven with the first in the text

24. It's not clear to me that intervention of the sort *Conferences* represents into the decisions of a bishop about whom to appoint to a particularly priestly office in his diocese is in fact a contribution to the political well-being of the ecclesial city. But it is clear that Pascal had that well-being in mind.

25. *Advocate* (*OC* 1/819–32).

26. *Advocate* (*OC* 1/824–27).

27. For example, *Provincials* 5 (*OC* 1/635).

but separable conceptually, is that Alexander's bull amounts to a prima facie illegitimate attempt to extend the teaching power of the Pope from matters of faith and morals to matters of fact.[28]

That question, of the propriety of the Church's bishops ruling, and requiring assent to their rulings, on matters of fact as well as on matters of doctrine, is a deeply political one, being in large part about the proper scope of magisterial authority. Pascal has no doubts or reservations about the fact of such authority; his questions, at least for a time, were about its proper scope. Magisterial decisions in the 1650s had already ruled not only that certain propositions on grace were false and heretical, but also that precisely those propositions had been advocated by Cornelius Jansenius in his *Augustinus*.[29] That work was of numinous importance for Pascal and the Port-Royalists. It was therefore a matter of some difficulty for Pascal to find Jansenius cast as a heretic by an authority he acknowledged, and his first response to that difficulty was to argue for a distinction between matters of fact and matters of doctrine pertaining to faith and morals, and to direct magisterial authority to the latter. In 1657, he restated (it had already been evident in his work from about 1650 onward) a clear distinction between two means of coming to assent to some claim. One is by reason, which means by deploying for oneself whatever methods of investigation are best suited to the claim in question; and the other is by reliance upon authority, which means faith or trust in those best equipped to rule on the topic. The second method, faith, is further subdivided: there's divine faith, which means faith in what the Lord God has entrusted to the Church, available to Catholics in Scripture and tradition, which latter means "what's proposed to

28. This is a matter also taken up in *Sorbonne* 5 (*OC* 1/957–58). *Sorbonne* and *Advocate* are mutually illuminating: the former is a theological analysis of the problem, and the latter a legal one. Pascal ventriloquizes both styles, and questions can reasonably be raised about whether these works are another example of Pascal writing as a fictional double with whose opinions he may not himself agree. See my brief discussion of pseudonymy in chapter 1, above.

29. See chapter 5, §5.1, above, on the five propositions.

us by the Church, with the assistance of the Spirit." The Church, Pascal writes, is infallible on those matters—*et c'est en cela qu'elle est infallible.*[30] And then there's human faith, which means faith in authoritative people, those best equipped to teach us truths about particular matters (historical, empirical, and so on).

And then he writes this:

> ⇒ Everything that has to do with a particular point of fact can only be assented to by human faith. That's because it's quite clear that such matters can't be founded upon Scripture or tradition, which are the two channels through which God's revelation, on which divine faith is founded, comes to us. And that's why the Church can be in error on questions of fact, as all Catholics recognize. (*Sorbonne* 3, *OC* 1/955)

And this:

> ⇒ To command those who are entirely persuaded of the truth of some point of fact to change their opinion in deference to papal authority would be to require that they abuse their reason against the order of God himself, who has given us reason to discriminate true from false so that we can prefer what we take to be true to what we take to be false. (*Sorbonne* 6, *OC* 1/959)

This makes the tension very clear. In spite of what Alexander's bull of 1657 says, Pascal continued to deny that particular matters of fact can be resolved by magisterial authority, and he did that because of an epistemology—an understanding of what knowledge is and how it's arrived at—that places conclusions about such matters in principle beyond the scope of magisterial teaching. The upshot is that if you should find yourself in the position, as Pascal did, of having what you take to be clear, even decisive, evidence in favor of some conclusion about a question of fact, you shouldn't

---

30. *Sorbonne* 3 (*OC* 1/955).

abandon your understanding of what you take to be true because a pope, or some bishops, say the opposite.

Pascal's part in this matter didn't end there. Following Alexander's bull, after much back-and-forth among the French bishops, the Roman consultors, and various political factions, to which Pascal contributed with the vigor you might expect, the situation by October 1661, nine months before his early death, was that the French vicars-general demanded, of at least priests, religious, and teachers of theology, signature of a formulary of submission to the bulls of 1653 and 1656, in wording designed to make it impossible to maintain a distinction between the condemned propositions and Jansenius's teaching of them. Pascal's last surviving written contribution to the difficulty, composed during the last months of 1661, speaks to a situation in which, as he sees it, the Port-Royalists have only three choices: sign the formulary without reservation, which would mean agreeing that the propositions are heretical and that Jansenius taught them; refuse to sign; or sign with the reservation that the signature has only to do with matters that concern the faith—that is, not with the question of what Jansenius did or didn't write or intend or teach, and only with the questions of substance about the workings of grace.

Pascal is explicit and excitable in his rejection of the third option. By now, he writes, "it's a point of doctrine and of faith to say that the five propositions are heretical in the sense given them by Jansenius (*au sens de Jansénius*)." What the formulary asks for submission to, then, is a denial of the-five-propositions-in-the-sense-given-them-by-Jansenius; that complex object can no longer be disaggregated into its components (the five propositions/Jansenius's teaching). Attempts to do so have been ruled out by *Ad sanctam* and the formulary. If the formulary is signed, the signature means submission to the whole; anything else would be bad faith. It would be "abominable before God and despicable before men."[31]

31. *Signature* (*OC* 1/997).

But it's not clear from this last surviving writing on the matter which of the other two possibilities—signing or not signing, each without reservation—he endorses. And there's nothing more from him on the topic before his death in August of the following year—nothing that survives, anyway; there's good evidence that he did write more on the topic, but whatever it was is lost to us.

It might seem at first blush clear that Pascal ought to have preferred not signing. If, as he'd been consistent in arguing for the preceding six years or so, the magisterium's authority doesn't, as a matter of principle, extend to matters of fact, and yet explicit submission to teaching on just such a matter was now being required of French Catholics, shouldn't he have refused to sign? Wouldn't signing have been acknowledgment of a kind of authority the bishops don't in fact have? Perhaps. But there's something else Pascal might have done, and some evidence to suggest that it's what he did.

The evidence: First, it's clear that by late 1661 Pascal was at odds with Antoine Arnauld and Pierre Nicole and others among the Port-Royalists on the question of the signature. The disagreements circled around whether the fact/doctrine distinction could be maintained; whether it was proper to sign with reservations; and whether it was proper to sign at all. Some of the disagreements are evident in Nicole's comments on Pascal's work on the signature,[32] but they surface in other places as well. That there were such disagreements shows at least that Pascal's final position wasn't identical with any of those held by prominent Jansenists in 1661–62, and since those positions were, essentially, sign with reservation or don't sign, it's at least possible that Pascal ended by advocating signing without reservation.

Second, there's some (disputed) evidence in support of the

---

32. Le Guern, as appears usual for editors of *Signature*, includes Nicole's comments with Pascal's words at *OC* 1/982–1000.

view that Pascal died in full communion with the Church, having confessed, received the last rites, and, during the last few days of his life, fully acknowledged to his confessor the right of the Church to require his assent to the claims of the formulary. That's the sworn testimony given after Pascal's death by the priest who attended him in his last days, testimony accepted by the bishop of Paris, who had commissioned an investigation into Pascal's death in response to a request that Pascal's remains be disinterred from their burial place on the ground that Pascal was a heretic who had died separated from the Church.[33]

And third, there's evidence (again, not probative) that close to the time of his death Pascal asked Jean Domat, to whom his papers were consigned, to destroy his writings on the signature if the religious of Port-Royal found themselves under persecution, but to preserve and publish them if they had submitted.[34] That report, if accurate, sits better with the thought that Pascal's final position was advocacy of signing without reservation than that he supported refusing to sign.

*

Pascal's case shows with unusual clarity what it is to hold together two judgments that might seem at first blush incompatible, and what it's like to act consistently with such a balancing act. The first judgment is: I'm convinced that p is the case; the second is: I see that the magisterium teaches *not-p*, and I acknowledge its authority to do so. Acknowledging that an authority teaches *not-p* doesn't require you to abandon your assent to p (Pascal never abandons his view that none of the five propositions is found in the *Augustinus*). What it does require is submission (the signature) to the authority of the teacher who teaches *not-p*. Not to acknowledge that authority would be, in the Catholic case, to separate yourself from the

33. Le Guern includes the relevant pages from Beurrier's *Mémoires* at *OC* 1/1017–19.
34. See the discussion by Le Guern at *OC* 1/1348–52. Compare Gouhier, *Commentaires*, 307–65.

form of life in part constituted by such acknowledgment. You may do that. But doing it comes with a price: it's the price of removing yourself from the form of life in which such laws exist and are enforced. That wasn't a price Pascal was prepared to pay in the Jansenius case. Within the form of life that Catholicism is, the magisterium does in fact have authority to do what it did in that case.

But acknowledgment and submission don't require pretense. If it seems to you that such-and-such is the case (that the five propositions aren't in the *Augustinus*), then clarity of thought and strength of conscience not only don't require you to pretend otherwise, but require the opposite: When occasion demands, you must say that what seems to you to be the case does in fact so seem, and when relevant you must give your reasons for so thinking. Theologians call this expressing a doubt: I see that the magisterium teaches *p*, but, so far as I can tell, *not-p* is the case, and here's why. We've seen Pascal doing this, *con brio*.

The modifier "so far as I can tell" is important. You might be wrong (that's always true), and, seeing that the magisterium seems to be teaching that you are, you ought place your sense of your own rightness under pressure. Pressure of that kind is usually a good thing for the intellectual life: it clarifies conviction by accentuating difference, as ghee is made from butter. And the exercise of affirming that *p* seems true to you when it's also the case, and you know it to be, that an authority you recognize affirms *not-p*, while it certainly produces tension, isn't difficult. We have partial analogues in secular life: representative democracy sometimes requires those holding elective office to advocate *p* because it's the will of those who've elected them (or, more dubiously, because party discipline and doctrine require it), even though they take advocacy of *not-p* to be the better course.

The clarity given Pascal's thought by the pressure of authority had one very clear yield. It brought him to see, or at least speculatively to suggest, that when the magisterium says that so-and-so's teaching of such-and-such is heretical, that claim is not best disaggregated (so-and-so's teaching/such-and-such), but, rather, treated as a complex whole—as Pascal advocates in his last writing on the signature. The nature of that complex whole then requires further clarification. Maybe it's heresies-about-grace-insofar-as-endorsed-by-Jansenius; or, whatever-Jansenius-wrote-that-comports-with-or-supports-grace-heresy; or, grace-heresies-best-labelled-"Jansenius's"—and there are more possibilities. I'm attracted by the thought that when the magisterium teaches about things such as "Nestorius's heresy" or "the heresy of Calvin" or "Milton's trinitarian errors" the function of the personal proper names in these labels is principally doxographic rather than exegetical: this, we're being instructed, is how to talk about mistakes of this kind. It's an instance of required Catholic talk, the rejection of which would be to mark yourself as exactly not someone who speaks rightly. Whether that, or something like it, is right or not, it's clearly the case that once disaggregation is rejected, new possibilities for thought open up, both for the speculative theologian (Pascal) and for the teaching Church. One such new possibility appeared, as we've seen, in Alexander's *Ad sanctam*: he develops what Innocent had written in *Cum occasione* by mentioning the sense in which Jansenius intended the (gravamen of) the five propositions. This, as I've noted, postulates an extra-textual something, and moves everyone's thought about the topic, to the extent that it's taken seriously, away from the textual particulars of the *Augustinus* and toward something else—a trajectory of thought, an implied grammar, or some such (let's hope not toward patterns of neuronal firing in Jansenius's brain). This magisterial move wouldn't have occurred without Pascal's polemics; and those, in turn, wouldn't have occurred without magisterial pressure. The benefit is mutual, and is the result of the magisterium doing what it should and the theologian (Pascal in this case) doing what he should.

The other question that Pascal's case raises and illuminates for us is about the place matters of fact have in magisterial teaching. Suppose we understand a matter of fact to be one capable, in principle, of exhaustive investigation by observation. One example: the presence of a sequence of words in a particular book—affirmed, as we've seen, variously, by Innocent X and Alexander VII in the case of Jansen's *Augustinus*. Another example: the involvement of a Roman official named Pontius Pilate in the trial, condemnation, and execution of Jesus-Christ—affirmed scripturally and credally ("suffered under Pontius Pilate").

Pascal came to see that his attempt to maintain an impermeable distinction between matters of this sort and matters of faith and morals couldn't be sustained. But the attempt is helpful to us in two ways. First, it shows that when the magisterium instructs about matters of fact, as it often does, it doesn't do so with any concern for those matters considered in themselves. Pontius Pilate is interesting to the Church only because he was involved with Jesus; had he not been, the Church would have had nothing to say about him. It follows from this that it's a misconstrual of the Church's Pilate-teaching to take it as an encyclopedia entry from which data about Pilate can be extracted and considered independently of the story about Jesus. This is compatible with the thought that some things said about Pilate are incompatible with the Church's teaching. That would be true, for example, of *Pontius Pilate was in Rome when Jesus-Christ was tried*, and the like. If you find yourself taking that to be the case—perhaps you're a historian whose life's work has been Pilate, and you've come to think that this is what the evidence shows—you'll then find yourself in something approaching the position just discussed, which is of at once taking as true something incompatible with what the Church teaches, while also (if you recognize the magisterium's authority) affirming the Church's authority to teach what it teaches.

But there is an interesting, if subtle, difference. Pascal's insistence on an impermeable distinction between matters of fact and matters of doctrine, and his probable eventual abandonment of that hard distinction, shows that the tension between the Church's teaching about Pilate and the historian's findings isn't best understood as a direct contradiction. It's not as it would be if you find the Church teaching *it's not possible for women to be ordained to the priesthood* while you find yourself taking as true *it is possible for women to be ordained to the priesthood.* That's a direct contradiction: *p* and *not-p.* But in the Pilate case, the Church teaches about Pilate only in his relation to and illumination of the figure of Jesus: Pilate has no significance for the Church outside that relation. His name serves as synecdoche for "empire-as-related-to-Jesus," or some such; the point and purpose of the Church's teaching about him isn't to make an entry into a chronicle of events, but to locate Jesus-Christ in time and place, and to show something about the significance of his trial and death. Those purposes can be served in other ways, and, so far as I can see, nothing much hinges upon whether the name of the Roman official who condemned Jesus-Christ was Pontius Pilate. That much remains of Pascal's insistence that no one's salvation rests upon belief about a matter of fact.

And that is the final gift that the Pascal case gives. It provides Catholics who want to think about matters of fact—what's written in the *Augustinus*; the biography of Pontius Pilate—spoken to in one way or another by the magisterium a fundamental guiding question: What is the significance, for the life of the Church, of the Church's teaching about this matter of fact? There will always be some such significance if, as I've suggested, the Church never teaches about matters of fact simply as such. And Catholics who find themselves in the tensive situation under discussion here should begin their thinking about the tension by trying to understand what that significance is and how, therefore, to move toward resolution of it.

*

Pascal's engagement with the magisterium illustrates the attitude to political advocacy outlined in §6.1—or at least it does in Pascal's better moments. That is, he recognizes the authority of the magisterium in the ecclesial city; he advocates, with vigor, a particular position with respect to one of its teachings; his advocacy is a battle, prosecuted with energy—combat, recall, is Pascal's preferred metaphor for political engagement and advocacy[35]—but it isn't aimed at victory. The engagement is the thing, and when it's clear that the fight is over, in this case by the magisterium's having made it impossible for Pascal's distinction between matters of fact and matters of doctrine to be maintained, serene submission is the thing, in accord with the view that the magisterium is more likely to be right than you are when it seems to you that it is wrong. All this provides an instance of the political attitude Pascal advocates; it also shows, vividly, a facet of life as a citizen of the ecclesial city.

Some further nuance with respect to this neuralgic political matter is to hand in these striking observations:

⇛ Our comparisons between what happened in the Church in the past and what's happening now are spoiled because we ordinarily consider St. Athanasius and St. Teresa [of Avila] as crowned with glory and their judges as black as demons. Now that the passing of time has clarified things, that's how it looks. But when they were being persecuted, the great saint was a man named Athanasius, and Saint Teresa was a daughter. Elias was a man like us, subject to the same passions as we are, wrote St. Peter, in order to disabuse Christians of the false idea that makes us reject the example of the saints as disproportionate to our condition. They were saints, we say, and it's not like that for us. But what was it that happened then? St. Athanasius was a man called Athanasius, accused as if he were no more than a dog, condemned by such-and-such a council for such-and-such a crime. All the bishops agreed, and so, in the end, did the Pope. What

35. See chapter 2, §2.3, and §6.1, above.

did they say to those who disagreed?—That they disturb the peace, as schismatic, and so on—Zeal, light—Four kinds of person: zeal without knowledge, knowledge without zeal, neither knowledge nor zeal, both knowledge and zeal—the first three condemn Athanasius; the last acquit him, and are excommunicated by the Church and nevertheless save the Church. (*Pensées* 510, *OC* 2/764)[36]

Sainthood and orthodoxy are apparent typically, and with assurance certainly, only retrospectively. We know that Athanasius and Teresa of Avila are saints only now that the passing of time has clarified things, and it's in the same way that we know their persecutors and those who condemned them, including councils and popes, to have been wrong. Episcopal (and papal) judgments about such things can be wrong and those who defend the condemned right, but from the viewpoint of the present the future perfect tense is the only one available to expose that state of affairs. It will be said in the present of those who defend them that they disturb the peace in schismatic fashion. Those were exactly the accusations brought against Pascal and others among the Port-Royalists, and there's no doubt where he places himself in this passage. It's clear, too, where he takes, or at least hopes, himself to belong among the four kinds of person listed at the end of the excerpt: those who are excommunicated by the Church and nevertheless save the Church (*sont excommuniés de l'Église, et sauvent néanmoins l'Église*).

Another passage to the same point, but a little more explicit in its location of Pascal and the Port-Royalists with respect to magisterial rulings and condemnations:

⇥ If my letters are condemned at Rome, what I condemn in them is condemned in heaven—*LORD Jesus, I appeal to your tribunal*—you are yourselves corruptible—seeing myself condemned, I feared I'd written badly, but the example of so many pious writings makes me

36. This *pensée* provides a sketch of materials worked up more fully in *Sorbonne*.

think the contrary, that it's no longer permitted to write well—the Inquisition is so corrupt or so ignorant—"It is better to obey God than humans."—I fear nothing and hope for nothing, unlike the bishops. Port-Royal fears, and it's bad politics to separate them [fear and hope] because then they won't fear and will make themselves more feared—I don't even fear your censures; they're [only] words if not founded on those of the tradition. (*Pensées* 714, *OC* 2/853)

Pascal's *Provincials*—presumably *mes lettres* of the excerpt— were placed on the Index in September 1657, and it seems reasonable to read this compressed and excited excerpt in light of and in response to that event. The first person in the excerpt is Pascal, it seems; the second person is the bishops; and the third person the Port-Royalists.[37] Pascal considers and rejects the thought that he hasn't expressed himself well in these writings, and was condemned because he'd been misunderstood. Rather, he self-regardingly writes, *il n'est plus permis de bien écrire* (it's no longer permitted to write well). He has been understood, and has been condemned because of what he's written. He stands by his writing, however, without fear and without hope, confident so far as is possible in the truth of what he's written. All that accords well with what we've so far seen from Pascal on the political dissent question. Even when the laws are those of the ecclesial rather than the secular city, the task is to continue to assert what seems to you to be the case, while at the same time prescinding from the desire to prevail in conflict, and from hope for (or fear of) a particular outcome. It's a razor's edge to walk, and Pascal sometimes falls off to one side or the other, as he does in part in this excerpt. That is, nonetheless, the position toward which he turns the gaze of his readers, and it's one worth a close look.

37. Pascal here, as often, separates himself rhetorically from the Port-Royalists. But this is one of the instances in which pseudonymy provides an interpretive difficulty. *Mes lettres* are Louis de Montalte's; and, perhaps, *je* is Salomon de Tultie. So perhaps the distancing from Port-Royal isn't of Pascal, but of these other two, fictions though they are.

7

JEWS

Understanding rightly the relation between the Church and Israel, and acting rightly upon that understanding, is a constitutive problem for Christianity in the sense that the differentiation of the Church from Israel was a necessary condition for the Church's coming to be. It's a problem that remains lively and continues to divide Christians, in part because it generates intractably difficult theoretical questions, the answers to many of which remain unclear. Catholic doctrine now requires it to be said that the covenant between the LORD and Israel remains in force, and will do so until the end of all things. This entails, among other things, that the halakhic lives of observant Jews are, still, a means of responding to the particular gift the LORD has given and continues to give to Israel. But how can this be, since all worship of the LORD is, as Christians see it, worship of the LORD-who-is-Jesus-Christ? The thought that the LORD Jews worship and the LORD Christians worship is not the same LORD is no longer open to at least Catholic Christians as a way to sidestep the problem: Catholic doctrine requires that the LORD Jews worship and respond to is one and the same LORD Christians worship and respond to, even though identified and

named differently, and even though Jesus-Christ is recognized neither as Messiah nor as LORD by (most) Jews. Catholic doctrine particularly, and Christian doctrine more generally, also requires that
anyone who is saved, where that means is brought by the LORD to
an indefectibly delightful intimacy with that same LORD, is saved
by Jesus-Christ alone, who is, exactly, the LORD. That claim needs
to be held together with those about the continued validity of the
covenant with Israel, and serious work is needed to do that. Serious
work is also needed to explain, Christian-theologically, how and
why it is that Jesus-Christ's flesh needs to be Jewish flesh, and what
the significance is of the fact that just such flesh is consecrated and
consumed at every Eucharist.

There are also numerous subsidiary questions, which include:
Should Christians evangelize Jews? If so, why? If a Jew is baptized,
may, or should, (s)he continue to live a halakhic life? Is it proper, or
even required, that a baptized pagan should live a life of that kind?
What's to be said about baptized pagans who undergo conversion
to Judaism? How should Christians respond to and think about
Jewish traditions of interpreting and commenting upon what Jews
call Tanakh, which is (or is it?) what Christians call Old Testament?[1] Have Christians standing to commend or criticize positions on any matters internal to Judaism since the parting of the
ways? How should Christians think, or should Christians think,
about the fact that since 1948 there has been a quasi-Jewish sovereign state in the world? And so on.

7.1 Christians of the Old Law

Pascal, inevitably, does not write about all, or even most, of
these questions. He could not have written about the State of Is-

---

1. There's no place in the Christian lexicon for "Hebrew Bible" as a label for these texts.
The Christian label is always and necessarily "Old Testament," since the works there collected
are given their meaning by the relation they bear to another collection called "New Testament." Christians, of course, have nothing to say about what Jews should call their holy books.

rael, of course; and he was neither aware of nor bound by the developments in Catholic doctrine signaled at the Second Vatican Council, and solidifed and further developed since. But he does write about some of them. Consider this instructive passage:

> ⇒ Pagan religion has no foundation today. They say that once it did, in the speaking oracles. But where are the books to assure us of this? Does the virtue of their authors make them worthy of belief? Have they been preserved with sufficient care that we can be sure they've not been corrupted?—Mahometan religion has the Alcoran and Mahomet as its foundations.[2] But was this prophet, who should have been the last the world expected, predicted? And what marks him that doesn't also mark everyone who'd like to call himself a prophet? What miracles does he say he's done? What mystery, according to his own tradition, has he taught? What morality? What felicity?—Jewish religion should be looked at differently in its popular tradition than in its holy books.[3] Among the people, its morality and felicity are ridiculous, but they are admirable in its holy books. Its foundation is admirable: it's the world's most ancient and authentic book, and whereas Mahomet forbade his book to be read in order to preserve it, Moses ordered everyone to read his in order to preserve it. And every religion is the same, for Christianity is very different in its holy books than it is in those of its casuists.—Our religion is so divine that another divine religion is nothing other than its foundation. (*Pensées* 227, *OC* 2/625)

Here, as is typical for Pascal in writing about these matters, "religion" provides the organizing category. There are four kinds of

---

2. I follow Pascal's renderings of Arabic and Hebrew words and names when translating him. In my own voice, I use the forms now standard in English.

3. I depart here from the text given in *OC*, reading *livres saints* for *leurs saints*, as also in the following occurrence of the phrase. The passage makes altogether better sense if there's reference to books rather than people at these places. Editors of *Pensées* differ about the proper reading here.

this: pagan, Islamic, Jewish, and Christian (*notre religion*). Two of these are of divine origin, which is to say the LORD's gifts, and those two are alike in another way as well, which is that what their *livres saints*, or holy books, contain is admirable, while in some other aspects (*la tradition du peuple / les casuistes*) they're ridiculous. Pascal doesn't here write that the books of the casuists are ridiculous, but since he spends many thousands of words in *Provincials* ridiculing them, it seems reasonable to extend the parallel in this way. Christianity and Judaism are then alike in being well founded and, on the ground, an admixture of the admirable and the ludicrous. They're contrasted with paganism and Islam, both of which, as Pascal sees it, are ill-founded without remainder.[4] The sole distinction between Christianity and Judaism in the excerpt under discussion is the formal one that Christianity has Judaism as its foundation, while the same is not true in reverse: *notre religion est si divine qu'une autre religion divine n'en a que fondement* (our religion is so divine that another divine religion is nothing other than its foundation). The implication of *n'en a que* is that Judaism has no other function than to serve as Christianity's foundation.

But Pascal is not consistent in that radically supersessionist view. Sometimes, he writes that true Christians and true Jews (the modifier "true" is important: for Pascal, just as not all the baptized are among the elect, so all the descendants of Abraham are not, properly speaking, Jews) have one and the same religion, which consists in nothing other than the love of God (*seulement en l'amour de Dieu*). He also lists the features that distinguish the Jews from other peoples: they have existed as a people for longer than any other; they have survived many attempts to delete them from the world; they are governed by "the most ancient law in the

---

4. Though Pascal does have some lingering fondness for the *oracles qui ont parlé*, as who can fail to? Even if the oracles have spoken, however, they don't provide the sure foundation that the LORD's gift to Israel and the Church does.

world, the most perfect, and the only one to have been uninter-
ruptedly protected within a state" (*la plus ancienne loi du monde,
le plus parfaite et la seule qui ait toujours été gardée sans interruption dans un État*); they gave the concept of law to the world; they
bear continuous witness to the one LORD whom Christians also
worship; and they bear witness also to the expectation of a coming
redeemer who will come not only for them but for all—"they've
been formed to be forerunners and announcers of this great coming, and to call all peoples to join with them in waiting for this redeemer." His encounter with this people, Pascal writes, astonishes
him (*m'étonne*), and he is sure that Jews will endure to the end of
the age, for that is the promise.[5]

Jews and Christians are also alike in another fundamentally
important way for Pascal. There are two kinds of people belonging
to each, as in this striking formulation:

> ≫ Among the Jews, there are the carnal, and also the spiritual, who
> were the Christians of the old law. Among the Christians, there are
> the grossly material, who are the Jews of the new law. Carnal Jews
> expect a carnal Messiah; grossly material Christians think that the
> Messiah has excused them from loving God. True Jews and true
> Christians adore a Messiah who makes them love God. (*Pensées* 269,
> *OC* 2/643)[6]

This excerpt deploys a standard trope—Jews as carnal/ fleshly,
Christians as spiritual—and transfigures it. Spiritual, or true, Jews
and Christians are at one in understanding and responding to the
Messiah as bringing them to the LORD's love, subjective and ob-
jective genitive both. Carnal, or grossly material, or false, Jews and

5. In this paragraph I quote and synthesize elements from *Pensées* 421–425 (*OC* 2/699–
707).

6. This is developed at *Pensées* 269–72 (*OC* 2/643–44). Compare *Provincials* 10 (*OC*
1/695–96), where the theme of being excused or excepted from the love of God is taken up in
the context of controversy with the casuists.

Christians are at one in understanding the Messiah to be about observances that need have nothing to do with love.[7] This way of putting things opens up avenues for further thought, though they aren't ones that Pascal chooses to walk down. He doesn't, for instance, go on to ask whether there can be or are spiritual Jews, in the sense he gives to that phrase, after Jesus-Christ's ascension, and what it would mean if there were. Neither does he consider whether the *chrétiens grossiers* and the *juifs charnels* are alike in ways other than their deafness to the LORD's love-offerings. But what he does do, decisively, is resist, at least most of the time, the long Christian tradition of identifying Israel *simpliciter et totaliter* with carnality. The division between carnal and spiritual cuts, for him, across that between Jews and Christians, and that is a significant, if under-theorized, move. He found it easy to make, I suspect, because of the importance to him of polemic against the (Christian) casuists. They, as he presents the matter, have badly misconstrued what the Christian life is, and the easiest and most summary way to state the nature of their mistake is to say that they have replaced delectation with heartlessly minimalist observance[8]—which is exactly the traditional way of saying what's wrong with Jews and Judaism from a Christian point of view. And once that error, with its concomitant division, has been placed within Christianity, it's easy, perhaps almost inevitable, for a dialectician like Pascal, to make it internal to Judaism as well. And that is how he arrives at the thought that there were Christians of the old law and are Jews of the new.

7.2 Supersession

So far I've canvassed Pascal's positive comments about the Jews. There are also plenty of the other kind. Sometimes, he for-

---

7. See the discussion of the Christian life in chapter 4, §§4.3–4.4, above.

8. This is the burden of *Provincials*, almost from beginning to end. See also *Comparison* (*OC* 2/103–7) for a similar way of contrasting the Christians of the early Church with those of the seventeenth century.

gets that he's entertained and affirmed that there are non-carnal Jews, and writes about them as if they're all carnal, and necessarily so.[9] And it is clear that when the topic suggests itself, Pascal is an utterly straightforward supersessionist, as here:

> ⇒ [C]ircumcision is only a sign ... which is why they weren't circumcised when they were in the desert, because there they couldn't be confused with other peoples. And after Jesus-Christ's coming, it's no longer necessary.... The Jews, lacking love, will be punished for their crimes, and the pagans elected in their place.... The sacrifices of the pagans will be received by God, and God will withdraw his acceptance from those of the Jews.... God will make a new covenant with the Messiah, and the old one will be rejected. (*Pensées* 423, *OC* 2/702–3)

And so on, until we arrive at "*le nom des Juifs serait réprouvé et un nouveau nom donné ... ce dernier nom serait meilleur que celui des Juifs, et éternel*" (the name of the Jews will be condemned and a new name given ... that latter name will be better than that of the Jews, and will be eternal).[10] The synagogue is ruined, the old covenant absorbed into the new or replaced by it, and the Jews have no more reason for being.

Except that Pascal also writes that the Jews continue in being for a reason, and that is to bear witness to Jesus-Christ and the Church. Their continued existence is necessary for that purpose, and not only their bare existence, but also their misery, for it is that combination that indicates both Jesus-Christ as Messiah and the Jews' responsibility for having killed him.[11] These, too, are utterly standard things that Christians write and say about Jews, and so there is nothing surprising in finding them in Pascal. These tropes

9. As, arguably, at *Pensées* 240 (*OC* 2/628). Compare *Pensées* 256 (*OC* 2/636).

10. *Pensées* 423 (*OC* 2/704).

11. As at *Pensées* 293 (*OC* 2/650–51). See also *Pensées* 370 (*OC* 2/669–70), and *Pensées* 505 (*OC* 2/762). On the Jews' blindness see *Pensées* 456 (*OC* 2/736–38).

don't, however, provoke or move him to flights of rhetorical excitement; they remain largely inert. Something different happens here:

>> The Jews reject Jesus-Christ, but not all of them: the holy ones accept him, not the carnal ones. This is far from telling against his glory—it is its culmination. Their reason for this rejection, which is the only one to be found in all their writings, in the Talmud and among the rabbis, is that Jesus-Christ did not subdue the nations by armed force—*your sword, O most mighty one.* Don't they have more to say than that?—"Jesus-Christ has been killed," they say, "he's succumbed and hasn't subdued the pagans by his power. He hasn't given us their spoils. He gives us no riches." Don't they have more to say than that? That's what makes me love him. I wouldn't want the one they figure to themselves. It's clear that it's nothing other than vice that prevented them from receiving him, and by this refusal they are irreproachable witnesses; what's more, they fulfil the prophecies in this way. (*Pensées* 506, *OC* 2/762)

Pascal of course claims more than he knows, and more than is true, when he writes that the only reason given for the rejection of Jesus-Christ as Messiah in all of Jewish literature (*la seule* [*raison*] *qui se trouve dans tous leurs écrits*) is that he didn't conquer the nations by force. That isn't even true of the reasons attributed in the New Testament to the Jews for demanding Jesus-Christ's crucifixion. And it's important to keep in mind that the Talmud and the rabbis show an almost complete lack of interest in Jesus-Christ. These reservations aside, the excerpt does show something important about Pascal's use of the idea of the Jew. It has to do with the epistemic significance, for pagans, of their witness, and, correspondingly, to do with the use of that witness in Christian apologetic directed not at Jews but at pagans. The thought is that everything about the gifts given to the Jews—their election, the Messianic prophecies, their particular history of rebellion, punishment, exile, return, subjugation by occupation, and so on, prior to the incarnation—ought to have disposed them to accept Jesus-Christ as Messiah. They nevertheless did not. And yet they have meticulously preserved the materials that, rightly read, show exactly that Jesus-Christ is the Messiah, and they continue to witness to him until now. They preserve and honor what at the same time they reject, and that is a *merveille* and a *miracle*, as Pascal goes on to write just after the excerpt quoted.[12] In this way, Jews are *témoins sans reproche* (a witness without reproach). It is, he writes elsewhere, that Jews love their prophecies so much, while at the same time being so opposed to their fulfilment.[13]

The excerpt also shows another theme in Pascal, also a standard trope in the tradition preceding him: that what (at least carnal) Jews find unacceptable in Jesus-Christ is exactly what Christians find most lovable. That is the fact that he did not establish his kingdom by force of arms—*c'est en cela qu'il m'est aimable*, as Pascal writes above. This trope moves almost entirely within the world of tropes: it has little to do with actual Jews or actual Christians.

7.3 Rabbinage

"Rabbinage" isn't a word in English, and not, it seems, in the French of Pascal's time, either. We'd write, I suppose, "rabbinism"; but Pascal's word is distinctive and flavorful, and it would be good to see it adopted into English. He uses it as a title for one of the bundles into which he sorted the fragments we know now as *Pensées*.[14] The matter contained under that heading is not especially interesting, being mostly Pascal's notes on the dates of composition and content of various Jewish texts—Mishna, Talmud,

---

12. *Pensées* 506 (*OC* 2/762).

13. *Pensées* 256 (*OC* 2/636).

14. *Pensées* 260–61 (*OC* 2/638–40) are the fragments so collected. The word is also used in Pascal's table of *liaisse*-titles (*OC* 2/543).

and so on—taken from the preface to a 1651 edition and commentary by one Joseph de Voysin of a thirteenth-century work by one Ramón Martí (Raymond Martin, I suppose, if Englished) called *Pugio fidei adversus Mauros et Iudaeos*, which is to say, *The Dagger of the Faith against the Muslims and the Jews*. That work is a compendium of arguments against its opponents, intended, probably, to equip Dominicans (Martí was one) to say what in the fourteenth century it was thought necessary for Christians to say about those people. De Voysin, the seventeenth-century editor, provides in his preface a conspectus of the Jewish literature about which Martí writes, and it's this that appears to have interested Pascal.[15] He's also interested in *midrashim* on this or that part of Scripture which show awareness, as he reads them, of a *tradition ample du péché originel selon les juifs* (rich tradition about original sin according to the Jews).[16] He copies down half a dozen of these, rendering them into French from Martí's Latin.

Why is he interested in this? He doesn't tell us. We can speculate, however. If Jewish exegetes at least sometimes saw in Scripture evidence that, as he quotes a certain Rabbi Moyse Haddarschan (I follow Pascal's method of romanizing Hebrew) as writing, "This evil leaven is put into us from the moment we are formed,"[17] then this shows how clear Scripture is about that matter. If even those who "hand on the books, and love them, but don't understand them"[18] can see this truth in them, at least sometimes, a truth that they are otherwise not disposed to acknowledge as Pascal sees the matter, then we have one more instance of the miracle discussed above, that the Jews hand on and witness to, sometimes with understanding, something that confirms a truth of central importance to Christianity. There may also be, in Pascal's interest

---

15. I draw this information from Le Guern (*OC* 2/1421).
16. *Pensées* 261 (*OC* 2/639).
17. *Pensées* 261 (*OC* 2/639).
18. *Pensées* 454 (*OC* 2/735).

in Jewish witness to original sin, a concern to gather ammunition against Christians who deny the doctrine—if even benighted Jews can see what's in Scripture about this, then surely you should. Perhaps, too, against pagans for whom the doctrine seems ludicrous—look, it's such a widespread idea, it's not just we Christians who see it, and so you should think again about it.

It's worth noting that nothing in the catena of rabbinic quotations Pascal provides supports anything like a developed Christian doctrine of original sin—not, anyway, if that doctrine includes a tracing back to what Eve and Adam did in the garden, or an explicit connection to the procreative sexual act as the means of sin's transmission. What the rabbinic texts do provide are statements that predicate damage of us when we're still in the womb—which is, however, a good way of stating an essential feature of the Christian doctrine.

This excursion into rabbinage is important for understanding Pascal in another way as well, and that is by providing a contrast. Ordinarily, for Pascal, the Old Testament is presented as a *chiffre*, a cipher or enigma, that is, whose meaning does not lie plain upon its surface but is veiled in figures that make it inaccessible to Jewish (and to most pagan) interpreters.[19] Jesus-Christ both is and holds the key to the cipher's interpretation. It is therefore remarkable when those who don't know Jesus-Christ are able to decipher it. But in the sequence of observations that Pascal devotes to this topic, his position isn't altogether straightforward.

Pascal's thought moves like this. If the Old Testament is a *chiffre*, then this means that the Old Testament's language is figurative, which is to say language that shows something (to those who can see) it doesn't explicitly say, or may even seem to contradict by what it does explicitly say. Much, though not all, as Pascal sees it, of

---

19. For the Old Testament as *chiffre*, see the collection of fragments bundled under the heading *Que la loi était figurative*, which are *Pensées* 229–59 (*OC* 2/626–38).

the Old Testament is like this. Figurative language relates to reality
much as a portrait does to what it's a portrait of. Portraits cannot
show all of what they represent; they must, just because they are
two-dimensional representations of three- or four-dimensional (if
we include time as the fourth) realities, leave something unshown.
They contain, as Pascal likes to put it, absence as well as presence,
whereas reality, what's depicted in a portrait, is fully present.[20]
The presence of prima facie contradictions in a text is one clear
sign that its language is figurative (a decisive one when that text is
scriptural); another is that the text itself declares that its meaning
is veiled or double or enciphered. Consider:

> ≫ A cipher has a double meaning. When we come across an im-
> portant letter whose meaning is clear, and in which it's nevertheless
> said that its meaning is veiled and obscured, hidden so that we see it
> without seeing it and hear it without hearing it, what are we to think
> except that it's a cipher with a double meaning? All the more so when
> we find manifest incompatibilities in its literal meaning. The proph-
> ets clearly said that Israel will always be God's beloved and that the
> Law will be eternal. And they said that we won't understand their
> meaning, and that it's veiled. (*Pensées* 243, *OC* 2/630)

In such cases, we need a key to interpret the text, a key that the text
itself won't provide.[21]

Much of the Old Testament is like this, as Pascal sees it. Many
of its surface-of-text recommendations and claims are figurative, and need deciphering. Without such deciphering, the text
remains the letter that kills;[22] and once its figurative nature has
been demonstrated, there's no longer any need to rely upon or ad-

20. See *Pensées* 243 (*OC* 2/629).
21. It's likely that Pascal has in mind the practices of code-users and code-breakers—a
topic in which he shows interest elsewhere—as well as the long Christian tradition of attrib-
uting multiple senses to Scripture.
22. *Pensées* 251 (*OC* 2/632).

vocate observance of what it seems to require:[23] "We say that the literal sense isn't true because the prophets themselves have said so."[24] But even this use of figurative interpretation doesn't yield the conclusion that only Christians understand that the text is figurative. Pascal's own explication of *chiffre* involves the prophets knowing and saying this, and he is happy to quote the rabbis as knowing and saying that parts of Scripture are figurative in just the sense he means. The breasts of the beloved mentioned in the Song of Songs are, he writes, read figuratively by the rabbis,[25] and he reports Maimonides himself as explicit in saying that Scripture has two faces.[26] But Pascal thinks that the Jews are nonetheless bedazzled by the literal sense much more than Christians, and therefore much less likely than they to see what Old Testament language figures—which is always Jesus-Christ.

So much for Pascal on rabbinage. As with the Jewish people in general, it seems, there are spiritual and carnal Jewish readers of Scripture. Christian readers and interpreters of the Old Testament can learn from spiritual Jewish exegetes of the Tanakh, though Pascal doesn't himself show much inclination to do so. There's also the possibility of using particular things Jewish interpreters of the Tanakh say, as in the case of apparent references to original sin, for Christian apologetical purposes—and that of course requires knowing enough about those particulars to make use of them. But for the most part, Pascal's excursions into rabbinage are an element in his defense of distinguishing Scripture's figurative sense from its literal sense. He's mostly concerned to use Jewish exegesis, imagined and real, in the service of that distinction, which, unlike the questions about Jews and Judaism, is of central importance to him.

*

23. So, almost, at *Pensées* 253 (*OC* 2/634–35).
24. *Pensées* 255 (*OC* 2/636).
25. *Pensées* 253 (*OC* 2/635).
26. *Pensées* 257 (*OC* 2/637).

Pascal's writing on the Jews is substantively unsatisfactory and difficult, perhaps impossible, to make coherent. His embrace of supersessionism, or at least of traditional supersessionist language according to which the halakhic life of observant Jews has no importance after the ascension other than as witness to Christianity, is difficult to square with his claim that Christianity and Judaism are alike in having spiritual and carnal adherents, and that spiritual Jews and Christians agree in loving the same God. He makes no attempt show how these positions relate to one another; rather, he uses the language of supersessionism when it suits his immediate purposes, and writes of spiritual Jews and Judaism—of some Jews as Christians of the new law—when that suits the topic at hand. The possible validity of the old law and the old covenant since the ascension does not engage him in the least as a question, even though he provides language that sits well with its affirmation.

Neither is his treatment of the figurative sense of Scripture anything more than flat-footed. He has a strong tendency, perhaps motivated by his adoption of the thought that the Old Testament is a *chiffre*, a cipher, to treat the figurative sense as something that, once uncovered, makes the literal sense no longer relevant—superseded, that is. Once you've seen that Old Testament talk of enemies can sometimes be read as talk of iniquities of one kind or another—that when there is an Old Testament prediction that the Messiah will deliver the Jews from their enemies it can be read to be about deliverance from the passions[27]—then the double meaning can be reduced to one, which is the figurative sense.[28] And then, when the code has been broken and the real meaning revealed, what's written in the coded text can be abandoned. A binary sequence of ones and zeroes can generate the appearance of words on your computer screen; but once those words have appeared, only a coder wants to know what the ones and zeroes are.

27. *Pensées* 253 (*OC* 2/634).
28. As, explicitly, in *Pensées* 252 (*OC* 2/633).

That, anyway, is what Pascal's statements about the figurative sense and figural exegesis often suggest. His practice, fortunately, is richer than his theory. Sometimes he takes wing, as here: "Even grace is only a figure of glory, for it's not the last end. It has been figured by the Law and itself figures glory; and so it is itself the figure and the principle or cause of glory."[29]

29. *Pensées* 258 (*OC* 2/638).

EPILOGUE

In 1982, the philosopher Saul Kripke published a book on Wittgenstein's understanding of rules and private language. In the introduction to that book, he writes that it should be thought of as "expounding neither 'Wittgenstein's' argument nor 'Kripke's': rather Wittgenstein's argument as it struck Kripke, as it presented a problem for him."[1] Kripke's book is, according to himself, not a work of Wittgenstein-exegesis but rather a collection of thoughts prompted in Kripke by having read Wittgenstein. It's not that Wittgenstein is unimportant to Kripke; he wouldn't have had the thoughts contained in the book had he not read Wittgenstein, and the thoughts are prompted and inflected by what Wittgenstein writes. But what counts for Kripke is the thoughts he's had and has written down, not the thoughts that Wittgenstein might have had. Those who've read both Wittgenstein and Kripke on Wittgenstein generally agree with Kripke that the relation between the thoughts of the one and the thoughts of the other is not always one of similarity. That state of affairs is a problem only if you think a book about Wittgenstein ought to re-present Wittgenstein's thoughts, or at least try to do so. If, by contrast, you allow that a book on Wittgenstein might properly be the literary deposit of an

1. Saul Kripke, *Wittgenstein on Rules and Private Language* (Cambridge, Mass.: Harvard University Press, 1982), 5.

engagement with the words of the person it's putatively about, an engagement that takes those words as a subliming catalyst, then there's no difficulty.

I mention this because it illuminates what it's like to read Pascal on Augustine, or Trent, or the Jesuits, or the Molinists. Pascal isn't re-presenting what those texts say; neither is he ventriloquizing their authors. Instead, he's offering you, for example, Augustine as he strikes Pascal. What you read when you read Pascal is the literary deposit of the thoughts prompted in Pascal by having read Augustine. It's important to keep this in mind as you read Pascal. If you don't, you're likely to get sidetracked into exegetical questions (has he said the right things about the works he discusses?) or questions about sources (What has he read? What is he quoting? What informs the line of thought here presented?). These are fine questions, of course; there's no ban on asking them. But asking them of Pascal tends to obscure the fabric of his thought and to dilute the benefit of reading him. That benefit, as it seems to me, is the offer of a line of thought drawn with vigor and clarity. You may accept or reject the line; the benefit of reading Pascal doesn't lie in being convinced that he's right (though, as this book has tried to show, he often is), but rather, first, in being shown by him what it's like to think about whatever the problem at hand happens to be; and then, second, in exemplifying a particular attitude to the Christian archive. That attitude is one of reverence and freedom combined: the archive is authoritative and to be treated as such; it requires, always, interpretation and commentary; and a principal point and purpose of the archive is to prompt in those who read and otherwise use it further word-work that extends, applies, and speculatively elaborates what's given in it.

Pascal is speculatively driven and speculatively bold, as is appropriate given his attitude to and use of the Christian archive. There is, I think, a single insight that lies at the root of his writing about Christianity and that explains the positions he takes on various controversial questions. It is an insight into strangeness and its correlate, for us, which is incomprehensibility. The nonhuman cosmos shows itself to us as devastated and mystifying, ordered and chaotic at the same time, vast in extent, endlessly variegated, and with a massive indifference to ourselves and an equally massive and ceaseless violence; what the microscope and the telescope show are phenomena to which we seem insignificant, and in light of which we appear insignificant to ourselves. What we've learned about the cosmos since Pascal's time accentuates this impression. We, too, are strange to ourselves, devastated, thrown into this cosmos, afflicted, mortal, ignorant, passionate, capable of comprehending neither the cosmos nor ourselves—but eminently and agonizingly capable of comprehending and theorizing exactly our own strangeness and being further afflicted by that capacity.

The human world, too, social and political and economic and scientific and literary and sexual and artistic, appears strange to us. It is death-inflected and death-driven, and we, as a creaturely kind, are ingenious in diverting ourselves from that fact in all the spheres just named. We construct polities, write books, perform experiments, prove theorems, compose symphonics, court and marry and procreate, explore the planet we find ourselves on, and try to understand what's around us. Sometimes, we succeed in that last, in part, spectacularly, but our successes typically open to us still more uncomprehended vistas. And above all, we are endlessly violent, to one another, to nonhuman living creatures, and to our nonhuman environment. We kill, we destroy, we rape, we torture: our passion for understanding is exceeded by our passion for domination, and both yield violence, a violence intensified by our sense that we are ourselves always and finally subject to that same violence.

This, as Pascal sees it, is not an encouraging situation. Its remedy is not obvious and the provision of that remedy beyond our ingenuity. There is, however, a remedy, and it is necessarily as strange as what it remedies. It is the triune LORD's *ex nihilo* creation of all that is, election of Israel, incarnation as Jesus of Nazareth, and establishment and guidance of the Church. Pascal shows no particular interest in these central claims of Christianity. He doesn't treat in anything other than incidental ways christology, trinitarian theology, mariology, or the doctrines of election, fall, and redemption. He assumes some version of all these, of course, and they do occasionally surface. But they don't drive his theological writing.

What does drive it is the depiction of Christianity as an incomprehensibly strange remedy for an incomprehensibly strange predicament. In order to meet that need, Pascal must and does emphasize the contrast between what the LORD gives and demands, on the one hand, and the norms and mores of the world, on the other. To be a Christian, for him, is to become incomprehensible to the world. It is, out of love for the LORD's gift, whose content is exactly the LORD, to bring both oneself and the norms of the human world to nothing. *Provincials* throws the contrast between the Church, which is the saturated presence of Jesus-Christ, and the world, into extraordinarily sharp relief. Those (the Jesuits) who make the Church recognizable to the world and the practice of Christianity accommodatable to the world's violence and concupiscence are remorselessly ridiculed because they have, in their accommodations, succeeded in making both the LORD and ourselves pleasantly pleasing, malleable, and comfortable. Pascal polemicizes against those who offer such views and perform such pastoral practices in an intense and ironical style because he sees them as *les chrétiens grossiers*, grossly material Christians who think that Jesus has dispensed them from loving the LORD.[2] Pascal's depiction of what Christianity is and how to receive it is aimed, above all, at making it possible to see Christianity as the gift of a LORD who makes Christians *incapables d'autre fin que*

2. *Pensées* 269 (*OC* 2/643).

de lui-même[3]—incapable of any end other than the LORD. And that can't be done in shades of gray.

The commitment to strangeness lies at the root, too, of Pascal's writing on grace. Can we do anything good of and by ourselves? No. Are we, once devastated by sin, deserving, by ourselves, of anything good, any gift of grace? No. Can we keep the commandments? Only if the LORD graces us. Will we be saved? Only if the LORD graces us. Do we, can we, know whether we will enter into eternal life? No. What does our coöperation with the LORD amount to? Self-annihilation, the bringing to nothing of all *amour-propre*.

Reading Pascal, then, is neither comfortable nor comforting. But it is bracing. If you let it, it can show you what it's like to be opened up, oyster-like, by conviction of your own misery and the LORD's love, evacuated, and then filled with the LORD. Pascal's writing is not free of error, not adequate to the riches of the Christian archive, often exaggerated, and always partial. But it shows, with an intensity rarely approached, how strange we are and how strange Christianity is, and how reciprocal those strangenesses are. It is, because of that, a gift both to the Church and to the world.

3. *Pensées* 419 (*OC* 2/698).

CONCORDANCE TO *PENSÉES*

The fragments collected as the work called *Pensées* are divided, ordered, and enumerated differently by different editors and translators. In this book I follow the order, division, and numbering given in Le Guern's edition. There are, however, other commonly used systems, notably those given in the editions made by Lafuma and by Sellier (these editions are listed in the bibliography). The concordance below has three columns. The first gives Le Guern's numbers; the second, Lafuma's; and the third, Sellier's. The concordance shows that sometimes text presented as a single fragment by Le Guern is distributed across more than one fragment by one or both of the other editors; and that sometimes text presented by one or both of the others as a single fragment is distributed across more than one by Le Guern. There are some instances, too, in which there are differences among the three in order and presentation of the text within a single fragment; I have not indicated those cases, since they don't ordinarily make it difficult to locate text quoted in one edition in another. And, finally, there are some instances in which the text of a fragment in Le Guern is altogether absent in one or both of the others; those cases are indicated by "xxx" at the relevant place. The three most widely used (at the time of writing) English versions of the *Pensées* depend upon the work of different editors thus: Krailsheimer on Lafuma; Ariew, and

Levi and Levi on Sellier. Judicious use of the concordance should make it easy to locate *pensées* quoted or discussed in this book in any of these versions.

Le Guern	Lafuma (Krailsheimer)	Sellier (Ariew; Levi and Levi)
1	1	37
2	2–4	38
3–30	5–32	39–66
31	33–34	67–68
32–41	35–44	69–78
42–53	46–57	79–90
54	58	91–92
55	59	93
56	60, 76	94, 111
57–70	61–74	95–108
71	75	110
72–75	77–80	112–15
76	81–82	116
77	83–84	117–18
78–90	85–97	119–31
91	98–99	132
92–93	100–101	133–34
94–111	103–20	135–52
112	121	153–54
113–23	122–32	155–65
124	133–34	166
125–29	135–39	167–71
130	140	172–73
131–38	141–48	174–81

Le Guern	Lafuma (Krailsheimer)	Sellier (Ariew; Levi and Levi)
139	149	182, 274
140–43	150–53	183–86
144	154–55	187
145–55	156–66	188–98
156	167	unnumbered title
157–72	168–83	199–214
173	184	215–16
174–78	185–89	217–21
179	190	222–23
180–82	191–93	224–26
183	194–97	227–28
184–85	198–99	229–30
186	200	231–32
187–94	201–8	233–40
195	209	241–42
196–10	210–24	243–57
211	225–26	258
212–26	227–41	259–73
227	242–43	275–76
228	244	277
229	245	unnumbered title
230–41	246–57	278–89
242	258–59	290
243–60	260–77	291–308
261	278	309–10
262–74	279–91	311–23

Le Guern	Lafuma (Krailsheimer)	Sellier (Ariew; Levi and Levi)
275	292–93	324
276–77	294–95	325–26
278	296, xxx	327, 741
279–93	297–311	328–42
294	312–13	343–44
295–304	314–23	345–54
305	324	355, 357
306	325	356
307–46	326–65	358–97
347	366	398–99
348	367	400
349	368–69	401
350–62	370–82	402–14
363	383–84	2–3
364–396	385–417	4–36
397	418–26	680
398	427	681
399	428	682
400	429	682
401	430	683
402	431	683
403	432	662, 684
404–9	433–38	685–90
410	439–40	690
411	441	690
412	442	690
413	443	690
414	444	690

Le Guern	Lafuma (Krailsheimer)	Sellier (Ariew; Levi and Levi)
415	445	690
416	446	690
417	447	690
418	448	690
419	449	690
420	450	690
421–23	451–53	691–93
424	454–55	694–95
425	456–57, 973	696, 698
426	458	697
427	459	697
428–31	460–63	699–702
432	464–66	703
433	467	704
434	468–69	705–6
435–38	470–73	707–10
439	474	711
440	475	711
441	476	711
442–50	477–85	712–20
451	486	721–33
452	487–88	734
453	489	735
454	490–99	736
455	500–501	737
456	502–3	738
457	504–5	672
458	506	673

Le Guern	Lafuma (Krailsheimer)	Sellier (Ariew; Levi and Levi)
459	506	674
460	507	675
461	508	676
462	508	677
463	508	678
464	508	679
465	509–11	669
466	512	670
467	513–14	671
468	515–24	452–53
469	525–29	454
470–71	530–31	455–56
472	532–35	457
473	536–43	458–59
474	544–49	460
475	550–52	461
476–77	553–54	462–63
478	555–56	464
479	557–58	465
480–84	559–63	466–70
485	564–65	471
486	566	472
487	567–69	473
488	570–71	474
489–95	572–78	475–81
496	579–80	482
497–98	581–82	483–84
499	583–84	485

Le Guern	Lafuma (Krailsheimer)	Sellier (Ariew; Levi and Levi)
500	585–87	486
501–4	588–91	487–90
505–6	592–93	492–93
507	594–95	491
508–12	596–600	493–97
513	601	498
514	922–24	499, 753
515	602–3	500
516	604	501
517	605–6, 610–11	502–3
518	607–9	504
519–41	612–34	505–27
542	635–36	528
543	637–39	529
544	640–44	529
545–50	645–50	530–35
551	651–52	536
552–58	653–59	537–43
559	660–63	544
560–61	664–65	545–46
562	666–68	547
563–91	669–97	548–76
592	698–99	577
593–12	700–719	578–97
613	720–21	598
614	722	600, 602–4
615	723	601
616–19	724–27	605–8

Le Guern	Lafuma (Krailsheimer)	Sellier (Ariew; Levi and Levi)
620	728	609–10
621–22	729–30	611–12
623	731–32	613
624–26	733–35	614–16
627	736–43	617
628	744–45	618
629–31	746–48	619–21
632	749–52	622
633–35	753–55	623–25
636	756–57	626
637–38	758–59	627–28
639	760–63	629
640	764	630
641	765–66	631
642–45	767–70	632–35
646	771–72	636
647–48	773–74	637–38
649	775	639–40
650–51	776–77	641–42
652	778–79	643
653	780–81	644
654	782–91	645
655	792–93, 931–32	646
656–58	794–96	647–49
659	797–98	650
660–61	799–800	651–52
662	801–6	653
663–66	807–10	654–57

Le Guern	Lafuma (Krailsheimer)	Sellier (Ariew; Levi and Levi)
667	811–14	658
668	815	659
669	816–17	659
670	818–20	660
671–75	821–25	661–66
676	826–27	667
677	828–29	668
678–79	830–31	419–20
680	832–33	421
681	834	422
682	835–36	423
683	837–39	424
684	840	425, 428
685	841	426
686	842–45	427
687	846	429
688	847–49	430
689–90	850–51	431–32
691	852–53	433
692–94	854–56	434–36
695	857–58	437
696	859	438
697	860–65	439
698	866–76	440
699	877–79	441–42
700–701	880–81	442–43
702	882–91	444–45
703–704	892–93	446–47

Le Guern	Lafuma (Krailsheimer)	Sellier (Ariew; Levi and Levi)
705	894–900	448
706	901–2	449
707	904–2	450–51
708–9	971–72	415–16
710	970	417–18
711–13	913–15	742–45
714	916–17	746
715	979	747
716	918	748
717	919	749, 751
718	920	750
719	921	752
720	925	754
721	926	755
722	927–29	756
723	930	757
724	980	760
725	933	761
726	934–35	762
727	936	751
728	937–38	763
729–30	939–40	764–65
731	941–42	766
732	943–45	767
733	946–47	768
734	948	769
735	981–82	770
736–37	949–50	787–88

Le Guern	Lafuma (Krailsheimer)	Sellier (Ariew; Levi and Levi)
738	952	789
739–43	953–57	790–94
744	958–59	795
745–47	960–62	796–98
748	963–64	799
749–50	965–66	800–801
751	967	599
752–53	968–69	802–3
754	xxx	813
755	974	771
756–57	975–76	739–40
758	978	743
759	983	804
760	984	781
761–67	985–91	805–11
768	992	782
769	993	812
770–78	xxx	772–80
779–82	xxx	783–86

BIBLIOGRAPHY

To read Pascal in French, I recommend Le Guern's edition of the complete works. It's reliable, relatively up to date, and thoroughly but not excessively annotated—altogether a delight to use. Lafuma's one-volume edition is a good second best: it's handy, and still easily and cheaply available, though less annotated than Le Guern's, and now superseded in some of its editorial decisions. The large annotated editions are those by Brunschvicg and Mesnard, the latter still incomplete and likely to remain so (Mesnard died in 2016): these are still very much worth consulting for their annotations and interpretations, but they're in many volumes, hard to find outside research libraries, and not designed for those who want to read Pascal rather than consult him. There are many more editions than these, some of individual works, some of the whole corpus, some scholarly, some popular, and some hard to classify. Le Guern's list (*OC* 2/1616–18) seems complete and reliable through the late 1990s. The translation of *Pensées* by Zoberman and Ferguson forthcoming from the Catholic University of America Press provides thorough bibliographic guidance to editions of that work in particular, and to Pascal studies more generally. The editorial enterprise will, I should think, continue to the end of the age.

Most of what Pascal wrote is available in English, though in versions widely varying in age and quality. Cailliet and Blankenagel, Eliot, Gleason, and Hutchins provide anthologies of translated texts, with considerable overlap—W. F. Trotter's version of *Pensées*, first published in 1904, appears in several of these volumes, for example. For the scientific and mathematical works, I recommend Popkin in general, and Spiers and Spiers for the experiments in physics. Buroker provides a complete translation of the Port-Royal *Logic*, of which some parts are by Pascal. For *Pensées,* the forthcoming translation under the direction of Zoberman and Ferguson will be definitive, and until then Krailsheimer's and Ariew's versions are both usable. For *Provincials*, Krailsheimer's is the most easily available English version, and it is good. The only rendering of the *Abrégé de la vie Jésus-Christ* appears to be that by Cailliet and Blankenagel; it is stilted and inadequate. The principal lacunae are: the *Écrits sur la grâce*, of which there still appears to be no complete English rendering (excerpts are in the selections rendered by Levi and Levi, and in Miel); the *Écrits des curés de Paris*, of which there is also no complete translation (excerpts are in the selections rendered by Cailliet and Blankenagel); the *Réflexions d'un docteur de Sorbonne*, of which there appears to be no English at all, because, it seems, it was long attributed to Antoine Arnauld rather than Pascal; and the works on the cycloid that appeared under the Dettonville name, of which again there seems to be no English at all. There are other more minor lacks. A desideratum is a complete Pascal in twenty-first-century English, rendered with an eye to consistency in translation of Pascal's principal terms of art, so that conceptual and rhetorical connections across the various domains in which he wrote might be more evident to monoglot anglophones than is possible now.

*

Attali, Jacques. *Blaise Pascal ou le génie français*. Paris: Fayard, 2000.

Auerbach, Erich. "On the Political Theory of Pascal." In *Blaise Pascal*, edited by Harold Bloom, 17–35. New York: Chelsea House, 1989.

Bloom, Harold, ed. *Blaise Pascal*. New York: Chelsea House, 1989.

Boeke, Kees. *Cosmic View: The Universe in Forty Jumps*. New York: John Day, 1957.

Buroker, Jill Vance, trans. *Logic or the Art of Thinking*. Cambridge: Cambridge University Press, 1996.

Cantillon, Alain. "Blaise Pascal ou la séparation béante." *Archives de sciences sociales des religions* 59, no. 166 (2014): 35–45.

Carraud, Vincent. "Remarks on the Second Pascalian Anthropology: Thought as Alienation." *Journal of Religion* 85, no. 4 (2005): 539–54.

———. *Pascal et la philosophie*. 2d ed. Paris: Presses Universitaires de France, 2007.

———. *Pascal: Des connaissances naturelles à l'étude de l'homme*. Paris: Vrin, 2007.

———. "Pascal's Anti-Augustinianism." *Perspectives on Science* 15, no. 4 (2007): 450–92.

———. *L'Invention du moi*. Paris: Presses Universitaires de France, 2010.

Cognet, Louis. *Le jansénisme*. Paris: Presses Universitaires de France, 1961.

Cole, John R. *Pascal: The Man and His Two Loves*. New York: New York University Press, 1995.

Conley, John J. *Adoration and Annihilation: The Convent Philosophy of Port-Royal*. Notre Dame, Ind.: University of Notre Dame Press, 2009.

———. *The Other Pascals: The Philosophy of Jacqueline Pascal, Gilberte Pascal Périer, and Marguerite Périer*. Notre Dame, Ind.: University of Notre Dame Press, 2019.

Connor, James A. *Pascal's Wager: The Man Who Played Dice with God*. New York: HarperCollins, 2006.

Cortese, João Figueiredo Nobre. "Infinity Between Mathematics and Apologetics: Pascal's Notion of Infinite Distance." *Synthese* 192, no. 8 (2015): 2379–93.

Courcelle, Pierre. *L'Entretien de Pascal et de Sacy, ses sources et ses énigmes*. Paris: Vrin, 1960.

Davidson, Hugh M. *Origins of Certainty: Means and Meaning in Pascal's Pensées*. Chicago: University of Chicago Press, 1979

———. *Blaise Pascal*. Boston: Twayne, 1983.

———. *Pascal and the Arts of the Mind*. Cambridge: Cambridge University Press, 1993.

Davidson, Hugh M., and Pierre H. Dubé. *A Concordance to Pascal's Pensées*. Ithaca, N.Y.: Cornell University Press, 1975.

Denzinger, Heinrich. *Enchiridion symbolorum definitionum et declarationum de rebus fidei et morum: Compendium of Creeds, Definitions, and Declarations on Matters of Faith and Morals*, 43rd ed. Edited by Peter Hünermann. San Francisco: Ignatius Press, 2012.

Descotes, Dominique. *L'Argumentation chez Pascal*. Paris: Presses Universitaires de France, 1993.

Doyle, William. *Jansenism: Catholic Resistance to Authority from the Reformation to the French Revolution*. New York: St. Martin's Press, 2000.

Duchêne, Roger. *Imposture littéraire dans les Provinciales de Pascal*. 2d ed. Aix-en-Provence: Université de Provence, 1985.

Eslin, Jean-Claude. "Pascal peut-il être pour nous une voie vers Dieu?" *Esprit* 333, no. 3/4 (2007): 266–78.

Ferreyrolles, Gérard. *Pascal et la raison du politique*. Paris: Presses Universitaires de France, 1984.

———. *Les reines du monde: l'imagination et la coutume chez Pascal*. Paris: Honoré Champion, 1995.

Garber, Daniel. *What Happens after Pascal's Wager: Living Faith and Rational Belief*. Milwaukee, Wisc.: Marquette University Press, 2009.

Gibbon, Edward. *The History of the Decline and Fall of the Roman Empire*. 6 vols. First published London, 1776–1789. Many printed and online editions.

Giono, Jean. *Un roi sans divertissement*. Paris: Éditions de la Table Ronde, 1947.

Goldmann, Lucien. *Le Dieu caché: Étude sur la vision tragique dans les "Pensées" de Pascal et dans le théâtre de Racine*. Paris: Gallimard, 1955.

Gouhier, Henri. *Blaise Pascal: Commentaires*. Paris: Vrin, 1966.

———. *Blaise Pascal: Conversion et apologétique*. Paris: Vrin, 1986.

Griffiths, Paul J. "The Quietus of Political Interest." *Common Knowledge* 15, no. 1 (2009): 7–22.

Hammond, Nicholas. *Playing with Truth: Language and the Human Condition in Blaise Pascal's Pensées*. Oxford: Oxford University Press, 1994.

———. "Mémoire et éducation chez Pascal." In *Pascal—New Trends in Port-Royal Studies*, edited by David Wetsel and Frédéric Canovas, 269–76. Tübingen: Gunter Narr, 2002.

———, ed. *The Cambridge Companion to Pascal*. Cambridge: Cambridge University Press, 2003.

Hart, David Bentley. *That All Shall Be Saved: Heaven, Hell, and Universal Salvation*. New Haven, Conn.: Yale University Press, 2019.

Hibbs, Thomas S. *Wagering on an Ironic God: Pascal on Faith and Philosophy*. Waco, Tx.: Baylor University Press, 2017.

Houellebecq, Michel. *Serotonin*. Translated by Shaun Whiteside. New York: Farrar, Straus and Giroux, 2019.

Hui, Andrew. *A Theory of the Aphorism: From Confucius to Twitter*. Princeton, N.J.: Princeton University Press, 2019.

Hünermann, Peter, ed. *Enchiridion Symbolorum definitionum et declarationum de rebus fidei et morum/Compendium of Creeds, Declarations, and Definitions on Matters of Faith and Morals*. 43rd edition. San Francisco: Ignatius Press, 2012.

Jansenius, Cornelius. *Augustinus*. 3 vols. Louvain: Iacobus Zegenus, 1640.

Koch, Erec R. *Pascal and Rhetoric: Figural and Persuasive Language in the Scientific Treatises, the Provinciales, and the Pensées*. Charlottesville, Va.: Rookwood Press, 1997.

Kolakowski, Leszek. *Chrétiens sans Église: La conscience religieuse et le lien confessionel au XVIIe siècle*. Paris: Gallimard, 1969.

———. *God Owes Us Nothing: A Brief Remark on Pascal's Religion and on the Spirit of Jansenism*. Chicago: University of Chicago Press, 1995.

Krailsheimer, A. J. *Pascal*. New York: Hill and Wang, 1980.

Kripke, Saul. *Wittgenstein on Rules and Private Language*. Cambridge, Mass.: Harvard University Press, 1982.

Le Guern, Michel. *Études sur la vie et les Pensées de Pascal*. Paris: Honoré Champion, 2015.

Lear, Jonathan. *A Case for Irony*. Cambridge, Mass.: Harvard University Press, 2014.

Logic or the Art of Thinking. Translated by Jill Vance Buroker. Cambridge: Cambridge University Press, 1996.

Marion, Jean-Luc. "*Mihi magna quaestio factus sum:* The Privilege of Unknowing." *Journal of Religion* 85, no. 1 (2005): 1–24.

Maritain, Jacques. "La politique du Pascal." *Revue universelle* XIV, no. 9 (1923): 29–41.

McDade, John. "The Contemporary Relevance of Pascal." *New Blackfriars* 91, no. 1032 (2010): 185–96.

McKenna, Antony. *Pascal et son libertin*. Paris: Classiques Garnier, 2017.

Melzer, Sara E. *Discourses of the Fall: A Study of Pascal's Pensées*. Berkeley: University of California Press, 1986.

Mesnard, Jean. *Pascal et les Roannez*. Paris: Desclée de Brouwer, 1965.

———. *Pascal*. Translated by Claude and Marcia Abraham. Birmingham: University of Alabama Press, 1969.

———. *La culture du XVIIe siècle: enquêtes et synthèses*. Paris: Presses Universitaires de France, 1992.

———. "Histoire secrète de la recherche pascalienne au XXe siècle." In *Pascal—New Trends in Port-Royal Studies*, edited by David Wetsel and Frédéric Canovas, 13–38. Tübingen: Gunter Narr, 2002.

Meynet, Roland. "'Les trois ordres' de Pascal selon la rhétorique biblique." *Gregorianum* 94, no. 1 (2013): 79–96.

Miel, Jan. *Pascal and Theology*. Baltimore: Johns Hopkins University Press, 1969.

Moriarty, Michael. "Pascal's Modernity." *The Seventeenth Century* 34, no. 2 (2019), 209–27.

Natoli, Charles. *Fire in the Dark: Essays on Pascal's* "Pensées" *and* "Provinciales." Rochester, N.Y.: University of Rochester Press, 2005.

Nelson, Robert J. *Pascal: Adversary and Advocate*: Cambridge, Mass.: Harvard University Press, 1981.

Parish, Richard. *Pascal's "Lettres Provinciales": A Study in Polemic*. Oxford: Clarendon Press, 1989.

Pascal, Blaise. *Oeuvres complètes*. Edited by Léon Brunschvicg. 14 vols. Paris: Hachette, 1904–14.

———. *Oeuvres complètes*. Edited by Louis Lafuma. Paris: Éditions du Seuil, 1963.

———. *Oeuvres complètes*. Edited by Jean Mesnard. 4 vols. (incomplete). Paris: Desclée de Brouwer, 1964–92.

———. *Oeuvres complètes*. Edited by Michel Le Guern. 2 vols. Paris: Éditions Gallimard, 1998, 2000.

———. *Pensées*. Translated by W. F. Trotter. London: Dent, 1904.

———. *Pensées*. Edited by Philippe Sellier. Paris: Mercure de France, 1976.

———. *Pensées*. Translated by A. J. Krailsheimer. 2d ed. London: Penguin Books, 1995.

———. *Pensées*. Translated by Roger Ariew. Indianapolis, Indiana: Hackett, 2005.

———. *Pensées*. Translated and edited by a team of scholars led by Pierre Zoberman and Gary Ferguson, co-editors. From the edition by Philippe Sellier based on Gilberte Pascal's Reference Copy. Washington, D.C.: The Catholic University of America Press, forthcoming.

———. *The Provincial Letters*. Translated by A. J. Krailsheimer. Harmondsworth: Penguin Books, 1967.

———. Selections in Harvard Classics, volume 48. Edited by Charles W. Eliot. New York: Collier, 1910.

———. Selections in *The Physical Treatises of Pascal: The Equilibrium of Liquids and the Weight of the Mass of the Air*. Translated by J. H. B. Spiers and A. G. H. Spiers. New York: Columbia University Press, 1937.

———. Selections in *Great Shorter Works of Pascal*. Translated by Emile Cailliet and John C. Blankenagel. New York: Westminster Press, 1948.

———. Selections in *Great Books of the Western World*, volume 33. Edited by Robert Maynard Hutchins. Chicago: Encyclopedia Britannica, 1952.

———. Selections in *The Essential Pascal*. Translated by Robert W. Gleason. New York: New American Library, 1966.

———. Selections in *Pascal: Selections*. Translated by Richard H. Popkin. New York: Macmillan, 1989.

———. Selections in *Pensées and Other Writings*. Translated by Honor Levi and Anthony Levi. Oxford World's Classics. Oxford: Oxford University Press, 1995.

———. *Short Life of Christ*. Translated by Emile Cailliet and John C. Blankenagel. Princeton, N.J.: Princeton Theological Seminary, 1950.

Pasqua, Hervé. *Blaise Pascal: Penseur de la grâce*. Paris: Téqui, 2000.

Pickstock, Catherine. *After Writing: On the Liturgical Consummation of Philosophy*. Oxford: Blackwell, 1998.

Pouzet, Régine. *Chronique des Pascal: "Les affaires du monde" d'Étienne Pascal à Marguerite Périer (1588–1713)*. Paris: Champion, 2001.

Rabourdin, David. *Pascal: Foi et conversion*. Paris: Presses Universitaires de France, 2013.

Rieger, Hans-Martin. "Wetten auf Gott? Die Wette des Blaise Pascal in religionsphilosophischer und theologischer Perspektive." *Zeitschrift für Theologie und Kirche* 104, no. 1 (2007), 84–116.

Sellier, Philippe. *Pascal et la liturgie*. Paris: Presses Universitaires de France, 1966.

———. *Pascal et Saint Augustin*. Paris: Éditions Albin Michel, 1995.

Soerensen, Jennifer L. "Search, Rest, and Grace in Pascal." *International Journal for the Philosophy of Religion* 76, no. 1 (2014): 19–40.

Topliss, Patricia. *The Rhetoric of Pascal: A Study of His Art of Persuasion in the "Provinciales" and the "Pensées."* Leicester: Leicester University Press, 1966.

van Fraassen, Bas C. "The False Hopes of Traditional Epistemology." *Philosophy and Phenomenological Research* 60, no. 2 (2000): 253–80.

Wetsel, David. *L'Écriture et le Reste: The Pensées of Pascal in the Exegetical Tradition of Port-Royal*. Columbus: Ohio State University Press, 1981.

———. *Pascal and Disbelief: Catechesis and Conversion in the Pensées*. Washington, D.C.: The Catholic University of America Press, 1994.

Westsel, David, and Frédéric Canovas, eds. *Pascal—New Trends in Port-Royal Studies*. Tübingen: Gunter Narr, 2002.

Wood, William. *Blaise Pascal on Duplicity, Sin, and the Fall: The Secret Instinct*. Oxford: Oxford University Press, 2013.

INDEX

Garber, Daniel, 123n81
geometry, 8, 18, 21–22, 60–62
Geometry (Pascal), 18n8
Gibbon, Edward, xii
glory, 56, 62, 114, 126, 135, 143, 152, 158,
    172, 192, 202, 209
God: as choosing an elect, 153–59; as
    departing from us, 143–44; as hid-
    den, 31–33, 61, 66, 154; as incompre-
    hensible, 65–67; as merciful, 35, 82,
    109–10, 123, 141–43, 154, 162, 172;
    as noncompetitive with us, 139–40,
    146, 149, 153, 156, 161; as obligated,
    148–49; as promising, 118–19, 138,
    148–49, 153, 159, 199; as willing abso-
    lutely, 135, 151–54, 157–58; as willing
    conditionally, 135–36, 152–54,
    157–58; as willing the salvation of
    all, 120–21, 132–33
Goldmann, Lucien, 34n33
Gouhier, Henri, 117n78, 130n83,
    187n34
grace: of creation, 127–28; as help,
    134–35; and human agency, 141–46;
    and love, 136; names for, 133–35; and
    perseverance, 137, 139, 148, 150; and
    predestination, 129, 132, 145n107,
    148–49, 155; and proximate power,
    133–39. *See also* help
Grace (Pascal), 24, 33n32, 34, 63,
    134–40, 143, 145, 148–50, 151–55,
    179

habit. *See* custom
Haddarschan, Moyse, 204
Hallé de Monflaines, Raoul, 181
Harlay, François de, 181
Hart, David Bentley, 159n124
help, 134, 135, 137–40, 145, 148, 153–54.
    See also grace
Houellebecq, Michel, 33n32
Hui, Andrew, 10n1
hunting, 91–94

In eminenti ecclesiae (Urban VII), 129
infinity, 19–20, 35, 54, 59–61, 65–66,
    73, 79–81, 95, 106, 115, 117–22, 147,
    169
Innocent X, 51, 129–30, 132–33, 136,
    189–90
Instruction (Pascal), 52n13
intention, direction of, 102–5
irony, 24–25, 38–40

Jansenius, Cornelius, 2, 23n22, 28,
    50–54, 129–30, 133, 183, 185, 188–89
Jesuits, 6, 23, 28–30, 100–105, 108, 132,
    146, 162, 182, 211, 213
Jesus-Christ, 15–16, 64, 77, 119, 193, 213;
    and affliction 83–87, 89, 116n74; as
    body of the Church, 106–9, 111–12,
    146, 162–63, 166, 178, 180; and Israel,
    159, 200–203; in the Old Testament,
    205, 207; and Pontius Pilate, 190–91;
    work of 56, 132, 155, 173–74, 195–96
Jesus-Christ (Pascal): 27, 56n2, 64,
    116n74
Jews: as carnal and spiritual, 199–200;
    and the Church, 195–96; distin-
    guished from other peoples, 197–99;
    on original sin, 204–5; as superseded
    by Christianity, 200–202; as witness
    to Christianity, 202–3
John (the Baptizer), 111
Jovinians (and Jovinianism), 138
justification (and the justified), 136–40,
    152, 168

kings, 25, 54–55, 64, 79, 91–93, 144,
    162, 169–70
Kripke, Saul, 210

law: and citizenship, 162–65; and
    controversy, 171–74; and force,
    166–68; and justice, 166–68; new
    and old, 198–200, 204, 206–9; and
    obedience, 168–69
Lear, Jonathan, 39n49

Why Read Pascal? was designed in Garamond with Requiem display type and composed by Kachergis Book Design of Pittsboro, North Carolina. It was printed on 55-pound Natural Hi Bulk and bound by Data Reproductions of Auburn Hills, Michigan.